ROUGH SKETCHES

OF THE

LIFE OF AN OLD SOLDIER:

DURING A SERVICE IN

THE WEST INDIES;

AT THE SIEGE OF COPENHAGEN IN 1807;

IN THE PENINSULA AND THE SOUTH OF FRANCE IN THE
CAMPAIGNS FROM 1808 TO 1814,

WITH THE LIGHT DIVISION;

IN THE NETHERLANDS IN 1815;

INCLUDING

THE BATTLES OF QUATRE BRAS AND WATERLOO:

WITH

A SLIGHT SKETCH

OF THE THREE YEARS PASSED BY THE ARMY OF OCCUPATION
IN FRANCE, &c. &c. &c.

By LIEUT.-COLONEL J. LEACH, C.B.
LATE OF THE RIFLE BRIGADE, AND PREVIOUSLY OF THE 70TH REGIMENT.

Published by

The Naval & Military Press Ltd
Unit 5 Riverside, Brambleside
Bellbrook Industrial Estate
Uckfield, East Sussex
TN22 1QQ England

Tel: +44 (0)1825 749494

www.naval-military-press.com
www.nmarchive.com

*In reprinting in facsimile from the original, any imperfections are inevitably reproduced
and the quality may fall short of modern type and cartographic standards.*

TO

THE 70TH REGIMENT,

AND

THE OLD 95TH,

(NOW THE RIFLE BRIGADE),

IN WHICH TWO CORPS

I PASSED ONE AND TWENTY EVENTFUL YEARS,

THE FOLLOWING PAGES

𝕬𝖗𝖊 𝕴𝖓𝖘𝖈𝖗𝖎𝖇𝖊𝖉

BY THEIR OLD AND SINCERELY ATTACHED COMRADE,

J. LEACH.

PREFACE.

As it is the fashion now-a-days for every one to become an author, I see no reason why I should not try my hand at it also, and let my book run the same risk of being criticised, lashed, and abused by the literati (if, indeed, they deign to peruse it), as is every day the case with some production or other, and to which every one, who is bold enough to make similar experiments, must make up his mind.

Such as mine is, forth it goes to the world; and it must be taken for better for worse.

During many years of active service, I kept a daily journal, in which I inserted matters and things as they appeared to me at the instant; and from which journals, aided by a tolerably fair memory, and some old notes and memoranda, the following pages were put together in a rough state many years ago, and may therefore, with great propriety, be styled "Rough Sketches."

I pretend not to any thing resembling a history of the Peninsular War. A very old Light Division comrade of mine, Colonel NAPIER, has already done it in so masterly a style, as to throw every other work on the same subject comparatively into the shade.

The operations of the Light Division of the Peninsular army I have detailed more minutely than those of any other. That division was, during a succession of campaigns, much detached from the mass of the army, having ample employment at the outposts. But I have not omitted to mention, also, the movements of other divisions, whenever an opportunity offered for my becoming acquainted with them.

It is unnecessary to remind my military readers, that as I never, for one hour in my whole life, held a staff appointment, but always did duty with my regiment, it was impossible that I could be acquainted, on every occasion, with the general combined movements of so large an army.

Those, however, who may have patience

to wade through my "Rough Sketches," will find in them a little about voyages, storms, shipwrecks, yellow fevers, musquitos, sangaree and sangarorum, sharks, dolphins, and flying-fish; night marches and day marches, camps and bivouacs, advances and retreats, skirmishes, battles, and sieges; signoras, waltzes, boleros, and fandangos; bull-fights, wild boar shooting, wolves, and red deer; British soldiers, and French, Spanish, and Portuguese, — all of which I have endeavoured to depict in their true colours.

If I have failed in my attempt, I am sorry for it; but my regret will be infinitely greater, if any of my brother-soldiers, whether of the cavalry, infantry, artillery, or engineers, either of the Peninsular army, or of that which fought at Waterloo, should accuse me of not having rendered due praise to the conduct of their respective divisions, brigades, or regiments, on particular occasions. Let me again remind them, that I was always regimentally employed; and that if any such omissions exist in my book, they are quite unintentional.

That they will be viewed in that light,

by the liberal-minded, I entertain neither fear nor doubt.

Forty-nine out of every fifty of the scenes which I have here endeavoured to describe, I was an eye-witness of; and, on one or two occasions, when agues and fevers placed me for a short period on the sick list, the events which took place in the interim I became acquainted with, by being allowed to have access to the log-books of some one or other of my brother-officers. The thread of the narrative is therefore unbroken.

CONTENTS.

Preface .... *Page* vii

CHAPTER I.

Join my regiment in Jersey. Embark for England. Winter at Chatham. The 52d regiment made Light Infantry. New system of drill introduced. Encamp at Shorncliffe in Kent. French camp and flotilla at Boulogne. Invasion threatened, and precautions taken by Sir John Moore. The Duke of York reviews the troops at Shorncliffe. Sudden order for our regiment to embark for the West Indies. Unfortunate occurrence on the march from Shorncliffe to Portsmouth. Remarks thereon. Embark and sail for Barbadoes. Tremendous storm. Various occurrences on the voyage. Arrive at Barbadoes. First impressions as to climate, &c. Death of the Commander-in-Chief of the West Indies. We proceed to Antigua. The harbour and dock-yard. Disembark at midnight. Lose my baggage. Scarcity of fresh water in Antigua. The regiment suffers dreadfully from yellow fever. Its losses. Hurricane. Officers' funerals. The military governor and his brigade-major die. A receipt for yellow fever. Dancing and other gaieties. Death of Sir William Myers, the new Commander-in-Chief in the West Indies. Terrible mortality in his family. Death of the new Governor of Antigua. Great mortality in the 96th regiment in Antigua. A French squadron. Dominica is attacked. The French are repulsed by the 46th regiment. We expect a visit from the same squadron at Antigua. Preparations for its reception. We are reinforced. Long marches. Sudden death of several soldiers from excessive heat. The 68th regiment is sent to Antigua. Its immense losses by climate. Horse-races and balls at St. John's. More funerals. Lord Nelson arrives in search of the French and Spanish squadrons. He returns to Europe. My health begins to suffer. A medical board orders me to Europe for its restoration. My own ideas as to *slavery*. Take my passage for Europe. Sail to Tortola. Large homeward-bound fleet. Dreadful gales and other mishaps on the voyage home. Anchor in Dublin Bay. Quarantine. Land at Dublin. Proceed to England.................................. *Page* 1

CHAPTER II.

Exchange into the 95th Rifle Corps. Expedition to Denmark. Sail tó Elsineur. Imposing appearance of our numerous fleet. Scenery on the Danish and Swedish coasts. A party to Elsineur. Cronberg castle. Hamlet's garden. Disorderly conduct of the Danes. Causes thereof. The army disembarks. The reserve commanded by Sir Arthur Wellesley. Advance towards Copenhagen. A sortie made by the garrison. Affairs between the Danish gun-boats and our advanced squadron. Ludicrous nocturnal affair at the outposts. The Danish pickets are driven in. The reserve is sent into the interior of the island of Zealand. Affair near Kioge with the Danish militia. A sortie from Copenhagen repulsed by Lieut. Light, of the 50th regiment. Bombardment of Copenhagen, and surrender of the Danish fleet and stores. Visit to the capital. Its deplorable appearance. The army re-embarks. List of Danish prizes. A large fleet of homeward-bound merchantmen joins us. We sail for England. A slight sketch of the

CONTENTS. xiii

Danes, and of the island of Zealand. Stormy passage to
England .... *Page* 26

CHAPTER III.

Four companies of our 2d battalion embark. Sail to Cork, and
join an expedition. Its destination. Boating excursions.
The expedition sails. We anchor in Mondego Bay. Bri-
gadier-General Fane's brigade. The army disembarks in
Portugal. Monks, friars, padres, and Portuguese females.
March to Lavaos. Joined by troops under General Spencer.
A present from the Portuguese junta. A Dutch concert.
The army advances. Features of the country. Reach
Lyria. Swiss deserters. Affair with the French near Obidos.
Battle of Roleia. A close shave and a narrow escape. Lieu-
tenant Cockrane. March to Lourinha. Reinforcements
join the army from England. Battle of Vimiera. Sir H.
Burrard arrives to take the command. A flag of truce.
Convention of Cintra. Reflections thereon. Sir John
Moore arrives. The British army encamps near Lisbon.
Amity between the French and English soldiers in Lisbon.
Lisbon. Its opera, &c. &c. An eccentric Highland chief-
tain. Fevers and agues; and by what means a person so
afflicted may be rendered still more miserable........ 40

CHAPTER IV.

The army under Sir John Moore leaves Lisbon. Marches to
Salamanca. Sir John Hope joins Sir John Moore near
Salamanca. Sir David Baird lands at Corunna. The
whole army is concentrated. Affairs of cavalry. The
army moves to attack Marshal Soult. Suddenly countermanded. Distribution of our first and second battalions.
Gallant affair of cavalry near Mayorca. General Crawford's
light brigade destroys a bridge. The French endeavour to

interrupt them in their work. General Crawford marches to Benavente. Brilliant action of cavalry near Benavente. Two light brigades sent to Vigo. Their march thither, and embarkation. Cursory view of Sir John Moore's retreat to Corunna, and his death. The army returns to England. Our third battalion is formed .... *Page* 59

CHAPTER V.

The Light Brigade composed of the 43d and 52d regiments of Light Infantry, and the 1st battalion 95th Rifle Corps. Embark for Lisbon under Brigadier-General Robert Crawford. Arrive at Lisbon. Proceed by water to Vallada. Santarem. Convents and nuns. March from Santarem to join Sir Arthur Wellesley. Sketch of the march. The Pass of Villa Velha, Castello Branco, Zarza Maior, Coria, Orapeza, &c. Extraordinary long march on 28th July, and want of water. We join the army at Talavera. Slight sketch of the field of action........................ 67

CHAPTER VI.

Scarcity of provisions. Horrid stench from the unburied bodies of men and horses. I lose my horse, and with him all my campaigning comforts. The British army marches on Orapeza to attack Soult. Conduct of General Cuesta at Talavera. The British army crosses the Tagus at Arzobispo. Desperate attack made by General Crawford's troops on a herd of swine. How to dress pork in the most expeditious manner. The army retires towards Delatosa. General Crawford's division proceeds to the bridge of Almaraz. Long and harassing marches thither. Parched peas and boiled wheat our food. A fortnight at Almaraz. Scanty diet of bran cakes and goat's flesh, without salt. How to reduce a corpulent person. The army falls back to the southern frontier of Portugal, and is cantoned near the Guadiana.

A short account of our retreat. Maravao. Castello de Vide. Jollification in the woods near it. Shooting party on the 1st of September. Portalegre. General Catline Crawford's brigade. Aronches. General Crawford's division reaches Campo Maior ....*Page* 87

CHAPTER VII.

The country near Campo Maior, and the climate of Alemtejo. The army becomes very sickly. Fate of General Cuestas' army after we parted company with it at Talavera. Various descriptions of field-sports near Campo Maior. How to keep off fevers, agues, &c. Shooting excursions in the forest of Albuquerque. Wild boars, wolves, and red deer. Bathing excursions of our battalion, and its march to and from the Caya. Destruction of hares, rabbits, and partridges. Riding down red-legged partridges. Lieut.-Colonel Sidney Beckwith's system contrasted with that of many commanding officers of regiments. Rumours of the army being about to return to England. The army continues sickly. The army leaves its cantonments on the Guadiana, and proceeds to the northern frontier of Portugal. Our march to that point. Students and young padres at the University of Coimbra uselessly employed. Sketch of the country between Coimbra and Pinhel, and our march through it. The 95th Rifle Corps and 1st German Hussars cross the Coa, and take up the outposts. The manner in which we passed our time in the outlandish regions between the Coa and Agueda, until the campaign of 1810 opened. Various amusements for the soldiers encouraged by Lieut.-Colonel Beckwith 104

CHAPTER VIII.

A skirmish with the French near Barba del Puerco. The whole of our battalion moves up to the Agueda, and occupies an extended line of posts. Massacre of a French soldier by some Spanish shepherds, near Almofala. Night attack made on four companies of our battalion at the pass of Barba del Puerco. The enemy is repulsed with loss. Observations. Letter from Lord Wellington to Colonel Beckwith, expressing his approbation of the conduct of his corps on the occasion. General Crawford also thanks the regiment in orders. The French force at San Felices reinforced from Salamanca. Character of General Loison. General Crawford withdraws the troops from Barba del Puerco. We occupy Villa de Ciervo. Our ten companies reduced to eight, and some officers sent to England to recruit. Fine specimens of crystal found near Villa de Ciervo. My establishment is augmented by a young wolf. Two Portuguese light battalions join General Crawford. We are reinforced also by a troop of horse artillery, the 14th and 16th Light Dragoons. Extensive line of posts guarded by General Crawford's corps. A large army under Marshal Massena assembles near Ciudad Rodrigo, intended to invade Portugal. The three different corps which composed it. By whom commanded. Massena's proclamation to the Portuguese. He lays siege to Rodrigo. The Light Division watch him closely, and are constantly getting under arms from various causes. Invidious feeling of certain persons in the army towards the Light Division. The French batteries open on Rodrigo. Their cavalry drive our pickets over the Azarva. Prognostications of some wiseacres in the army that the siege of Rodrigo would be raised by Lord Wellington. General Junot crosses the Azarva to reconnoiter our force. Captain Krauchenberg, of the 1st German Hussars, distinguishes himself. General Crawford retires across the Duas Casas, and takes up a position behind the Touron. General Junot's cautious manner of advancing. Query: Why did Massena never attempt to cut off the Light Division from the Coa with his numerous cavalry? Rodrigo surrenders to the French. General Crawford surprises a French detachment. Colonel Talbot, of the 14th Light Dragoons, killed. Gallantry of his regiment. Exemplary conduct of the French infantry in square. Observations..............*Page* 123

CHAPTER IX.

General Crawford falls back to Junsa, on the Coa. The French advance. Fort Conception is destroyed by mines. Action of the Coa, 24th July, 1810. Major M'Leod of the 43d regt. French grenadiers storm the bridge, and are destroyed. General Crawford retires at night to Valverde. Reflections on the events of the day. We march to Celerico, and make huts near the town. The Light Division is divided into two brigades. Massena besieges Almeida. The Light Division moves up to support the cavalry. The powder magazine in Almeida explodes and destroys the town. The garrison capitulates. Affair between our cavalry and the French near Freixadas. The army retires towards Coimbra. Excursion to the summit of a mountain to see a lake. Discussion with a padre as to the qualities attributed to its waters. We continue the retreat. The Light Division arrives at Mortagoa. Affair of cavalry. We fall back on Buzaco, engaged with the French advanced guard. Sketch of the position 144

CHAPTER X.

Battle of Buzaco. Flag of truce. General Simon's baggage brought in. Wounded of the two armies removed from the field. Terrible carnage in and near Sula. The light troops constantly engaged. Deserters come over to us. Their reports of Massena's intentions. The French army breaks up, and marches away to our left. Lord Wellington retires from Buzaco to the lines of Torres Vedras. Occurrences on the march. Stores destroyed at Pombal. King John's coffin in the cathedral at Battalha. Affair between our rear-guard and the French advanced guard. Our habitation takes fire, and we are nearly burnt out of it,—horses, mules, donkeys, and baggage. Affair of cavalry near Alcoentre. Speculations on Massena not having pursued us more vigorously in the retreat. The Light Division reaches Alemquer. The French turn us out of it without our dinners. We retire to Arruda in bad humour and in dreadful weather. An agreeable surprise. A word or two relative to the lines of Torres Vedras. Gun-boats on the Tagus. Jack Tar's zeal. Great sufferings of the Portuguese from the French invasion. Reconnoissances made by Massena, and skirmishes brought on by it. Sharp affair between Sir Brent Spencer's division and the enemy. Scarcity of provisions in the country in our front. Our employments whilst we remained in the lines. The French army falls back to a position behind the Rio Maior. Sentries of straw. We march in pursuit, and take some prisoners. Dead Frenchmen, horses, mules, and donkeys, on the road-side. The Light Division comes up with the enemy near Cartaxo. We are preparing to attack, when Lord Wellington arrives and countermands it. Causes thereof. The French retire across the Rio Maior. Rough sketch of their position. General Hill crosses the Tagus. The Light Division bivouac in a pine-wood. Washed out of a water-course by the rain. Lord Wellington makes demonstrations against the French position. The Light Division engaged with the enemy's light troops on the left. The troops are withdrawn.. *Page* 164

CHAPTER XI.

The Light Division holds the outposts at the bridge of Santarem. General Junot wounded near Rio Maior. The allied army is put into cantonments. How we passed the winter. Sufferings of the French army from want of provisions and forage. They are harassed by the armed peasantry and militia. Shooting and coursing parties close to the French videttes. Their courteous conduct on those occasions towards us. Anecdote of a dragoon and his cloak. Burlesque on horse-racing in the cantonments of the Light Division. Flags of truce. Conversation with French officers at the bridge of Santarem. Theatrical performances. The Marquis de la Romana dies. The Duke of Brunswick's corps joins the Light Division. They desert by wholesale to the French. Several are shot by sentence of a court-martial. The corps is sent out of the Light Division. Lord Wellington contemplates relieving the Light Division for a time at the outposts, to give the men rest. This is not carried into effect. Some regiments join the army from England. The 7th division of infantry is formed. I go with a brother-officer on a frolic to Lisbon for five days. Return to our old post at the bridge. Lieutenant Strenowitz, of the 1st German Hussars, surprises a French cavalry post. Marshal Mortier defeats a Spanish army near Badajoz, and lays siege to the place. Massena commences his retreat out of Portugal. State of Santarem. The 1st battalion 95th Riflemen drives the French from a village. The Light Division and cavalry come up with the French near Pombal. The castle is attacked. Action near Redinha. Reach Condeixa. The Portuguese militia gain possession of Coimbra. Massena changes his line of retreat. Lord Wellington attacks Marshal Ney. He falls back to Miranda de Corvo. Conduct of the French army during the retreat. The French leave numbers of baggage-animals on the road much lacerated. The Light Division finds the enemy on the Ceira. Action near Foz d'Aroce. Remarks. The army out-marches the commissariat. Major Stewart of the 95th Rifle corps. His character. Lord Wellington crosses the Alva. Massena retreats towards Celerico. Affair near Freixadas. The 95th loses its adjutant. His character. The army marches on Guarda. Massena falls back behind the Coa. Action near Sabugal. Colonel Beckwith .... *Page* 185

CHAPTER XII.

The French army re-enters Spain. They leave a garrison in Almeida, which is blockaded. The Light Division and 1st German Hussars take up their original line of posts. Skirmishes at Marialva bridge. Some companies of our corps are sent to shoot the cattle at Almeida. Massena assembles his army to relieve Almeida. The Light Division and 1st German Hussars fall back and join the army in position, near Fuentes d'Onoro. Battle of Fuentes d'Onoro. Flag of truce in the evening. The wounded removed. Conversation with some French officers. A sprig of nobility in the French army at the head of one of their Hussar regiments. Colonel Beckwith's brigade occupies Fuentes d'Onoro for the night. Precautions for its defence. The hostile armies remain close to each other for many days. Waggon-loads of wounded Frenchmen sent to Rodrigo. Marshal Marmont arrives from France. Assumes the command of the army in our front, and supersedes Massena. He inspects the infantry of the Imperial Guard within view of our position. The French army retires behind the Agueda. We resume our original line of outposts. Almeida is blown up, and the garrison escape. Marmont sends a cavalry force to reconnoiter Colonel Beckwith's brigade. We send them back faster than they advanced. Intelligence reaches us of the battle of Albuera. We celebrate the king's birth-day. Sudden order to march in the midst of our festivity. Affair between the 1st Royal Dragoons and the

French cavalry. We march into Alemtejo. A few lines relative to the march thither. Encamp on the Caya. Gallant but unsuccessful attempts against Fort San Christoval. The army offers battle to the united armies of Soult and Marmont. They decline the challenge, and fall back to Seville and Placentia. Terrible sickness in our army. Action of cavalry near Campo Maior. Fort La Lippe. I receive a present from a Portuguese don. Starved state of our horses. The army marches back to the northern frontier of Portugal. A bee-hive captured. Staff characters .... *Page* 209

CHAPTER XIII.

The Light Division crosses the Agueda. Lord Wellington reconnoiters Rodrigo. Don Julian Sanchez. The French governor taken prisoner by Guerillas. A picket of our light cavalry made prisoners in the Sierra de Gata. The Light Division reinforced by the third battalion of the 95th Rifle corps from Cadiz. Deaths by Alemtejo fever. I cross the mountains with my own company and one of Portuguese. Wild scenery. Goatherds. Their dress, language, and habitations. Rejoin the Light Division. Marmont advances to Rodrigo. The Light Division in position on the Vadillo. Gallant conduct of General Colville's brigade. The Light Division joins the 3d and 4th near Guinaldo. The army falls back to Aldea de Ponte. The Light Division engaged with the French cavalry and dismounted chasseurs. Brilliant charge of the Fusileer brigade. General Picton's light troops engaged. The army retires to Soita. Marmont follows the allied army no further, and falls back to Placentia. Our army goes into cantonments. Comparative merits of Spanish and English greyhounds. A new governor arrives at Rodrigo. Winter quarters in Spanish villages. Libraries not in vogue. An essay on cigars, and their utility in campaigning. A party made to shoot wild deer. General Hill surprises a French division. A shooting party in the mountains. Boleros, fandangos, and Irish jigs. Capital sport with the woodcocks. A good dancer and a particularly bad shot. Excursion to Robadillia. Just punishment inflicted on a demi-brigade of padres. The Light Division invests and lays siege to Ciudad Rodrigo. Redoubt of San Francisco stormed and taken. The siege and storming of Rodrigo. Death of Generals Crawford and M'Kinnon. Remarks on the defence made by the French governor. Contrast between the siege of 1810 and that of 1812. The army marches to the southward and besieges Badajoz. Difficulty of keeping our horses alive during the march. Siege of Badajoz. Storming of the place............ *Page* 227

CHAPTER XIV.

Marmont penetrates into Portugal during the siege. Lord Wellington marches back to the north. General Alten appointed to command the Light Division. The army advances to Salamanca. Takes up a position. Marmont's army opposite. A fortified convent in Salamanca is besieged by the 6th Division. It is set fire to, and the garrison capitulates. Marmont retreats behind the Douro. We follow him. A dance at Navis del Rey. Arrive at Rueda. Wine vaults. French soldiers assassinated by the Spaniards. Marmont is reinforced. The Light Division falls back to Castrejon. The French cross the Douro. Attack the troops at Castrejon. We fall back behind the Guarena, closely followed by Marmont. Beautiful evolutions of the two armies. The 27th and 40th regiments repulse the French with loss. Deaths from want of water and excessive heat. British six-pounders and French nines, with their respective advanced guards. Observations on the fire-arms of French and British dragoons. The two armies march within cannon-shot of each other for several days in succession. The Light Division crosses the Tormes, by a ford at night, in a tremendous thunder-storm. Battle of Salamanca. Marmont's promises to the Spaniards of destroying Lord Wellington's army not fulfilled. Opinions of certain British officers in the Portuguese army, as to the comparative merits of Portuguese, British, and French soldiers. Gallant attack of General Bock's cavalry brigade on the French rear-guard. We pursue the French many days. Various reports of Marmont's death. Corpse of the French General Ferez dug up and exposed to view by the Spaniards. We cross the Douro. Valladolid. Mode adopted of raising the wind to purchase bread, &c. The army marches on Madrid. Segovia. A beautiful Castilian. Palaces of El Rio Frio and San Ildefonso. Pass the Guadaramma mountains. Encamp in the park of the Escurial. The palace. Affair between some Portuguese and French cavalry. The army enters Madrid. Its reception. French garrison in the Retiro capitulates. A word or two about the capital. Its palace, streets, public walks, Castilian women, &c. Pheasant-shooting in Joseph Bonaparte's park. A grand ball. A bull-fight. Extravagant fondness of the Spaniards of both sexes for this amusement. Four divisions march to Burgos, and lay siege to the castle. Soult raises the siege of Cadiz and marches on Madrid. General Hill and Colonel Skerrit join the troops at Madrid. Colonel Skerrit repulses Soult's advanced guard at the bridge of Aranjuez. The Light Division marches to the front from Madrid. Soult passes the Tagus. We bid adieu, with great regret, to Madrid...... *Page* 260

CHAPTER XV.

Commence the retreat to Salamanca. A wild boar killed. The armies from Burgos and Madrid unite near Salamanca.

The army retreats to the Agueda. Sketch of the retreat. Rations of acorns and oak-leaves for man and horse. The Light Division engaged at San Munos. General Paget taken prisoner. We arrive at Rodrigo. The campaign of 1812 concludes. A few lines relative to it. We go into winter-quarters. Establish a regimental mess in an old barn. A supply of Douro wine. Vocal performers. Circular letter to officers commanding regiments, relative to the late retreat. The Light Division establish theatrical performances. Lydia Languish and Julia drink punch and smoke cigars behind the scenes. Coursing, woodcock-shooting, and Lord Wellington's fox-hounds. Boleros, fandangos, waltzes, &c. &c. in our village. Hot punch by no means disapproved of by our fair partners. Lord Wellington proceeds to Cadiz for a short time. The French general Foy makes an attempt to surprise General Hill's advanced post at Bejar, and is repulsed. General Kempt is appointed to command a brigade in the Light Division. Preparations for the campaign of 1813. Lord Wellington reviews the Light Division and 1st German Hussars. The Hussar Brigade, the Life Guards, and Blues, join the army, from England. The eight divisions of infantry, and by whom commanded.......... *Page* 289

CHAPTER XVI.

The campaign of 1813 opens. The 2d and Light Divisions march on Salamanca. Sir Thomas Graham, with the six other divisions, crosses the Douro. He advances to the Esla and crosses it. The Light Division encamps at San Munos. Contrast between our situation then with that of the 17th of November, 1812, on the same spot. We reach the Tormes. The French retire from Salamanca, and are pursued towards the Douro. They suffer from our horse artillery and cavalry. The Light Division crosses the

Douro at Toro. Brilliant affair of cavalry, wherein the Hussar brigade distinguishes itself. We follow the French to Palencia, and from thence to Burgos. The French blow up the castle of Burgos, and retreat behind the Ebro. We pass the Ebro at Puente Arena. Magnificent scenery. Appearance of the troops descending the pass. Language, dress, and appearance of the people northward of the Ebro. Beautiful scenery at every step. The Light Division surprises a French division near St. Millan. The French army assembles near Vittoria. Sale by auction in the camp of the Light Division. Ladies' dresses, &c. &c..... *Page* 304

CHAPTER XVII.

Battle of Vittoria. The Light Division and some cavalry pursue the French rear-guard on the road to Pampeluna. Engaged with them several days. Two French ladies restored to their husbands. Baron Alten directs the movements of the advanced guard with great judgment and effect. We take the last piece of artillery but one in possession of the French rear-guard. The country between Salvaterra and Pampeluna favourable for a retreating army. Reflections on approaching the Pyrenees. Lord Wellington marches with the 3d, 4th, and Light Divisions against General Clausel. A Spanish priest apprises that general of our movements, and mars our plans. Our benedictions on the said padre. We return to Pampeluna, and assist in the blockade. March into the Pyrenees. Splendid scenery. Sir Rowland Hill's corps engaged in the passes. Vale of San Estevan. A week spent there. Dress, language, &c. of the Spanish Basques. Trout-fishing on the Bidassoa. The Light Division advances to Vera. Drives the French out of it into the pass. The first view of the ocean for four years. Cheers of the soldiers on seeing it. Rough sketch of the position of our army in the Pyrenees. Quadrilles danced by our French neighbours in their encampment opposite to us. Sir Thomas Graham besieges St. Sebastian. The French entrench themselves in our front. An attempt to storm St. Sebastian fails. Marshal Soult attacks our right wing. It falls back towards Pampeluna. Defeats the French, and drives them again into France, with great slaughter. The 7th and Light Divisions fall back from Vera and Echelar. Soult's proclamation to his army before he attacked the allies in the Pyrenees. The Light Division makes forced marches to reach the bridge of Yanci. The Riflemen inflict a severe loss on the retreating columns of the French. General Kempt's brigade drives the enemy from a high mountain into France. Gallant attack made by General Barnes' brigade. The hostile armies occupy their former positions .... *Page* 317

CHAPTER XVIII.

We celebrate the anniversary of the formation of our corps. St. Sebastian is stormed and taken. The French pass the Bidassoa near Vera. Part of the Light Division engaged in that town. The French attack the Spaniards, and are repulsed. They retreat to the Bidassoa, and force the bridge of Vera at night. Movements of the Light Division on this occasion. Lord Aylmer's brigade joins the army from England. The left wing of the army passes the Bidassoa. The Light Division and Spaniards storm the entrenchments in the pass of Vera. Gallantry of Lieut.-Colonel Colbourne's brigade. A French gun-brig destroyed by British cruisers, in sight of both armies. Horrible weather in our mountain encampment. Tents continually blown down. Violent snow-storm. Two Portuguese soldiers of the pickets die from cold. Pampeluna surrenders. The army invades France. Battle of the Nivelle. Approach Bayonne. French entrenched camp. Position of the allied army. Soult reconnoiters our line of pickets. Skirmishes. The Light Division drives back the French advanced posts in its front .... *Page* 336

CHAPTER XIX.

Sir Rowland Hill passes the Nive. Battles of the Nive. The French are beaten in every attempt against us. We dance-in the New-year of 1814 at Arcanguez. Reflections on the past and present situations of the two armies. Soult manœuvres near Dax. We take the field for a few days in very inclement weather. Return to cantonments. Heavy fall of snow in the Pyrenees. Capital woodcock shooting. The army moves to its right. Our battalion marches to St. Jean de Luz for its new clothing. Sir John Hope blockades Bayonne. He passes the Adour. The Guards repulse a sortie from the garrison. We march from St. Jean de Luz to rejoin the army. Orthes. Handsome peasantry. We rejoin the Light Division. Soult makes demonstrations against Sir Rowland Hill's corps. The 15th Hussars attack a French cavalry post and take some prisoners. The 7th Division is detached to Bourdeaux. Lord Wellington marches on Tarbes. Affair near Vic Bigorre. Action near Tarbes. The French retreat towards Toulouse. We follow them. A pontoon-bridge is established below Toulouse. The army crosses............................... *Page* 351

CHAPTER XX.

Battle of Toulouse. The French retreat to Carcassone. The allied army enters Toulouse. Despatches reach Lord Wellington from Paris relative to Bonaparte's abdication, and his

CONTENTS.

departure for Elba. He transmits this information to Soult, who declines a cessation of hostilities. We march from Toulouse towards Carcassone. Count Gazan meets us with a flag of truce. Soult acknowledges the new order of things. Hostilities cease. The dismay of fire-eaters at the termination of the war in the Peninsula and south of France. Sortie of the French garrison from Bayonne. Some regiments embark at Bourdeaux for America. Five weeks at Castel Sarrazin. Soult's army reviewed at Montauban by the Duke d'Angoulême. We march to Bourdeaux. Take leave of our Portuguese allies. The parting. Arrive at Bourdeaux. Lord Wellington reviews the 43d, 52d, and 95th regiments. We embark for England .... *Page* 363

CHAPTER XXI.

CAMPAIGN OF 1815 IN FLANDERS.

Embark for Ostend. Proceed to Brussels. We are appointed to Sir Thomas Picton's division. Battle of Quatre Bras. Ligny. Predictions and foretellings *after* things have occurred, no uncommon practice. Fire-side tacticians and critics. The army falls back from Quatre Bras to Waterloo. The cavalry are engaged 372

CHAPTER XXII.

Sketch of the battle of Waterloo, but more particularly of the operations of Sir Thomas Picton's division. Death of Sir Thomas Picton. The 27th regiment. Advance of the Prussians. General attack on the French position, and their total defeat and route. The morning after the battle 383

CHAPTER XXIII.

March to Paris. Cambray is taken by escalade. Letters from Highlanders to their friends in the North. Half a dozen lines only relative to Paris. Another half dozen as to the three years spent by the army of occupation in the north of France. On the distribution of medals. The army evacuates France, and is dispersed all over the globe. Reflections on this breaking up of old friends and comrades. A campaign amongst the Glasgow radicals. Proceed to Ireland. Guarding jails, hunting stills and White Boys. A few words at parting with my military friends.. *Page* 396

ROUGH SKETCHES

OF THE

LIFE OF AN OLD SOLDIER.

CHAPTER I.

Join my regiment in Jersey. Embark for England. Winter at Chatham. The 52d regiment made Light Infantry. New system of drill introduced. Encamp at Shorncliffe in Kent. French camp and flotilla at Boulogne. Invasion threatened and precautions taken by Sir John Moore. The Duke of York reviews the troops at Shorncliffe. Sudden order for our regiment to embark for the West Indies. Unfortunate occurrence on the march from Shorncliffe to Portsmouth. Remarks thereon. Embark and sail for Barbadoes. Tremendous storm. Various occurrences on the voyage. Arrive at Barbadoes. First impressions as to climate, &c. Death of the Commander-in-Chief of the West Indies. We proceed to Antigua. The harbour and dock-yard. Disembark at midnight. Lose my baggage. Scarcity of fresh water in Antigua. The regiment suffers dreadfully from yellow fever. Its losses. Hurricane. Officers' funerals. The military governor and his brigade-major die. A receipt for yellow fever. Dancing and other gaieties. Death of Sir William Myers, the new Commander-in-Chief in the West Indies. Terrible mortality in his family. Death of the new Governor of Antigua. Great mortality in the 96th regiment in Antigua. A French squadron. Dominica is attacked. The French are repulsed by the 46th regiment. We expect a visit from the same squadron at Antigua. Preparations for its reception. We are reinforced. Long marches. Sudden death of several soldiers from excessive heat. The 68th regiment is sent to Antigua. Its immense losses by climate. Horse-races and balls at St. John's. More funerals. Lord Nelson arrives in search of the French and Spanish squadrons. He returns to Europe. My health begins to suffer. A medical board orders me to Europe for its restoration. My own ideas as to *slavery*. Take my passage for Europe. Sail to Tortola. Large homeward-bound fleet. Dreadful gales, and other mishaps on the voyage home. Anchor in Dublin Bay. Quarantine. Land at Dublin. Proceed to England.

THE same year in which the British army gained never-fading laurels in Egypt, I obtained a commission in the 70th regiment, and shortly after seeing my name in the Gazette, was ordered to join in the island of Jersey. I felt that delight which I fancy is experienced by most youngsters, on making an escape from school, putting on a scarlet coat, epaulet, cocked hat, and a tremendously long feather, to say nothing of the false queue affixed to a head of hair plastered with pomatum and well powdered (the custom of those days), together with sundry et ceteras too well known to military men to need a further detail.

The regiment had recently returned from service in the colonies; the officers in general were very young; and the soldiers, with the exception of a small number of old hands, were recruits, and on the whole a very fine body of men.

Jersey is rather better known than either the interior of Africa, or New Holland. A description of it would, therefore, be superfluous. During the eleven months which I spent in it, I made a tour round the island with some of my brother-officers, and we had every reason to be satisfied with our excursion. The roads, at the time I mention, scarcely deserved that name; but I understand that very excellent ones have been since made, in various directions.

Towards the end of October, 1802, the 3d regiment, or Buffs, arrived from England to relieve us, and we sailed in ships of war to Deal, where we disembarked, and marched to Dover Castle, in which we remained three weeks, and from thence proceeded to Chatham. The garrison consisted of my own regiment, the Royal Staff corps, and the first and second battalions of the 52d regiment. Sir John Moore commanded here.

To the winter which we passed in Chatham, with little to vary the scene except dock-yard guards, main guards, and sundry other guards, on which I constantly found myself posted, I do not look back with any particularly pleasurable recollections.

In the early part of the spring of 1803, Sir

John Moore picked and culled the finest and most effective men of the two battalions of the 52d regiment, the first of which Lieutenant-Colonel Kenneth M'Kenzie was appointed to command, and to organise as Light Infantry. The second battalion was then gazetted as the 96th regiment, and almost immediately afterwards sent to Ireland, under the command of Lieutenant-Colonel Conran.

The new system of drill which Lieutenant Colonel M'Kenzie introduced at this period, and which has been adopted by other light infantry regiments, it will scarcely be denied by the most prejudiced persons, has been attended with the most complete success. I allude to the ease and correctness with which the regiments drilled according to that system marched and manœuvred ever after.

In the month of June, 1803, we found ourselves encamped on the heights of Shorncliffe, in Kent, under Sir John Moore's command, the following regiments composing the brigade: the 4th or King's Own, the 52d Light Infantry, the 59th, the 70th, and five companies of the 95th Rifle Corps, with two pieces of light artillery. Every one knows, or ought to know, that at this time Bonaparte threatened our shores with a visit from his numerous army and flotilla, which were in and about Boulogne. We had no difficulty in seeing the immense mass of white tents on the French coast, when the day happened to be clear. Whether Sir John Moore entertained the same apprehension of invasion which the majority of the nation did, it is not for me to decide; but certain it is that every precaution was taken at night, by patrolling constantly along the beach until morning,—and by having the quarter and rear guards under arms one hour before day-break, and remaining so until we could clearly ascertain that our French neighbours had not ventured on the high seas with their flotilla. We were constantly practised to strike and pack our tents at the shortest notice, and occasionally to load the bât horses with them, and to make every preparation for a march. Thus passed the summer and autumn. The Duke of York reviewed the brigade on the heights of Shorncliffe in the course of the summer.

Towards the end of October, a sudden, and, on our part, unexpected order arrived for our regiment to march immediately to Portsmouth, to embark for the West Indies. This intelligence caused some long faces among a few of our old hands who had previously served in that part of the world; but the greater part of us being young and thoughtless, the order for moving, being a novelty, was received with pleasure rather than dislike.

We reached Portsmouth early in November,

but not without an occurrence having taken place on the march thither, which I have never forgotten. We halted one night at Battle, in Sussex. Some time after midnight, the officers were called out of their beds in consequence of an affray between some of our soldiers and a party of artillerymen; but before we could reach the small public-house in which the disturbance had arisen, most unfortunately two artillerymen were shot by our people, and another was bayoneted in the body. A corporal and two soldiers, who had committed this act, were left in the hands of the civil power. They were subsequently tried and acquitted; it having been proved that they used their muskets and bayonets in defence of their lives, which must have been sacrificed had they not done so, as the artillerymen, in great numbers, attacked them with bludgeons, and had already broken open the door of the public-house in which they were billeted. The three men in question joined us in the West Indies twelve months after. Some dispute as to the respective merits or demerits of certain regiments, led to this unhappy affair. A more dangerous subject cannot possibly be agitated by any military men, from the drumboy to the commandant of a regiment. No man is worthy to wear the uniform of his corps, be that corps what it may, who is not as tenacious of its good name as of his own individual character, and as ready to stand forward in its defence.

Early in November we embarked at Portsmouth in the Pandour (an old Dutch-built tub of a 44, armed *en flute*, and fitted up as a troop ship) and in the Comet transport. The Alexander transport also sailed under our convoy, taking out detachments for different regiments in the West Indies. A few days after our departure from Portsmouth, we encountered, in the skirts of the Bay of Biscay, a most tremendous gale, which lasted without intermission three days and nights, during the greater part of which the helm was lashed down; every stitch of canvass which we attempted to carry was torn to atoms in an instant —the pumps were choked—several feet of water were in the hold—and we had an accumulation of other nautical grievances and disasters, so numerous as to baffle a landsman's description of them. On the morning of the fourth day the gale abated considerably, and land was discovered; but, as no observation had been taken for several days, it seemed a matter of doubt what land it was. It proved to be the Start, or the Bolt, or one of the other iron-bound headlands eastward of Plymouth. The wind having come fair, we stood on again for the West Indies, although our commodore had it in contemplation, at one time, to put into Plymouth, and repair the damages sustained in the late gale.

Who does not know, that on reaching certain latitudes, one falls in with sharks, dolphins, flying fish, and various other kinds both of fish and birds, not found in the colder regions? I used to sit hour after hour endeavouring to harpoon the dolphins and other large fish, but generally with indifferent success. Somewhere between Madeira and Barbadoes we caught a large shark, to the infinite delight of myself and the other youngsters who had never previously navigated those seas. The operation of ducking, shaving, &c. &c., so scrupulously observed by the sailors in passing the tropical line, we avoided, by a liberal donation of rum to the sea-god.

In the course of the voyage, the old Pandour chased, brought to, and examined several vessels, all which proved to be Portuguese. One of them was a large and beautiful ship, bound from Lisbon to the Brazils, which, on first discovering her, was pronounced by our naval men to be a frigate. Our ship was cleared for action; the grenadier company was posted on the forecastle, and the light company on the poop; the remaining companies were ordered below, until they should be called up to board our supposed antagonist; but, after a chase of many hours, she turned out to be a neutral, and all our golden dreams of prize-money vanished in an instant.

Once fairly in the trade winds, we glided

smoothly along day after day, at six, seven, and eight knots an hour; nor did any thing occur worthy of notice until two or three days before arriving at Barbadoes, when a suspicious-looking, schooner-rigged vessel was discovered far to windward, on which our little convoy closed, by signal, to the commodore. The schooner followed many hours in the wake of the Pandour, but with a certain degree of caution. We had been running the whole day directly before the wind, and our commodore, getting tired, at last, of having this wasp of a vessel hovering about him, without being able to shake her off, or to put his paw on her, suddenly hauled the Pandour to the wind, as near as she could lay, which manœuvre the schooner performed as rapidly as ourselves, flew away into the wind's eye, soon distanced us, and put all chance of coming up with her out of the bounds of possibility, unless we might, by some good chance, injure her masts or rigging by our fire, which we kept up as long as any chance remained of its being effectual; but, as she outsailed us, we soon gave up the chase, and stood on our original course. All this was quite new, and very interesting to the fresh-water sailors on board.

After a six weeks' voyage from Portsmouth, we anchored on Christmas-day in Carlisle Bay, Barbadoes. The sky was cloudless, and the heat sufficiently intense to satisfy a salamander.

We could scarcely, at first, be reconciled to the idea of its being Christmas, with such a blazing sun over our heads; every tree and plant seen on the island being as green as we have them in England at Midsummer; and, above all, the total absence of snow, frost, and the dark and lowering clouds emblematic of that season in Europe. The Commander-in-Chief of the Windward and Leeward Islands, General Greenfield, died whilst we were on our passage out.

During the few days which we passed at anchor in Carlisle Bay, parties of our officers went ashore at Bridgetown, where we were hospitably entertained at the mess of the 64th regiment. Between the noise of lizards, musquitoes, and other tormenting devils, which sing and bite throughout the night, and unite all their efforts to destroy one's slumbers, I got but a small allowance of sleep, in spite of the liberal potation of old Madeira imbibed at the 64th mess. I may here remark, that during the whole of my stay in the West Indies, I suffered less than the generality of my brother-officers from the bites of musquitoes, although their eternal singing has tired my patience many a night.

Every thing which met the eye on our landing was, of course, quite new, and, for a time, interesting to the *Johnny Newcombes* of the regiment; but the novelty soon wore off, and I cannot say that any thing I saw, with the exception of the fine, bold, and striking scenery which many of the West India Islands present in passing them at sea, (or, in the nautical phrase, running down the islands), excited much interest in my mind. The 87th regiment, which was stationed at St. Kitt's, was ordered home on our arrival.

We sailed from Barbadoes about the 28th or 29th of December, and on the evening of the 31st anchored in English Harbour, in the island of Antigua. Entering this harbour from the ocean, by an extremely narrow and rocky passage, the effect is quite magical, as you instantaneously find your ship in a calm and well-sheltered basin, surrounded by high, rocky hills, studded in various parts with the houses and wigwams of the blacks and coloured people. The king's dock-yard is at the inner extremity of the basin. Soon after midnight we commenced disembarking in the dock-yard, from whence we marched to the Ridge and Shirly Heights Barracks, which we reached soon after day-break on the 1st of January, 1804. We relieved a detachment of the 64th regiment, which embarked a few days afterwards for Barbadoes. By the negligence of the guard left in charge of the baggage at the dock-yard, or by some other mishap, I lost every article of my baggage except one portmanteau. Few subalterns possessed a better kit than that which I lost on this occasion; but I never could gain any intelligence of it, nor was any remuneration allowed me to replace it. This was an inauspicious commencement in such a climate, where an abundance of linen and wearing apparel is so desirable.

It is singular that in the island of Antigua there is not one spring of fresh water. Consequently the inhabitants are dependent for their supply of this necessary article on the rains, which fall at certain periods in torrents, and are caught in tanks, with which the barracks, as well as the generality of the better class of houses, are provided. From January until June 1804, scarcely a drop of rain fell; so that for many weeks we were on an extremely small allowance of water. Even this would have been still more limited, had not several sloops been constantly employed, during this drought, in bringing barrels of water from the neighbouring island of Montserrat, and thereby replenishing the tanks. Although the members of the corps to which I had the honour to belong, were by no means addicted to the use of water as a beverage, we nevertheless suffered severely from its scarcity.

During the first five months after our arrival, the regiment continued comparatively healthy;

but in the month of June we were suddenly visited with an attack of yellow fever, that eternal curse and scourge of Europeans, which in a few days filled the hospitals to such an excess as has, perhaps, never been exceeded in any regiment, and but rarely equalled. Between the months of June and October we buried two-thirds of the officers who came out with the regiment from England, six of whom were captains. The ravages occasioned by this infernal pestilence amongst the soldiers, their wives, and children, bore a full proportion to that of the officers; nor did there appear any symptom of the fever subsiding, until the islands were visited, in the month of October, by one of the most violent hurricanes which had been experienced for many years. Intermitting fevers and agues now took the place of the yellow fever, which seemed to have nearly expended its fury. In short, by the end of 1804, the regiment was a perfect skeleton, and could with great difficulty furnish men to perform the regimental duties.

We buried also, at this period, the military governor, General Dunlop, and his brigade-major, Captain Vans, both of whom came out with us from England in the Pandour. The deaths were so frequent, that General Dunlop directed the procession and forms usually observed at military funerals to be discontinued, and that the coffins of officers deceased should be carried to the grave on the shoulders of the soldiers, without band or drums, and without a party to fire over them. This I have ever thought a most prudent order; for what can so much tend to depress the spirits as the constant recurrence of that imposing ceremony. The general expressed a wish that, in the event of his own death, he should be buried precisely in a similar manner. This order was obeyed to the letter; and both he and his brigade-major, who died within a few days of each other, were taken to their graves in a light waggon, attended by the few of our officers and soldiers who were able to do duty, and by a small party of artillerymen.

As a proof that this dreadful fever visits Europeans newly arrived with tenfold virulence, the three companies of the 37th regiment, in garrison with us at this time, had not more than two or three men in hospital, whilst our men were dying at the rate of eight and ten daily. The 37th had been several years in Trinidad and other islands, and were seasoned to the climate. In 1805, the survivors amongst us were, in some measure, seasoned, and the deaths consequently were not so frequent.

For the benefit and edification of the faculty, I must commit to paper the following fact, for the accuracy of which I pledge myself, although

I fear there are but few living witnesses to bear me out in my assertion.

At the time when almost every officer was on the sick-list, and the fever raged with the utmost fury, I felt every symptom which I had heard described by so many of my friends who had been attacked, and had fallen victims to the disorder. Violent pains, flushed face, my eyes burning as if ready to start from their sockets, excessive languor and thirst, made me think it more than probable that my turn had at length arrived to be carried to the little town of Falmouth, and my bones to be deposited in the churchyard. This attack, which took place in the evening, was extremely sudden, for I was in rude health two hours before. I instantly went to bed without consulting any one, ordered my servant to bring me a jug of boiling Madeira, which I swallowed, and soon fell into a sound sleep; from which I did not awake until six or seven hours afterwards. The fever had entirely left me, but I was so debilitated as not to recover from its short attack in less than ten days or a fortnight. I must endeavour to throw a light on this case of mine, by explaining to my medical friends, that I attribute the preservation of my life to the boiling Madeira, inasmuch as it produced a most violent perspiration, which, with my youth and a strong constitution, proved an overmatch for the fever, and rescued me from its grasp. It was a kill or cure business, and worthy only of a wild youth, who, in after-years, has often looked back with astonishment at his folly, and at the success which attended his mad-brained remedy. If a constant exposure to the sun in shooting, boating, riding, &c. &c., contrary to the repeated advice of old and experienced West Indians, were causes likely to produce effects fatal to a newly-arrived European, I most certainly did deserve to suffer.

West Indians are proverbially fond of dancing, and are not satisfied either with a moderate allowance of it. Often have we retired at day-break from private dances, bathed, and dressed for parade, without attempting to procure a moment's sleep until the following night. Such frolics as these, aided by liberal potations of sangaree, cold punch, and other fluids, throughout the evening, cannot long be played off with impunity, even in climates less destructive than the one in question.

Sir William Myers, the Commander-in-chief of the Windward and Leeward Islands, came out to take the command whilst I was in the country; and out of fifteen or sixteen members of his family, including servants, who accompanied him from England, eleven, besides himself, died at Barbadoes in an incredibly short space of time.

Brigadier-general Vandeleur, who came out from Ireland in 1804, and was appointed to command the troops in the Island of Antigua after General Dunlop's death, survived but a few months. The mortality in the 96th regiment, which arrived at Antigua from Ireland in 1805, was quite dreadful; and perhaps but little less so than that of our own corps the preceding year. Antigua was at this period, indeed, almost a certain grave for newly arrived Europeans. Bad as it still is, however, it cannot be doubted that the troops stationed there of late years have suffered in a comparatively trifling degree.

About this period a French squadron appeared in those seas with some thousand troops on board. They disembarked in considerable force at Dominica; but the Governor, General Prevost, repulsed them in various engagements, and finally compelled them to re-embark with loss, and to return to Guadaloupe or Martinique. The conduct of the 46th regiment throughout the whole business was particularly gallant.

At Antigua we were for some time afterwards in expectation of a visit from the French squadron, and every preparation was made for its reception which our slender means afforded. We were reinforced by the flank companies of the 11th regiment, from some of the neighbouring islands: we made several long marches and counter-marches, from one part of the island to another, in consequence of various false alarms; but the enemy never landed. Five of our soldiers died on the road from *coup de soleil*, during one very long march in the heat of the day. Their deaths were almost instantaneous. My servant, a young, active, and healthy man, was one of those who died in this manner.

The 68th regiment was sent to Antigua in 1805, with its ranks sadly reduced by the climate. It had arrived in the West Indies about five years before, with two battalions, each 1200 strong; and I have understood from their officers, that they had buried in those five years 2400 men and sixty-eight officers. The regiment had, of course, received repeated drafts of men from England during that period.

Towards the end of October 1804, the air being somewhat cooled by the rains which fell during the hurricane, several days were devoted to horse-racing, in the vicinity of St. John's, the principal town of Antigua. The course is circular, and not bad. A little thorough-bred chestnut English horse won every thing, and found no difficulty in beating all the American and Creole horses which started against him. The amusements of the day were followed by balls at night, which were kept up until day-break each morning.

Two officers of our regiment died in consequence of having partaken too freely of the gaieties of the race week. They were remarkably fine-looking men, and both grenadiers. One of them was a most intimate friend of mine, and I have ever regretted his loss.

In June or July 1805, Lord Nelson arrived in the West Indies, in pursuit of the combined French and Spanish squadrons, and remained for some hours off the island of Antigua. That he instantly returned to Europe, not having found the object of his search in those seas, is well known; as is also the terrible example which he made of the combined fleets a few months afterwards off Trafalgar.

The effects of constant exposure to the sun, with other peccadilloes not warrantable in a climate such as this, having begun to shew themselves on me in the shape of a slow and debilitating fever, a medical board, which assembled to consider my case, decreed that an immediate removal to Europe was the only chance of my health being re-established.

Before I bid adieu to the spot where so many of my earliest and much-valued military friends and companions were taken prematurely to their long homes, I must say a word or two on the idea which I formed of the system of slavery. I am well aware that different persons look at this question in different points of view; but I am willing, nevertheless, to believe, that the numbers in England who view it with the same degree of indignation, horror, and disgust, which I ever have done, preponderate beyond all comparison; and that the time is not far distant, when the voices of those will be silenced who are not ashamed to declare, that an unfortunate negro, writhing under the lash of the merciless slave-driver, for laying aside his spade for a few minutes in the heat of a tropical sun, or for some offence equally trivial, is infinitely better off, decidedly more happy, and in a more enviable situation, than the labouring peasant in the mother country. Facts are stubborn things; and although many years have rolled over my head since I left the West Indies, I have not yet forgotten what the system of slavery was in 1803, 1804, and 1805. The first exhibition of the kind which met my eye a few days after landing in Antigua, was a huge slave-driver flogging most unmercifully an old decrepit female negro, who appeared bowed down with misery and hard labour. I know not what her offence was, but she was one of a gang, as they are termed, of negroes of different sexes and ages, working with spades under a midday tropical sun. A brother-officer, who was with me on a shooting excursion, felt as astonished and indignant at this unnatural and inhuman proceeding as myself; and our first impulse was to threaten to shoot the driver if he did not desist. I am not ashamed to say, that, after drawing off to such a distance that our small shot could not seriously injure the vagabond, we peppered his legs pretty handsomely. That we should have adopted so summary a mode of punishment, had we lived twice as long in the world, I will not say; but my conscience has never reproached me for the steps which we took to shew our disapprobation of the diabolical act. I adduce this as only one of the numerous instances of flogging which I had ocular demonstration of. I have too often witnessed the application of the lash to old and young, male and female, and have too frequently heard their cries and lamentations, ever to forget it:—nor shall I ever cease to hold in utter detestation and abhorrence this infernal system. I have several times been on board vessels laden with slaves from the coast of Guinea; and I have no hesitation in saying, that the most highly coloured description of this vile traffic ever given, falls short of the reality of the sufferings of those cargoes of ill-fated human beings. Emancipation of the negroes must necessarily be gradual; but I am one of those who hope most sincerely that it will in due time be effected.

Having taken my passage with two officers of the 18th and 96th regiments, in a merchantman, bound to Dublin, I bade adieu to Antigua, and sailed under convoy of the Netley schooner to Tortola, the grand rendezvous of the homeward-bound fleet, which amounted to 260 sail. Here we remained at anchor two or three days, and then took our final departure for Europe, under a strong convoy of ships of war. It was a magnificent sight, when the whole of this immense fleet weighed and stood out of the harbour. In consequence of adverse winds, constant gales, and so forth, our passage home occupied thirteen weeks, which was more than double the time we were in making the passage out from Portsmouth to Barbadoes in 1803. This unusually long and tedious voyage, in a dirty old sugar-ship, during the last five weeks of which we were on an extremely short allowance of fresh water and provisions, was unmarked by any occurrence worthy of notice, except that, somewhere about the latitude of the Western Islands, we encountered a terrible storm, which lasted two days, during which seven vessels of the fleet foundered, and three individuals only of all their crews were saved, who were picked up by the Ramillies, 74, clinging to a piece of a wreck. One note more on the disasters of our tedious voyage, and I have done with the subject.

In the month of September, about two hours after midnight, it blowing very fresh, we were almost thrown out of our berths by a sudden shock, as if the ship had struck on a rock. In an instant we bolted on deck, where all was dismay and confusion. A vessel, considerably larger than our own, had run aboard us, and the two ships were hanging together by the yards and rigging, as if they had been lashed for the purpose of boarding; nor did any chance appear of their being extricated. Every swell of the sea caused the ships to thump against each other, and to give such frightful shocks, as can only be fully understood by those who have been in a similar situation. I confess, that when I saw the master of our ship, who was a Catholic, on his knees crossing himself and giving up all for lost, instead of stimulating his crew, as his mate fortunately did, to make some efforts to cut away parts of the yards and rigging, in order to disengage us from our unwelcome neighbour, I thought I might just as well have left my bones in Antigua, as become a prey to sharks. Thanks to our mate and the exertions of our little crew, the vessels at length got clear of each other. We sustained serious injury in the rigging, yards, &c., and had our jib-boom carried away. In addition to these disasters, a leak was sprung, which kept our pumps constantly going during the remainder of the voyage; and every one on board, passengers and all, was obliged to take his turn. One of the frigates seeing our signal of distress flying at day-break, sent an officer, with a party of men and some carpenters, to repair our damages, who remained with us two days.

In the winter of 1805 we anchored in Dublin Bay, the beauties of which are universally known and acknowledged, and have been a thousand times described by far abler pens than mine. Had we not been doomed to perform quarantine in this magnificent bay for many days, I believe my retrospective view of it would have been infinitely more pleasing. To us landsmen, after a three months' voyage, wishing the yellow flag at the devil, and looking wistfully at the shore without being permitted to land, it was no small delight to be informed, after six or seven days' penance thus performed, that we were at liberty to go ashore.

I spent several days very pleasantly at Dublin, with the two officers who came home with me from Antigua. One of them returned to the West Indies the following year, and fell a victim to the climate; the other was promoted into the 45th regiment, and died in Portugal some years afterwards.

I embarked in the packet, and reached Holyhead after a stormy passage of thirty-six hours, and proceeded to my home, from which I had been absent four years.

CHAPTER II.

Exchange into the 95th Rifle Corps. Expedition to Denmark. Sail to Elsineur. Imposing appearance of our numerous fleet. Scenery on the Danish and Swedish coasts. A party to Elsineur. Cronberg castle. Hamlet's garden. Disorderly conduct of the Danes. Causes thereof. The army disembarks. The reserve commanded by Sir Arthur Wellesley. Advance towards Copenhagen. A sortie made by the garrison. Affairs between the Danish gun-boats and our advanced squadron. Ludicrous nocturnal affair at the outposts. The Danish pickets are driven in. The reserve is sent into the interior of the island of Zealand. Affair near Kioge with the Danish militia. A sortie from Copenhagen repulsed by Lieut. Light, of the 50th regiment. Bombardment of Copenhagen, and surrender of the Danish fleet and stores. Visit to the capital. Its deplorable appearance. The army re-embarks. List of Danish prizes. A large fleet of homeward-bound merchantmen joins us. We sail for England. A slight sketch of the Danes, and of the island of Zealand. Stormy passage to England.

THREE months out of the six which had been granted me to return to Europe for the recovery of my health, were already expended on the voyage home, and it consequently became indispensably necessary that one of two measures should be decided on without loss of time. Either to rejoin my regiment, and spend some of the best years of my life in a sugar island, where cold punch, sangaree, cigar-smoking, musquito bites, and every now and then a friend swept off by yellow fever, were the only varieties I had to calculate on; or to exchange into one of the regiments in England or Ireland, whereby I should stand a fair chance of participating in any service going on in Europe or elsewhere, as the fates might decree.

When encamped, in 1803, at Shorncliffe, with the 95th Rifle Corps, I took a particular fancy to it, and ever afterwards wished most ardently to wear a green jacket. On my return from the West Indies, this wish being by no means lessened, I lost no time in feeling the pulse of the captains of that corps; and, to my great joy, found one of them disposed to exchange his green jacket for a red coat, and to try his fortune in Antigua. I was shortly afterwards gazetted, and found myself fully accoutered as a rifleman, and stationed with my regiment in Kent, early in the spring of 1806.

Towards the end of that year, the battalion to which I belonged received orders to be in readiness for immediate embarkation. Report said that the Marquess of Hastings was to command the expedition; but we received counter-orders, and no embarkation took place that year.

In the summer of 1807, government having decided on sending a powerful fleet and army to the island of Zealand, in order to get possession of the Danish fleet, the battalion to which I belonged embarked in July at Deal—sailed the latter end of that month—passed the Sound on the 8th of August—and anchored between Elsineur and Copenhagen. The strikingly bold and romantic scenery which the coast of Sweden presents before reaching the Sound, afforded us much pleasure. From the fishing-boats which came off we were abundantly supplied with excellent fish, and at an inconceivably moderate rate.

Between Elsineur and Copenhagen our numerous fleet of line-of-battle ships, frigates, sloops of war, gun-brigs, bomb-vessels, and transports, containing upwards of twenty thousand troops, lay at anchor; and a more magnificent and imposing sight cannot well be conceived.

The fine beech forests on the Danish coast, growing in many places down to the water's edge; the bolder and more marked scenery on the Swedish side; the distant view of Copenhagen, with its formidable floating batteries; and, in an opposite direction, the castle of Cronberg, with the towns of Helsenburg on the Swedish shore, and Elsineur on the Danish,—form a picture which I can scarcely imagine to be exceeded in beauty and interest.

During the six or seven days after our arrival, which were spent in negotiations, and before it was finally resolved that our army should be landed, to obtain by force that fleet which the Danish authorities refused to place in our hands, I went ashore with a party of our officers at Elsineur. Of Cronberg castle, we were, of course, not permitted to see more than the exterior, which appeared extremely formidable. In the town of Elsineur I can remember to have seen but little either to amuse or interest. We lost no time in procuring a person to conduct us to Hamlet's garden, which is in the vicinity of Elsineur; and our guide, who was an antiquated female, affected to point out with great precision and exactness the identical spot where the old king of Denmark slept at the time he met his death by the hands of his brother. I recollect nothing peculiar in the garden itself, it being like a hundred other gardens which I have seen elsewhere.

On returning to the boat, about sunset, to go on board our transport, a large concourse of Danish sailors, and of the lower orders of inhabitants of Elsineur, assembled in a tumultuous manner on the pier, and were by no means nice or scrupulous as to the manner in which they conducted themselves towards any Englishman then ashore. A captain of our navy and his boat's crew were maltreated, and some of them thrown into the water. Our party did not escape without being hustled and jostled and pushed into our boat. We effected our retreat, however, in good order, and reached our ship without any serious mishap.

That the Danes should have conducted themselves so uncourteously on this occasion, is not to be wondered at;—for it appeared that the final answer from the Danish authorities in Copenhagen had been received on that day by Lord Cathcart and Admiral Gambier, the commanders of our fleet and army, refusing to deliver the Danish fleet into our hands. The alternative was consequently soon known at Elsineur, that hostilities would immediately commence. It may also easily be imagined that the conflict which took place a few years before, between the British fleet under Lord Nelson, and the Danish fleet and floating batteries at Copenhagen, was still fresh in the recollection of thousands of the inhabitants, who had witnessed it from the shore; nor is it probable that they had yet forgiven us for the destruction of their fleet, and the dreadful carnage occasioned by their brave defence of it.

On the 15th of August the army received orders to land on the following morning. The reserve was under the command of Major-general Sir Arthur Wellesley, and consisted of the 1st battalion 43d Light Infantry, the 2d battalion 52d

Light Infantry, the 92d Highlanders, with five companies of the 1st and five of the 2d battalion 95th Rifle Corps. The remainder of the two battalions of our regiment were, at this time, in South America, under Generals Whitelock and Sir Samuel Auchmuty.

Before day-break, on the 16th of August, we were in the boats and launches, and rowed rapidly towards the shore, over a sea as smooth as a mirror. We landed, without opposition, on a sandy beach; and some large woods being in the vicinity, Sir Arthur Wellesley immediately directed the companies of our corps to penetrate them and reconnoitre the different roads and paths. This having been done, the division advanced in the direction of Copenhagen, and bivouacked at night near a village, without having encountered any thing more formidable than a few armed peasants, who fled at our approach.

The next morning, at day-break, we again moved forward, and, with other divisions of the army, occupied the different roads leading to the capital, and took possession of such houses as were eligible, from their situation, for quartering the troops. As the army closed on the city, the fleet approached it also.

A day or two after we had taken post round the city, a sortie was made from the garrison, its principal force being directed towards the left of our position, near the sea, whilst some light troops kept us in play by skirmishing with our centre. This movement of the Danes was supported on the left by their gun-boats, which cannonaded our posts near the shore, and were also warmly engaged with the vessels of our advanced squadron. They were driven back, without much loss on our part. There were several sharp affairs between the Danish gun-boats and the brigs, bomb-vessels, &c. &c. of our fleet, at various times, the whole of which we could distinctly see from the shore. The sea appeared quite alive with the incessant plunging of shot and shells in various directions.

A ludicrous occurrence took place a few days after we landed. Shortly after dark, the reserve got under arms in great haste, in consequence of some firing in our front from one of the pickets of the division. Sir Arthur Wellesley and his staff were soon on the spot; and the alarm was found to have been occasioned by some unfortunate Danish horses which had strayed from their farm-yard. These animals came galloping down the road which led to the picket, with their collars, chains, and other apparatus, with which they had been fastened all day to the plough or harrow, and from which they had not been disencumbered. The officer who commanded the picket, hearing the galloping and clanking of chains, hesitated not a moment to open a fire on the road where the ill-fated quadrupeds were amusing themselves with kicking, frisking, and various other gambols, after their day's labour. "Blaze away, my brave fellows! we are attacked by cavalry!" was the order promptly given, and instantly executed by the picket; and blaze away they did, to the no small annoyance of friend and foe: for we may conclude that the Danish out-posts, as well as our own, got under arms, and remained so until matters were explained. The return of killed and wounded of the Danish cavalry, in this nocturnal affair, was never clearly ascertained.

On the 24th of August, at break of day, the whole army drove in the Danish out-post, each division clearing its own immediate front, and causing the Danish pickets to take shelter under the guns of the town. We had some skirmishing with them amongst the gardens and suburbs, but with a trifling loss on our side.

A day or two afterwards, the reserve was ordered to march into the interior of the island, to disperse a large body of militia and armed peasantry which had assembled. Some troops, commanded by General Linsingen, were also placed under Sir A. Wellesley's command, consisting of hussars, light infantry, and light artillery, of the German Legion. On the 29th of August, after three or four days' march, we found this body of

Danish militia in a position near the village of Kioge, with many pieces of artillery, indifferently appointed. Sir A. Wellesley lost no time in attacking them; nor did he experience much difficulty in defeating and dispersing this ill-disciplined force. We took from them their artillery, fifteen hundred prisoners, and some ammunition, stores, &c. &c. Our loss in this affair was very trifling, as it was impossible that the Danes could offer any effectual resistance to disciplined troops. Their numbers have been rated as high as fifteen thousand; but I believe it to have been vastly exaggerated. In order to render the dispersion of this body complete, and to prevent it from reuniting, our division and General Linsingen's corps occupied different towns and villages in the interior of the island; but the inhabitants evinced no disposition to disturb us. Sir A. Wellesley enforced the strictest discipline in his division, which may, in a great measure, account for the good understanding which existed between the troops and the inhabitants. In October, the reserve was still more scattered and detached in towns and villages on the Belt.

Whilst Sir A. Wellesley was carrying on those operations in the interior, the siege of Copenhagen was prosecuted with vigour by the other divisions of the army, aided by the fleet. A sortie was made before daylight one morning, and was stopped by Lieut. Light, of the 50th regiment, whose gallant conduct at the head of his picket merited every encomium. On the 2d of September, our mortar-batteries and the bomb-vessels of the fleet opened a tremendous fire of shells and rockets, with such effect, that the unfortunate city was soon in flames in various places; and the wooden steeple of a large church or cathedral fell down, and spread the flames still farther around, thereby increasing the danger.

To save the ill-fated capital from total destruction, the Governor, General Peymaun, sent out a flag of truce on the 5th of September, and a capitulation was drawn up, by which the citadel was to be placed in the hands of our troops, together with the dock-yard, and the whole of their fleet and stores. The news of the capitulation reached us a few days after it was concluded, our division being at this time several marches from Copenhagen. I obtained leave of absence to visit the capital, which the British officers were allowed to enter with passports signed by a general officer. Having procured one, signed by General Ludlow, of the Guards, I spent five days with a party of my brother-officers at a capital hotel.

Callous and insensible must he have been who could have walked through the streets and witnessed the horrors occasioned by the bombardment, and the misery inflicted on thousands of the unoffending inhabitants, without bitterly regretting that our government should have considered it necessary to adopt such rigorous measures. The museum and observatory escaped the conflagration. From the ground to the summit of the observatory, the passage is extremely broad, and gradual in its ascent, and it commands a magnificent view of the city, the sea, and the country around to a considerable extent. One-third of the city was destroyed by the bombardment; consequently there was an appearance of confusion and irregularity in the parts which had suffered most.

About the middle of October, the working parties from the fleet and army having cleared the dock-yard of all the stores and the whole of the Danish fleet, preparations were made for the embarkation of the army, and our return to England. The reserve was withdrawn from the interior; and before the end of October the whole army was on board ship. The first and second battalions of our regiment embarked in the Princess Caroline, a Danish prize of 74 guns.

Eighteen Danish ships of the line, sixteen frigates, nine gun-brigs, and twenty-five gun-boats, being the whole of their naval force, were taken possession of and carried to England, with the exception of three or four, which were destroyed as not sea-worthy, or in too unfinished a state for the voyage.

By the time the embarkation was completed, a numerous fleet of homeward-bound merchantmen, from different parts of the Baltic, joined us, to take advantage of the convoy; and at length we set sail for England, with a fleet which, including ships of war, prizes, transports, and merchantmen, amounted to nearly five hundred sail; the largest, perhaps, ever assembled in the Baltic or elsewhere.

The castle of Cronberg did not fire on the fleet as we passed out of the Sound; and, indeed, had the Danes been disposed to do so, we could, by keeping near the Swedish shore, have avoided any ill effects from their batteries. We had every reason to be satisfied, during our stay in Denmark, with the conduct of the inhabitants, who, although they did not attempt to conceal their displeasure at our having landed, burnt their capital, and taken possession of their fleet, behaved uniformly with civility towards us; and, with the exception of the circumstance which took place at Elsineur two days before we landed, to which I have already alluded, I did not hear of an individual having been abused or ill-treated, even in the capital, notwithstanding that swarms of British officers were there throughout the day and night, and even before the flames which had consumed their houses were thoroughly extinguished. There are few capitals, similarly circumstanced, in which assassinations would not have taken place without number, particularly in the southern parts of Europe.

From our short sojourn in Denmark, I am well inclined to respect the Danes as a brave, honourable, and manly people. Their peasantry are quiet, orderly, and industrious; and as totally free from the preposterous pride of the Spanish peasant, as of the cringing servility of the Portuguese. The parts of the island of Zealand through which Sir A. Wellesley's division marched, in our little expedition into the interior, is by no means without interest. There appeared to be no lack of cultivation, nor any symptom of want among the peasantry. The features of the country are, in general, not marked or bold; but the fine forests of beech, with various lakes, form altogether a pleasing picture.

After a passage of about four weeks from the Sound, in which we experienced a succession of heavy gales, and in which some vessels of the fleet foundered, or were wrecked on the coast of Holland, we anchored in the Downs; and our regiment disembarked in large pilot-boats, in a very heavy sea, which broke over us the moment we touched the beach at Deal. We marched the following day to Hythe barracks, in Kent, where we were stationed during the winter: here we were shortly afterwards joined by the companies of our two battalions which returned from South America, after the storming of Monte Video, under Sir Samuel Auchmuty, and the subsequently disastrous and ill-fated expedition to Buenos Ayres, under General Whitelocke. Their loss in officers and men had been very severe.

CHAPTER III.

Four companies of our 2d battalion embark. Sail to Cork, and join an expedition. Its destination. Boating excursions. The expedition sails. We anchor in Mondego Bay. Brigadier-general Fane's brigade. The army disembarks in Portugal. Monks, friars, padres, and Portuguese females. March to Lavaos. Joined by troops under General Spencer. A present from the Portuguese junta. A Dutch concert. The army advances. Features of the country. Reach Lyria. Swiss deserters. Affair with the French near Obidos. Battle of Roleia. A close shave and a narrow escape. Lieutenant Cockrane. March to Lourinha. Reinforcements join the army from England. Battle of Vimiera. Sir H. Burrard arrives to take the command. A flag of truce. Convention of Cintra. Reflections thereon. Sir John Moore arrives. The British army encamps near Lisbon. Amity between the French and English soldiers in Lisbon. Lisbon. Its opera, &c. &c. An eccentric Highland chieftain. Fevers and agues; and by what means a person so afflicted may be rendered still more miserable.

In the spring following (1808), four companies of our battalion, of which my own was one, embarked at Dover and sailed to Cork, the grand rendezvous appointed for an expedition, to be commanded by Sir Arthur Wellesley; but of its destination we knew nothing certain. The general opinion was, that South America was the point against which the expedition was to be directed. Indeed, we provided sea-stock for a long voyage. During the four or five weeks which we remained in the Cove of Cork, waiting the arrival of Sir A. Wellesley from England, we amused ourselves with boating parties to Glanmyre, and other places of considerable beauty on the river, and in frequent trips to the city.

About the second week in July the expedition sailed, and at the expiration of a fortnight we were off the coast of Portugal, near Oporto, whence we steered to Mondego bay and anchored. Although the weather was perfectly calm, I never remember to have experienced more motion in a gale of wind, than we felt during the six days spent at this anchorage. The long and heavy swell made the yards of the ship at times almost touch the water, as she rolled from side to side, which caused some awful breakages amongst our wine-glasses and crockery-ware.

On the 1st of August, Brigadier-general Fane's brigade, consisting of the 45th regiment, the 5th battalion of the 60th (German riflemen), and our own four companies, disembarked at the mouth of the Mondego river. The disembarkation of the whole army followed as rapidly as the boats could accomplish it; and the process of passing the bar of sand, on which there is, even in the finest weather, a dangerous surf running, was effected, I believe, without any thing more serious than some wet jackets. Whilst we were drawing up our men near the landing-place, and waiting for further orders, we were beset with a host of padres, friars, and monks, of all ages, each carrying a huge umbrella of the most gaudy colour imaginable; intended, no doubt, to protect their complexions, which vied with those of chimney sweeps. These gentry welcomed us with *vivas*, and protested that, with our assistance, every Frenchman in Portugal should speedily be annihilated. Our visitors were not confined to the male sex; for some olive beauties, with sparkling eyes and jet black hair, were induced to take a peep at us; and, before we parted, some of the more favoured of us were presented with flowers and fruit from the hands of these damsels.

Keeping our right towards the sea, we marched several miles over an uninterrupted plain of white sand, hot enough almost to have dressed a beef-steak, into which we sunk ankle deep at every step. The troops having been on board ship so many weeks, were much fatigued with this their first day's march. We encamped near the village of Lavaos, where the whole of the army assembled as soon as the disembarkation was effected. Here we remained upwards of a week, during which several regiments, that had been some time before embarked, under General Spencer's command, landed and joined us.

The Portuguese Junta, at the head of which, I believe, was the Bishop of Oporto, or of Coimbra, sent a present to our army, consisting of pigs, sheep, poultry, cart-loads of fruit, vegetables, and wine, the arrival of which at camp was highly acceptable; but the squeaking of pigs—the bleating of sheep — the various and discordant notes of geese, ducks, fowls, and turkeys—with the diabolical groaning of the carts, the wheels of which are never greased in Portugal, created such a concert of vocal and instrumental music, as no description could do justice to. The first week after our disembarkation was employed in landing provisions, ammunition, and stores, and in making the necessary preparations for our advance on Lisbon, which was occupied by General Junot, the Duke of Abrantes, with the main body of the French army.

About the 9th or 10th of August the army moved forward, the advance guard being formed by some squadrons of the 20th Light Dragoons and General Fane's brigade. Large pine woods, growing on an arid, white, sandy soil, occasionally varied by uncultivated heaths, with here and there a vineyard, constituted the chief features of the country through which we passed, in our march of two or three days, from the camp of Lavaos to

Lyria. We remained in bivouac a day near this city, which had, a short time before, been visited by a considerable French force, detached from Lisbon to levy contributions on the different towns. Here they were guilty of atrocities which exceeded belief. The town bore every mark of recent depredation, plunder, and excess of all kinds. The walls of a convent, into which I went with some other officers, were covered with blood and brains in many places; damning proofs of the scenes which had been recently acted there, in spite of the attempts made by some persons to exculpate the French, and to prove the assertions of the Portuguese exaggerated. What unprejudiced person, who has served in the Peninsular war, will say, that an exaggeration of facts is necessary to rouse feelings of indignation against the French for their countless acts of merciless cruelty towards the people of Spain and Portugal?

Leaving Lyria, we marched in the direction of Lisbon, our advanced guard being in constant expectation of coming up with detached parts of the enemy, who were known to be falling back gradually as we advanced. As yet, the only specimens of the French army which we had seen, were five Swiss deserters, from their infantry, clothed in scarlet, and remarkably fine-looking men. The time, however, was at hand, when we were to see and to have a brush with them.

On the 15th of August, after a long march, a party of French cavalry and infantry were found near the town of Obidos, where there is a Moorish castle. Four companies of ours and of the 60th regiment instantly attacked and obliged them to retire. In the ardour of pursuit, our people pushed on a considerable distance from any support, and were met by a very superior body of the enemy, sent forward to support their advanced party. A sharp skirmish ensued, in which we lost some few in killed, wounded, and missing. The Honourable Captain Pakenham, of our regiment, was wounded, and Lieutenant Bunbury killed, the first British officer who fell in the Peninsular wars. He was much regretted by us all. Our companies, with some of the 60th, occupied during the night, as an advanced post, an extensive knoll near the road by which the enemy had retired. We remained on the *qui vive* until daybreak, when we prepared to extract as much comfort, by way of toilet and breakfast, from our havresacks, as their narrow compass would admit. We carried every thing on our own shoulders, so that we were by no means superabundantly supplied with necessaries or luxuries. Our baggage remained on board the transports.

We halted on the 16th at Obidos, and on the 17th the army advanced to attack General Delaborde, who was in a position with six thousand men, near the village of Roleia.

BATTLE OF ROLEIA.

After a march of two or three hours, we found the enemy occupying a formidable position, with a plain in his front, where his cavalry, to the amount of about five hundred, were drawn up; and in his rear was Roleia, behind which village were several passes through the mountains, by which was his line of retreat, if defeated. The British army was formed into several distinct columns of attack, each brigade having a portion of work cut out for itself. We were very soon warmly engaged with the French light troops, who contested the rough and mountainous ground in which we attacked them, with great obstinacy; and it was not without many severe struggles, and a considerable loss, that we succeeded in dislodging and driving them from mountain to mountain, and in rooting them out from amongst the thick brushwood and high heath, from which they kept up an invisible and destructive fire as we advanced. Whilst our brigade was thus engaged, the others were not idle. The 9th and 29th regiments, in attacking some passes in the mountains on our right, encountered difficulties, from the nature of the ground, and the gallant resistance made by the enemy, which the most determined resolution and valour only could have surmounted. The Honourable Colonel Lake of the 29th, and Colonel Stewart of the 9th, fell at the head of their regiments.

As the captain of a company, with abundance of work on my own hands at the time, I pretend not to detail the particular feats of each brigade and regiment. That six thousand veteran French troops, commanded by a brave and experienced general, were driven successively from one formidable position to another by an inferior number of British, the majority of whom had never before seen gunpowder burnt in earnest, few will deny to have been an exploit of which the army had reason to be proud. True it is, that the British far outnumbered the French; but the numbers *actually engaged* fell short of those of our opponents. Neither before nor since do I remember to have felt more intense and suffocating heat than we experienced in climbing the mountains to the attack; every mouthful of air was such as is inhaled when looking into an oven.

Having driven the enemy from one of the highest mountains, and in the act of collecting our men on its summit to renew the attack on a second position, to which they had retired, one of my brother-officers, whilst holding his canteen to my mouth to give me some wine, *well mulled by the sun*, received a musket shot through his hand, and through the canteen, which latter it split, splashed my face thoroughly with wine, spoiled my draught, gave me a sharp blow, which cut my mouth, and spun me round like a top. For a few moments I concluded that I was wounded; but the mystery was soon explained by seeing my friend on the ground, bleeding profusely, and the broken canteen at his side. I sent a soldier with him to the rear; and, notwithstanding that his wound was for a length of time afterwards painful and troublesome, we had the pleasure to see him rejoin us in a few weeks. A more gallant soldier, sincere friend, or a more independent, straight-forward, manly fellow than Cockrane, never wore His Majesty's uniform. In proof of the high estimation in which he was held by his corps, suffice it to say, that his brother-officers erected a monument to his memory in Ireland, where he died a few years after the termination of the war in the Peninsula and Waterloo, in both of which he was actively engaged. An egotist being a character for which I never had a predilection, this trifling anecdote should not have found a place in my memoranda of occurrences, if its narration tended to place a feather in my cap; but as it was within an ace of lowering me five feet seven inches, I have ventured to note it in my log-book.

The French, being much superior to us in cavalry, were enabled to effect their retreat in good order, as the plains beyond the mountains were favourable for that arm. This success was not gained without a heavy loss on our side. The French left three pieces of artillery in our possession, and a considerable number of wounded, which, from the nature of the ground and the rapidity of our advance, they could not carry off. Their loss must have been severe. We bivouacked this night on the plains beyond the mountainous position from which the enemy had been expelled.

On the 18th the army bivouacked near Lourinha. About this time the 50th regiment was appointed to our brigade, in place of the 45th, which was moved to General Catline Crawford's.

On the 20th, several regiments which had arrived on the coast from England, under Brigadier-generals Ackland and Anstruther, landed at Maceira bay and joined the army, which was in position near the village of Vimeira. Amongst the newly arrived regiments were the 2d battalion 9th; 2d battalion 43d Light Infantry; 2d battalion 52d Light Infantry; the 97th, or Queen's Germans; and two companies of the 1st battalion 95th Riflemen.

BATTLE OF VIMEIRA.

Our brigade, under General Fane, composing the advanced guard of the army, occupied a hill ot no considerable height above the valley in which Vimiera is situated. We had several pieces of artillery at this point. On our right were the 97th in line. Some squadrons of the 20th Light Dragoons, drawn up at the back of the hill, were ready to support us, and to take advantage of any favourable opportunity which might offer. The 2d battalions of the 9th and 43d were likewise in reserve at or near this point, in column, if I mistake not, fronting the village of Vimeira. This, I believe, to have been nearly the disposition of the troops on our part of the position on the morning of the 21st of August, when the cavalry of General Junot's advanced guard appeared in force, particularly towards the left of our position, which the brigades of Generals Ferguson and Nightingale were destined to defend.

The night before the battle I belonged to a picket of about two hundred riflemen, of our own regiment and the 60th, under the command of Major Hill, of the 50th regiment. We were posted in a large pine wood, to the right and front of General Fane's brigade. About eight or nine o'clock in the morning of the 21st, a cloud of light troops, supported by a heavy column of infantry, entered the wood, and assailing the pickets with great impetuosity, obliged us to fall back for support on the 97th regiment. In our retrograde movement, Major Hill, who commanded the pickets, was severely wounded. As soon as we had got clear of the front of the 97th, and passed round its right flank, that regiment poured in such a well-directed fire, that it staggered the resolution of the hostile column, which declined to close and measure its strength with them. About the same time the 2d battalion of the 52d, advancing through the wood, took the French in flank, and drove them before them in confusion. On the pickets being driven in, I joined my own brigade, which was on the left of the 97th. Here the business was beginning to assume a serious aspect. Some heavy masses of infantry, preceded by a swarm of light troops, were advancing with great resolution, and with loud cries of "Vive l'Empereur!" "En avant!" &c. against the hill on which our brigade was posted. In spite of the deadly fire which several hundred riflemen kept up on them, they continued to press forward with great determination, until the old 50th regiment received them with a destructive volley, following it instantly with a most brilliant and decisive charge with the bayonet, which broke and sent back, in utter dismay and confusion, and with great loss, this column, which a short time before was all confidence and exultation.

In this charge the enemy lost seven pieces of artillery and a number of prisoners. The road by which this column moved on to the attack was choked with killed and wounded, the greater part of whom lay in a small compass. I have understood that the first trial of Shrapnell shells in the field, took place on that day, and that they answered every expectation which had been formed of their efficacy.

The French column, when broken and turned back by the quick and accurate fire of our artillery, which was never better or more gallantly served, and by the fire and charge of General Fane's brigade, was assailed in its retreat by the 20th Light Dragoons, who dashed gallantly in amongst the fugitives, and, in the ardour of the moment, following them to a distance from any support, encountered a very superior body of French cavalry, which obliged the 20th to fall back with some loss. Lieutenant-colonel Taylor fell, whilst gallantly leading on his regiment in this charge.

During the attack on our brigade, the French, in some force, got round the left flank of the 50th regiment, and endeavoured to penetrate into the village of Vimeira; but the 2d battalion 43d being let loose at them, a desperate conflict ensued in and near the road which leads into the village. The 43d highly distinguished itself, and repulsed the enemy; but there were many broken heads on each side. The particulars which I have endeavoured to detail, relate to what took place on our part of the position.

On the left, the troops under Generals Ferguson and Nightingale were assailed with similar impetuosity; but the discipline and bravery of the different regiments at that point baffled the veterans of France, and took from them six pieces of artillery, and a great number of prisoners, leaving the ground covered with their killed and wounded. The 36th, 40th, 71st, and 82d regiments were principally engaged at this point.

It is but justice to our opponents to admit, that no troops could have advanced with greater determination and valour to the attack, or have sustained with greater courage the deadly fire to which they were exposed.

Our loss, although much inferior to that of the French, was severe; but not more so, perhaps, than might be expected, where so complete a victory was gained. Thirteen pieces of artillery were taken; six by the brigades of Generals Ferguson and Nightingale, and seven by our own, besides a number of ammunition-waggons, powder, &c. &c. When it is remembered that scarcely one-half of the British army drew their triggers, and that every corps in the French army had, in the course of the action, been engaged, it will not be denied that this battle shed additional lustre on the British arms.

Lieut.-general Sir H. Burrard, who had been sent from England to supersede Sir A. Wellesley in command of the army, landed after the action had commenced; and, with feelings highly honourable, did not interfere in the command, but allowed Sir Arthur to conduct matters, and to bring the battle to a favourable termination. Sir H. Burrard did not approve of our instantly following up the discomfited troops of the French, as was recommended by Sir A. Wellesley in the strongest terms, it being the opinion of the former that it would be more prudent to remain in our position at Vimiera until some reinforcements, which were hourly expected from England, should arrive.

On the 22d, a flag of truce came in from the French, which General Kellerman accompanied, who was authorised to treat for the evacuation of Portugal by the French. It is needless to add, that this overture led to the convention of Cintra, on which pages and volumes having been written, little remains for me to say on the subject.

The wisdom and propriety of the government in sending out Sir H. Burrard to supersede Sir A. Wellesley, and immediately afterwards ordering Sir Hew Dalrymple to supersede Sir H. Burrard, is a question which I shall leave others to decide. My own opinion on the business has long since been formed. The old and homely adage, that "too many cooks spoil the broth," I conceive to have been verified on this occasion. Much having been said as to the propriety and consistency of Sir A. Wellesley having ever consented, as far as he was concerned, to the convention of Cintra, the simple question appears to be this,—Had Sir A. Wellesley retained the command of the army after the battle, and followed up, as he unquestionably would, with a certain number of his brigades, the French army, without allowing it time to rally and re-form, whilst, with the remainder of his force, he had pushed on with all haste by another route, and thereby gained possession of the passes leading to Lisbon before Junot's army could reach them, *would the convention of Cintra have taken place?*

That Sir Arthur was sanguine in his expectation of reaching the passes before the French, is, I fancy, well known; and the nicety and exactness of his calculations, in a variety of marches and military movements, during a succession of brilliant campaigns, can leave but little doubt on unbiassed minds, that, in the present instance also, he would not have miscalculated. It must be borne in mind, that every minute, nay, every second, was of the last importance to us, if the enemy was to be followed up after his defeat, and the passes gained before he could reach them. The aspect, therefore, of affairs was totally changed on the

22d, when the flag of truce came in. The enemy then had possession of all the defensible positions between us and Lisbon, independent of the citadel and different forts near the capital. This would have enabled General Junot to protract the contest for a length of time; whilst the game of the British clearly was to root out their opponents with as little delay as possible, and to gain possession of the capital; not only on account of the lateness of the season, but because the presence of our army would be desirable in Spain.

Soon after the cessation of hostilities between Junot's army and our own, Sir John Moore arrived from Sweden with the troops which composed the expedition to that country. The British army closed towards Lisbon about the end of September, and encamped near it before the French army had embarked, which, agreeably to the convention, was to be conveyed to Bourdeaux in British ships. The best possible understanding existed between the soldiers of the two armies, who were to be seen drinking, carousing, shaking hands, and walking arm in arm about Lisbon.

The French infantry were encamped in the squares of the city whilst the transports were preparing for their reception. At length, when the embarkation was completed, and the national flag of Portugal once again waved on the citadel and forts in place of the tri-coloured, there was such a combination of *vivas,* sky-rockets, ringing of bells, singing, dancing, screeching, crying, laughing, old and young embracing in the streets, added to the curses and execrations uttered by the populace against their late masters, as must render every attempt at description hopeless.

Of Lisbon, suffice it to say that it is a city which swarms with monks, friars, and ecclesiastics of all ages, sorts, and kinds, and is filled with every species of filth and dirt, in spite of the measures taken by the French to prevent it. The opera, which was thronged every night with British officers, had lost the claim to which it at one time pretended, of being the first in Europe. Soon after our arrival at Lisbon, the four companies of our regiment were moved to another brigade, which was composed of a certain Highland regiment and ourselves. The colonel of the Highlanders commanded this brigade, having been appointed a brigadier-general a few weeks before On hearing that our four companies were to be under his command, this gallant but eccentric old chieftain declared, " he did not want a *parcel of riflemen,* as he already commanded a thousand Highlanders, who would face the devil." Had our corps been raised *northward of the Tweed,* it is more than probable that our brigadier would have set a higher value on us; but we were removed to another brigade before he had an opportunity of judging of the merits or demerits of the *Southerns* in the field.

The army began to feel the effects to which all troops are liable at the close of a burning summer's campaign, in a climate to which they are not seasoned. Fevers and agues were extremely prevalent, and I was one of the many so attacked, which confined me to my bed many weeks, and reduced me to a mere skeleton; so that it was more than probable I should find my grave in Lisbon. The intolerable stench of the small fish called Sardinias, frying in villanously bad oil under the windows of the hotel where I lingered some weeks in a sad plight, called forth maledictions on the miscreants so employed which need not be committed to paper, but which will be fully understood by those whose olfactory nerves have been put to a similar test, by inhaling that detestable odour whilst on the bed of sickness.*

---

* From the memoranda of my brother-officers, I give an outline of what took place during my short absence from the regiment, which the sickness alluded to rendered unavoidable.

CHAPTER IV.

The army under Sir John Moore leaves Lisbon. Marches to Salamanca. Sir John Hope joins Sir John Moore near Salamanca. Sir David Baird lands at Corunna. The whole army is concentrated. Affairs of cavalry. The army moves to attack Marshal Soult. Suddenly countermanded. Distribution of our first and second battalions. Gallant affair of cavalry near Mayorca. General Crawford's light brigade destroys a bridge. The French endeavour to interrupt them in their work. General Crawford marches to Benavente. Brilliant action of cavalry near Benavente. Two light brigades under General Crawford sent to Vigo. Their march thither, and embarkation. Cursory view of Sir John Moore's retreat to Corunna, and his death. The army returns to England. Our third battalion is formed.

THE British army under Sir John Moore marched from Lisbon in the direction of Salamanca, towards the end of October. The roads northward of the Tagus having been reported impracticable for artillery, Sir John Hope proceeded with the cavalry, artillery, and several regiments of infantry, through Alemtejo to Talavera de la Reina, and from thence to the Escurial. The other brigades of the army marched by Abrantes and

Coimbra to Almeida, a fortress on the northern frontier of Portugal, and from thence by Ciudad Rodrigo to Salamanca, where they arrived about the middle of November.

Sir John Hope having passed the Guadaramma mountains, which divide New from Old Castile, joined Sir John Moore early in December, in the neighbourhood of Salamanca, and shortly afterwards the army advanced towards the Douro. The cavalry, under the command of Lord Paget, occupied some towns and villages on that river. Sir David Baird had arrived from England at Corunna, and landed there with several thousand troops; and having formed a junction with Sir John Moore, the whole army was concentrated near Mayorca about the third week in December.

The weather was exceedingly severe, and deep snow was on the ground. The cavalry under Lord Paget and Brigadier-general Stewart surprised several of the enemy's out-posts in the open country, near Valladolid. Our hussars had a brilliant affair near Sahagun, which ended in the defeat and dispersion of a superior force of the enemy's cavalry, and in our taking a number of prisoners.

Marshal Soult being in position behind the river Carrion, Sir John Moore made every arrangement to attack him. The army was put in motion for that purpose on the night of the

23d of December, which had a most exhilarating effect on the spirits of the soldiers, who had become impatient to meet their antagonists; but Sir John Moore having received positive intelligence that numerous French columns were in full march against him, from various points, with a view of cutting off his retreat from the coast, the attack was immediately countermanded, and not a moment was lost in withdrawing the army across the Esla.

The four companies of our 2d battalion, which sailed from Cork the preceding summer with Sir Arthur Wellesley, and were with him at the battles of Roleia and Vimeira, were joined by the remainder of the battalion, which came out with Sir D. Baird to Corunna; and the whole were placed in Brigadier-general Robert Crawford's light brigade. Our first battalion was in in the reserve, commanded by Sir E. Paget. General Crawford's light brigade was left in a position on the left bank of the Esla, to protect the passage of the bridge of Castro Gonzalo. Some troops of our hussars, near Mayorca, attacked a superior body of French cavalry, which were advantageously posted, and beat them in gallant style, taking many prisoners.

The light cavalry of the enemy hovered about General Crawford's brigade, and used every endeavour to interrupt it whilst employed in the destruction of the bridge of Castro Gonzalo. It was not an idle moment; for whilst a certain portion of the brigade was busied in demolishing the arches of the bridge, in a tempestuous night of snow and rain, the remainder kept watch, and covered the working parties, which, as already stated, were close to the enemy's advanced pickets, who were in force, and by whom repeated attempts were made to interrupt them in a work so important to the whole army. Planks having been laid across some arches of the bridge which had been broken, General Crawford's brigade retired over them, on the night of the 28th, to the opposite bank, unperceived by the French; and then, springing a mine, dismantled the bridge. The brigade then marched to Benavente, a good town situated on the Esla, where the cavalry and the reserve were stationed.

On the following day, the reserve and General Crawford's brigade retired from Benavente, following the march of the army, and leaving Lord Paget with the cavalry to guard the passage of the Esla, which was fordable at different points. A most brilliant action took place in the plain near Benavente, between our hussars and several hundred cavalry of the Imperial Guard, under the command of General Lefebre, and (it has been asserted) within view of Napoleon himself, who, from the heights opposite, directed that general "to cross the Esla, and to bring him those English cavalry prisoners." General Lefebre passed the river at a ford, and obliged the pickets of the British cavalry to fall back; but being reinforced, they became the assailants in turn, and in a short space of time sent back the enemy across the Esla, at a much more rapid pace than they had advanced.

General Lefebre was wounded and made prisoner, with many other officers and soldiers; in addition to which, the French suffered considerably in killed and wounded. This gallant action was not gained without the loss of about fifty of our own cavalry. It was a salutary lesson to the imperial gentry; and if their emperor witnessed their defeat, so much the better. The artillery, which was attached to the cavalry, cannonaded the French as they re-formed on the opposite bank of the Esla, and obliged them to retire. General Crawford's light brigade, and that likewise which was composed of the light battalions of the German Legion, under Brigadier-general Alten (which was also placed under Crawford's command), were ordered to separate from the main body of the army, and to proceed, on the 31st of December, by cross roads to Vigo; whilst the remainder continued their retreat towards Corunna.

The brigades under General Crawford were not harassed by the enemy, after their separation from the army, in their long and dreary retreat to Vigo; but they suffered, nevertheless, severely from constant marching, in snow and rain, through the worst of roads, from want of rest, and other privations and hardships inseparable from all retreats, and particularly when made during such an inclement season. Finally they reached Vigo, the men and officers mostly without shoes to their feet; and embarking on board transports, arrived in England in the latter end of January, 1809.

Volumes have already been written on the subject of the retreat to Corunna, which shew that the sufferings experienced by the British army were exceedingly great. Constant marching through snow and over miserable roads, by day and night; the uncertain and irregular supply of provisions; the enemy's advanced guard constantly galling the rear guard of the British; and the feelings of irritation naturally produced in the soldier when retreating before an exulting foe, were causes sure to bring with them irregularities to a certain extent. That the retreat from the Esla to Corunna was rendered indispensably necessary for the preservation of the British army, and that it was most ably conducted, the prejudiced, and those ignorant of such matters, only will deny. In the various actions in which our cavalry and infantry were engaged during this long and arduous retreat, their superiority over their opponents was incontestably proved. I trust I shall be exculpated from the charge of trumpeting the fame of my own corps, if I observe that our first battalion, which was in the reserve under Sir E. Paget, always forming the rear guard of the infantry, and constantly engaged with the French advanced guard, acquitted itself much to the satisfaction of Sir John Moore, who was an eye-witness of its conduct in the various trying actions in which it was engaged, and who repeatedly eulogised it.

In spite of the hardships and sufferings which beset the British army in the retreat, its discipline, which in many instances had become exceedingly impaired, was in great measure suddenly restored when drawn up to offer battle to the enemy at Lugo, and subsequently at Corunna. In the hardly contested battle of Corunna, although fighting under manifold disadvantages, the army gained a glorious victory; and proved to the world that, in the day of trial, it was an overmatch for the veteran troops which had overrun and paralysed the whole continent of Europe. On this occasion the army lost its brightest ornament, by the fall of its gallant leader, Sir John Moore, who died in the arms of victory. He was buried on the ramparts of Corunna. Sir David

Baird lost an arm in the battle; and the command of the army devolved on Sir John Hope.

The night after the battle the army was embarked; and towards the end of January 1809, the whole of the troops from Vigo and Corunna reached different ports in England. The two battalions of our corps went into barracks in Kent.

I have attempted to give merely the outline of the operations of our army, from the time of its departure from Lisbon to its embarkation at Corunna and Vigo.

Early in the spring of 1809, we received orders to form a third battalion to our corps, by volunteers from the militia. This was effected in a very short space of time; and had not the order from Sir David Dundas (at that time commander-in-chief) arrived for us to discontinue receiving more men from the militia, we could easily have raised a fourth battalion.

The formation of a 3d battalion causing some trifling promotion in the corps, I became effective in the 1st battalion, and joined it from the 2d.

CHAPTER V.

The Light Brigade composed of the 43d and 52d regiments of Light Infantry, and the 1st battalion 95th Rifle Corps. Embark for Lisbon under Brigadier-General Robert Crawford. Arrive at Lisbon. Proceed by water to Vallada. Santarem. Convents and nuns. March from Santarem to join Sir Arthur Wellesley. Sketch of the march. The Pass of Villa Velha, Castello Branco, Zarzo Maior, Coria, Orapeza, &c. Extraordinary long march on 28th July, and want of water. We join the army at Talavera. Slight sketch of the field of action.

A VERY short time had elapsed after the return of the army from Corunna and Vigo, when orders were transmitted to the three light regiments, the 43d, 52d, and the first battalion of our own corps, to prepare for service again, with the least possible delay, and to form a brigade under Brigadier-General Robert Crawford. Our destination was Portugal. The losses which we had sustained in the late campaign were filled up from our 2d and 3d battalions; and I conclude that the 43d and 52d were completed in a similar manner. On the 25th May, 1809, our battalion embarked at Dover in the Malabar, Fortune, and Laurel transports, and sailed immediately to the Downs, where we remained at anchor several days, in very boisterous weather. On the 3d of June we sailed under convoy of La Nymphe frigate and the Kangaroo sloop of war, and anchored at St. Helen's.

In consequence of adverse winds, we were detained between St. Helen's, Spithead, Ryde, Cowes, and Yarmouth in the Isle of Wight, until the 18th of June, during which we contrived to kill time by various excursions to Portsmouth, Ryde, Newport, Carisbrook Castle, Yarmouth, and Leamington. [N. B. We all agreed that the women of the Isle of Wight were particularly handsome.]

On the 18th of June we passed the Needles with a fresh breeze; and the order of the day on board our transport was, to bombard the sea-fowl which swarm at this season on the rocks. Rifles and fowling-pieces, with ball, slugs, and swan-shot, were brought into full play on this occasion.

On the 19th, we were abundantly supplied with fish by the Torbay fishermen; and, moreover, opened another heavy and destructive fire on such unfortunate gulls and other sea-birds as ventured within reach. We pursued our course with favourable winds and heavenly weather, and entered the Tagus on the 28th of June, and the same day anchored abreast of Lisbon. The pilot who conducted our vessel into the Tagus related some marvellous stories of the Marquis of Romana having recently played the devil with one of the French armies. We placed, however, but little reliance on his report.

As we entered Lisbon last year, after the convention of Cintra, by the roads leading to it from Vimeira, we had not until now so fair an opportunity of judging of its magnificent appearance from the Tagus. The country houses and convents on the sides of most picturesque hills, thickly planted with vines; the legion of windmills near Belem; and, finally, the city itself, form altogether so enchanting a picture, that any attempt of mine to do it justice must inevitably fail *in toto*. Besides, Lisbon and its river have been often described by far more able pens. How sadly is a stranger disappointed when he lands and traverses the dirty, rascally streets of this priest-ridden city, and wades, hour after hour, through one uninterrupted accumulation of disgusting filth, in which the inhabitants appear to glory and rejoice! Instead of being the most disreputable and dirty place in Europe (or perhaps on the globe), it might most assuredly be the very reverse. Above the city is one of the finest aqueducts in the universe, from which almost every street might, with good management, be constantly washed, and every thing offensive carried down to the Tagus. But this, it appears, is quite foreign to Portuguese taste. Let them therefore vegetate in the old way, and luxuriate in the effluvia to which they have ever been accustomed.

We were busily employed, from the moment of our arrival on the 28th of June, to the 2d of July, in purchasing horses, mules, donkeys, pack-saddles, cigars, and various other odds and ends, indispensable in campaigning. We were to proceed, without delay, to join Sir Arthur Wellesley, who was at this time in Spanish Estremadura. He had arrived at Lisbon from England about a couple or three months after Sir John Moore's army returned from Corunna to England, taking out with him some troops, with which, in addition to the regiments left by Sir John Moore in Portugal the previous autumn, he immediately commenced operations against Marshal Soult; and, by a series of rapid and masterly movements, advanced to the Douro — forced the passage of that river — completely defeated the French army at Oporto, and drove them out of Portugal, with the loss of their artillery, baggage, ammunition, &c. &c.; and occasioned them a heavy loss also in killed, wounded, and prisoners.

The particulars of this brilliant exploit are too well-known to render it necessary for me to enlarge on it. Having cleared Portugal a second time of its invaders, Sir Arthur turned his attention in a southerly direction, and was, at the period of the arrival of our brigade at Lisbon, co-operating with the Spanish General Cuesta in Spanish Estremadura. Instead of landing the light brigade at Lisbon, and marching it to Santarem, it was determined that we should be conveyed in boats to the village of Vallada, forty miles above the capital, and that our baggage-animals should be sent by land to Santarem.

About midnight on the 2d of July, the tide serving to take us up the river, we were put into flat-bottomed boats and launches, and the tedious operation of towing us against the current commenced. After twenty-four hours spent in this bewitching manner, every man's legs terribly cramped by being crammed so tight into the boat, we reached Vallada, near which place we bivouacked on the bank of the river. I never entertained the smallest doubt that all the frogs in the Peninsula had assembled, by common consent on this occasion, to welcome us to Portugal; for such an eternal croaking I never heard before or since. It failed, however, to spoil our night's rest, as sleep the previous night had been quite out of the question, owing to our being constrained to sit upright in the boats.

The three regiments composing the light brigade having now landed, I may observe, that unprejudiced persons, and those neither directly nor indirectly connected with it, have pronounced it the finest and most splendid brigade that ever took the field. I will venture to go so far as to assert, that if it has been *equalled*, it has never been *surpassed*, in any army, whether the materials of which it was composed, its fine appointments and arms, its *esprit du corps*, its style of marching and manœuvring, and, in short, every requisite for a light brigade, be considered. Each regiment was nearly eleven hundred strong; there were many hundreds in each battalion to whom the smell of *gunpowder in earnest* was no novelty; for they had served with Nelson at Copenhagen, with Auchmuty at Monte Video, with Whitelock in the ill-fated and bloody business at Buenos Ayres, with Sir A. Wellesley at Roleia and Vimeira, and with the ever-to-be-lamented Sir John Moore at Corunna. If, therefore, they were not veterans in age, they had at least some claim to the appellation from their services.

4th.—After a few hours' sleep near Vallada, we bade adieu to our bivouac and the frogs, and marched to Santarem, where we halted until the 7th, waiting for our baggage-animals, ammunition, and commissariat arrangements. Santarem is a a good town, beautifully situated on a high hill, clothed with the finest olive groves, on the right bank of the Tagus, overlooking its fertile banks to a considerable distance, both above and below the town. Like all towns of any size in Portugal, it is full of churches and convents. With the fair inmates of the latter we had a deal of chit-chat, although the close iron gratings which separated us from our inamoratas obscured them in great measure from view. That they all were blessed with sparkling black eyes, I am ready to swear; the rest was left to the imagination. By means of the *whirligig* concern in which various matters find their way out of and into the convent, these fair ladies presented us with preserved fruits, nosegays, and all sorts of fine things; in return for which, certain little notes or love-letters, written in villanously bad Portuguese, were transmitted by the same mode of conveyance to them. They appeared much interested as to the result of the campaign in which we were about to take a part; and two of them, who were heartily tired of their unnatural prison, declared to myself and a brother-officer, that they were ready and willing to make their escape, with our assistance, and to share our fortunes in the " tented field." When one considers that by so doing they would have brought down on them the vengeance of monks, friars, padres, and mother-abbesses, and that these black-eyed damsels must have calculated on being buried alive, or broiled on a gridiron, had they been detected in such an adventure, we must admit that they were heroines of the first class.

General Crawford having decided that his brigade should proceed independently by regiments, our battalion moved on the 7th from Santarem; and after a broiling march reached Golegao, a small town prettily situated on the Tagus, but almost entirely deserted by the inhabitants. Junot's army had plundered and ravaged it thoroughly the preceding year.

We marched on the 8th to Punheite and Tanchos, small towns on the right bank of the Tagus. On a small island in the river near the latter place stands a Moorish ruin, called Almeira, to which we paid a visit.

9th.— Reached Abrantes, a dirty town, but situated similarly to Santarem, and commanding a most extensive and diversified prospect. We did not halt in the town, but crossing to the left bank of the Tagus by a pontoon bridge, bivouacked in some large woods.

On the 10th we halted on the same ground. General Crawford at this period issued a long string of standing orders and regulations to his brigade: many of them were undoubtedly excellent, and well calculated to insure regularity, on the march, in camp, and in quarters; but they were so exceedingly numerous, and some so very minute and tedious, that a man must have been blessed with a better memory than falls to the general lot of mortals to have recollected one half of them. I shall here remark that, in consequence of the suffocating heat of the weather, our march from Santarem into Spanish Estremadura was chiefly performed in the night, or very early in the morning. We usually started soon after midnight, and were thereby able, in general, to finish the day's work by eight or nine in the morning, and to rest during the heat of the day. In some instances, when we did not commence the march until dawn of day, we had, of course, the full benefit of a southern sun the greater part of the way.

I was, unfortunately, one of those restless beings who, after a night spent in marching, could not sleep in the bivouac during the day; and many a time have I envied the happy fellows who lay down like dogs, under a cork-tree, and slept most soundly, until the rations of tough beef (perhaps killed only a few hours before), boiled into an *omnium gatherum*, with an onion or two, some rice, and a mouldy ship biscuit, were pronounced in a fit state for the table; the said dinner-table being neither more nor less than the turf at the foot of a tree, with a soldier's knapsack by way of camp-chair; a japanned half-pint tin cup stood for wine glass, which, with a pocket-knife, fork, and spoon, and a tin plate, constituted the whole of our dinner service. It being utterly impracticable to have a regimental mess whilst in the field, the officers of each company formed a little mess of their own. Candlesticks not being the fashion of the day, we substituted an empty bottle in their place; and a most bandit-like appearance the interior of our tents presented after dark, filled generally with such clouds of smoke from our cigars, that I have often since wondered we were not smothered in our sleep from such an atmosphere, in which we reposed rolled up in our cloaks.

At midnight of the 10th we harnessed for the night's march, and poked our way in the dark towards Gavion, a poor town. Near it are some Moorish ruins, which I would willingly have visited, had not my marching propensities been fully satisfied for one day; having been thirteen hours under arms, many of them under a scorching sun.

12th. — We reached, after a tedious march, Neza, a dirty town, where there are some Moorish walls and ruins, on which multitudes of storks build their nests. Both old and young birds were perched on the walls in great numbers, and were fully as tame as pigeons. These birds are held sacred in the Peninsula, and to shoot one of them is considered nothing short of sacrilege.

13th. — Long before dawn of day we were again on our legs, and in due time approached the awfully grand and terrific pass of Villa Velha, leading down to the Tagus by a zig-zag mountainous road, so well known to all old Peninsula men.

It would be presumptuous beyond measure for any one less gifted with descriptive powers than Anne Radcliffe, to fancy he could do justice to the wild beauties of this pass; suffice it, therefore, to say, that its features are as bold and terrific as are to be found any where short of the Alps or Pyrenees. There is scarcely a vestige of cultivation on either bank of the river, which rushes with great rapidity through its rocky bed at the foot of the pass. Eagles and vultures are abundant in those regions; and their constantly soaring above the summits of the mountains, which frown over the river, gives an additional interest to the picture.

On the summit of a mountain rising abruptly from the Tagus on the opposite bank, and clothed with gum cistus, stands a Moorish watch-tower, an object which the admirers of fine scenery cannot fail fully to appreciate. We bivouacked on the right bank of the river, having passed it by a curious flying bridge, large enough to carry only a company or two at a time, which made it a long and tedious process.

After two days' march from Villa Velha over a bad description of mountainous roads, and through an uncultivated country, prolific only in stones, gum cistus, and cork-trees, we reached Castello

Branco, a place of considerable size, but, like the generality of Portuguese towns, extremely dirty, with narrow streets, where tens of millions of flies were amusing themselves. We halted here on the 16th and 17th, to allow the 43d and 52d regiments to join us. Three men of the latter corps died between Santarem and this place, from the excessive heat and fatigue. We tried in vain, during our short sojourn there, to get a peep at the nuns; but, as we afterwards learnt that they were old and ugly, it ceased to be a disappointment. Leaving Castello Branco soon after midnight, the light brigade bivouacked in some large woods of Spanish oak and cork near Ladouira; and on the 19th, after toiling through many leagues of a most barren, desolate, parched, uninteresting country, we constructed huts for the day near the wretched village of Zebreira, a few miles distant from which stand the town and Moorish castle of Monte Santo — fine, wild-looking objects, perched on the summit of a mountain.

On the 20th we crossed the Elga, which river is here the boundary between Portugal and Spain, and encamped near Zarza Maior.

A stranger is forcibly struck, on entering Spain from Portugal, by the superior neatness and cleanliness which he finds, not only in the dress of the Spanish peasantry, but moreover in their cottages; to say nothing of the independent manly manner of the Spaniard, which, contrasted with that of his Portuguese neighbour, throws the latter inevitably into the shade. It was no trifling luxury to be able to purchase to-day some of the excellent white bread of Spain, after grinding, day after day, a short allowance of ship biscuit, or the very inferior bread of Portugal.

After two long and burning marches, through a country not particularly attractive, we arrived at Coria on the 22d. On the 21st I shot, in a large wood where we encamped, a beautiful bird, the name of which I am ignorant of, never having seen one of the kind before or since. It was of the crow genus, but much smaller, and the plumage variegated. On the 23d we halted at Coria. We made a fruitless effort to see and converse with the nuns in one of the convents, who, we were assured, were young and handsome. We undoubtedly had to thank the lady-abbess for their non-appearance at their prison gates. Coria is a city of great antiquity, situated in a country affording a variety of interesting scenery. From the summit of a castle, now in a dilapidated state, but once perhaps formidable, is an extensive and delightful prospect, with mountains in the distance, forming an amphitheatre round the plains watered by the Allagon, and bearing abundance of corn, vines, and olives. The cathedral is a fine building, having, nevertheless, too much gingerbread work in the interior. The streets of this city are exceedingly clean and regular when compared with those of the towns which we had recently marched through in Portugal.

During the 24th, 25th, 26th, and 27th, we continued our march, under a burning sun. In those four days we passed from Coria to Naval Moral, many miles of the route being through extensive and very thick forests of ilex and cork. Half a pound of bread per man was served out on the 27th, which was instantly consumed, as, since our departure from Coria, we knew of such a thing only by *name*.

On the evening of the 27th, vague rumours reached us at Naval Moral relative to the hostile armies. We knew nothing certain further than that Sir Arthur Wellesley and the Spanish General Cuesta had united their forces in the plains some leagues in our front; and as the French under Marshal Victor, the Duke of Belluno, were known to be not far distant from the allied army, a general action might be expected daily.

28th.—Before day dawned we were off again, and ere long, something like a distant cannonade was heard. Our suspense and anxiety can easily be imagined, aware as we were of the proximity of the hostile armies to each other. We arrived at Orapeza at mid-day, where General Crawford considered a short halt indispensably necessary.

He then directed the commanding officers of regiments to select and leave at Orapeza such men as were thought incapable of enduring the forced march which he determined to make, and not to halt until he reached the British army, which was known to be engaged in our front, as the distant but unceasing cannonade plainly announced. Having rested his brigade in this burning plain, where water was not to be procured, General Crawford put it in motion towards Talavera de la Reina. It may well be conceived it was a march productive of the highest degree of feverish anxiety and excitement. The one only feeling was to push forward, to throw our mite into the scale, and to lend a helping hand to our brothers in arms.

We soon met *wounded* Spanish soldiers, and Spanish soldiers *not wounded*, bending their course in a direction from the field of battle. I wish I could assert with equal truth that this retrogression was confined to our Spanish allies; but the truth must be told; and I regret to say, that stragglers from the ranks of the British army, some without a wound, were also taking a similar direction to the rear. As they passed our column they circulated all sorts and kinds of reports of a most disheartening nature: "The British army was utterly defeated, and in full retreat;" "Sir Arthur Wellesley was wounded;" and, by others, "he was killed." In short, all was suspense and uncertainty. One thing was, nevertheless, certain — that the cannonade continued without cessation.

We pressed forward until ten o'clock at night, when, having reached a pool of stagnant water near the road, in which cattle had been watered during the summer, and where they had constantly wallowed, a halt was ordered for an hour or two. Those who have never been in similar situations may be inclined to doubt my veracity when I state, that the whole brigade, officers and soldiers, rushed into this muddy water, and drank with an eagerness and avidity impossible to describe. The use of such an execrable beverage, except on extreme occasions, like the one in question, where we had been the whole day without water, under a sun as oppressive as can be experienced in Europe, might indeed be deemed extraordinary; but excessive thirst knows no law.

After a short repose on the banks of this horse-pond, we again got under weigh, and without another halt joined the British army in its position at Talavera. Here we learnt that a most sanguinary contest had taken place the day before, wherein the British army gained immortal glory, the particulars of which are generally known; and as the light brigade arrived too late to take a share in the fight, I shall not be expected to describe them. To shew that our brigade did all men could do to reach the field of action in time, suffice it to say, that in twenty-four hours it passed over upwards of fifty miles of country; as extraordinary a march, perhaps, as is to be found on record; particularly when it is remembered that each soldier carried from sixty to eighty rounds of ammunition, a musket or rifle, a great coat, and (if I recollect rightly) a blanket, a knapsack complete, with shoes, shirts, &c. &c.; a canteen and haversack, bayonet, belts, &c. &c. Such a load, carried so great a distance, would be considered a hard day's work for a horse. The heat was intense, as every soldier who has served in the Peninsula well knows is the case in the month of July, in the heart of Spain, on its sun-burnt, arid plains. Water was scarcely to be had, and of such quality that the quadrupeds doomed to drink it need not have been envied, much less the bipeds. It must also be added, that for some days before we had been very scantily supplied with provisions. Very few men, comparatively speaking, were left on the road. The constant cannonade heard in front was a stimulus which had a most beneficial effect, and made them forget, for a time, their extraordinary fatigue.

It is not my intention to question the propriety or necessity of the light brigade having been halted two days at Santarem, one day at Abrantes, two days at Castello Branco, and one day at Coria, on its march to Talavera; certain, however, it is, that one day's rest at Santarem instead of two, and one day's rest at Castello Branco instead of two, would have brought a reinforcement of more than three thousand light troops to Sir Arthur Wellesley, before the bloody battle of the 28th; and that such an addition to his force would have been highly acceptable, particularly as he was deficient in the number of his light troops. Could General Crawford have foreseen that by those halts his brigade would have arrived a *few hours too late* at Talavera, I feel thoroughly convinced that he would have pushed on, *péle-méle*, without a single halt between Santarem and the field of battle.

On our arrival at the position, we were immediately sent to occupy some woods in front, and to take charge of the outposts. Hundreds of wounded were still on the field; but parties were actively employed in taking them to the hospitals in the town of Talavera. Very many of the wounded of both armies who had been so injured as not to be able to crawl back into their own lines during the battle, were, most unfortunately, burnt to death by the dry grass and brush-wood catching fire from the explosion of the shells. A more horrid death can scarcely be imagined. This occurred on what might properly be termed the *neutral ground*, in front of the two armies, where the light troops had been engaged, and when knocked down, could not be carried from the field so long as the contest continued.

The Spanish army commanded by General Cuesta was strongly posted on the right of the British, on intersected ground, and took but little share in the battle; as the game of the French commander evidently was, to crush and annihilate Sir Arthur Wellesley's troops with overwhelming numbers, whilst he contented himself with keeping the Spaniards in check with a very inferior force. Although the loss of the British was extremely severe, that of their opponents was infinitely greater; nor were the sterling qualities of our soldiers on any occasion put more severely to the test, or the character of the British army more nobly upheld, than on this bloody and memorable day.

The allied army remained in the position on which it had fought until the 3d of August, during which time no movement of consequence took place on its part. The enemy kept a strong rear guard on the Alberchè (a river flowing into the Tagus near the town of Talavera), which the cavalry and the light brigade had an eye to.

About the 1st of August Marshal Victor fell back some leagues towards Toledo. The Spanish cavalry pickets caused frequent false alarms in the camp, by blazing away in a most unmeaning and useless manner at the French videttes.

I have but little to relate of occurrences from the day our brigade joined the army, on the 29th of July, to the 3d of August.

CHAPTER VI.

Scarcity of provisions. Horrid stench from the unburied bodies of men and horses. I lose my horse, and with him all my campaigning comforts. The British army marches on Orapeza to attack Soult. Conduct of General Cuesta at Talavera. The British army crosses the Tagus at Arzobispo. Desperate attack made by General Crawford's troops on a herd of swine. How to dress pork in the most expeditious manner. The army retires towards Delatosa. General Crawford's division proceeds to the bridge of Almaraz. Long and harassing marches thither. Parched peas and boiled wheat our food. A fortnight at Almaraz. Scanty diet of bran cakes and goat's flesh, without salt. How to reduce a corpulent person. The army falls back to the southern frontier of Portugal, and is cantoned near the Guadiana. A short account of our retreat. Maravao. Castello de Vide. Jollification in the woods near it. Shooting party on the 1st of September. Portalegre. General Catline Crawford's brigade. Aronches. General Crawford's division reaches Campo Maior.

The Spanish authorities had failed most shamefully in their promise of procuring supplies for the British army; and I do not believe that more than one day's allowance of bread was issued from the 29th of July to the evening of the 2d of August, nor were the rations of wine, spirits, and meat, forthcoming either. Dollars we had in our pockets, it is true; but they soon became totally useless.

In Talavera every thing was soon bought up at an enormous price, as may readily be imagined when it is considered that 35,000 hungry Spanish troops, and 20,000 British, were encamped near the town, every one scrambling for bread, chocolate, wine, and, in short, for whatever was eatable or drinkable, at any price.

The feelings which constant hunger produces were, however, in some degree counteracted two days after the battle, by the insufferable stench arising from the hundreds of dead bodies of men and horses still unburied. The Spaniards at length were ordered to collect the bodies in heaps and to burn them; and even to the present moment I am undecided whether the horrid smell arising from those funeral piles was not more trying than that which we had previously experienced.

The 31st of July proved an ill-fated day to me. I lent my saddle-horse to a brother-officer, to ride from the camp into Talavera, to purchase whatever he could lay his hands on; and, to my utter horror and dismay, I saw my friend return to the bivouac late in the afternoon, *not* on horseback, but on foot, and with a face longer than my arm. I was soon put out of suspense by learning that a rascally Portuguese or Spanish boy, to whose care he had intrusted my charger in the town whilst he went into a shop, had disappeared with him. No Peninsula soldier need be told that this was a serious mishap. The *prad* was a capital one; and the saddle, bridle, the cloak affixed to the saddle, the *valise*, containing all the articles of the toilet, a blanket under the saddle, and the various *et ceteras*, which in those days constituted the sole comfort of campaigners, were not to be replaced for love nor money on the plains of Talavera. Instead, therefore, of having a chestnut quadruped to carry me on the retreat from Talavera to the frontiers of Portugal, and having the benefit of a cloak and blanket at night in the bivouac, (our tent was thrown away, by the by, in consequence of death, by starvation and fatigue, of my baggage mule) I had the felicity to tramp it on foot from the Tagus to the Guadiana, no trifling distance either, and to stretch myself at the foot of a tree every night, with no covering but the sky and a green jacket.

August 3d.—Before day-break this morning the whole British army was put in motion towards Orapeza. The occasion of our backs being thus turned towards the army of Marshal Victor, which had experienced so signal a defeat on the 28th of July, was this: Sir Arthur Wellesley had received information that Marshal Soult, with a powerful army, had crossed the mountains which divide Leon from Estremadura, and was bearing down, by forced marches, on the rear of the British, with a view of cutting off their communication with Portugal, by the bridges of Almaraz and Arzobispo; thus hemming them up in the narrow valley of the Tagus, and placing them between two fires, viz. Victor in front and himself in their rear. Not a moment was to be lost; and Sir Arthur formed the daring resolution of counter-marching the British army and attacking Soult, in spite of his superior force, whilst General Cuesta, with his thirty-five thousand Spaniards, who had been almost untouched in the battle of the 28th, should remain at Talavera and keep Marshal Victor in check.

In pursuance, therefore, of this plan, such of our sick and wounded as could not be moved were left in hospital at Talavera, the Spanish general having faithfully promised to protect them. A march of twelve hours brought the British army to Orapeza; but, owing to the intense heat of the weather, the want of water, and the scarcity of provisions for many days before, the road was covered with stragglers, who were quite exhausted. Soon after our arrrival at Orapeza, the mortifying intelligence reached Sir Arthur, that General Cuesta, instead of remaining at Talavera to observe Victor, had abandoned that

ATTACK A HERD OF PIGS.

town and our hospitals, with the intention of making the best of his way to the left bank of the Tagus. No alternative now remained for the British commander but to cross the Tagus at Arzobispo, and to defend the line of that river, or to fall back towards the southern frontier of Portugal.

About this time Colonel Donkin's brigade, consisting of the 45th, 88th, and 5th battalion of the 60th (Germans), was placed under General Crawford's orders, and, with the light brigade, formed a division numbered the 3d. We halted the remainder of the 3d of August at Orapeza, and on the 4th the whole army crossed at the bridge of Arzobispo. Our battalion was attached to the cavalry, and formed the rear-guard.

As neither bread, meat, nor rations of any kind, were to be had, General Crawford ordered that any animals in the shape of cattle, sheep, or pigs, which could be found in the extensive woods in which we halted for the evening, should forthwith be put in requisition for the troops; and never do I remember having seen orders so promptly obeyed. A most furious attack was instantly made on a large herd of pigs, which, most fortunately for us, little dreamt of the fate that awaited them, or, I presume, they would have absconded on our first appearance in the forest. It would be useless to attempt a description of the scene of noise and confusion which ensued. The screeches and cries of those ill-fated swine, as they met their death at the point of the bayonet, the sword, or sergeant's pike, and the rapidity with which they were cut up into junks, with the hair on, and fried on the lids of camp-kettles, or toasted at the fire on a pointed stick, to allay the cravings of hunger of some thousands of half-famished soldiers, was quite incredible, and, I must add, truly ludicrous. As neither bread, salt, nor vegetables were to be procured, it must be confessed that the repast was a singular one, although it was eaten with the greatest *goût*, and was washed down with some water from a rivulet hard by.

At midnight we resumed our march, the main body of the army proceeding by the road towards Truxillo, and our division taking its route through a mountainous tract of country, with orders to reach the bridge of Almaraz with the least possible delay. After a thirteen hours' march through a mountainous, barren, unproductive country, affording no provisions of any sort except now and then a large, coarse description of pea, parched to a cinder by the sun, and an occasional God-send of wheat, found in the ungleaned fields near the line of march, we took up our ground for the night in a wild, uncultivated ravine, from which, I am inclined to think, the most enthusiastic admirer of romantic scenery would have made his escape without delay, from the fear of starvation. Our battalion was pushed forward to some woods in the direction of Almaraz. The heat was intense.

6th.—Day-break found us again in the act of scrambling over the mountains, and with pretty nearly the same sort of diet as on the preceding day,—boiled wheat and dried peas, without salt, bread, or meat. Spring water tolerably abundant, as rivulets were found in the numerous ravines. I cannot call to my recollection having ever witnessed a day's march where so many men left the ranks from fatigue. Many hundreds of the division were left in the mountains to find their way to Almaraz at their leisure, or, rather, as soon as exhausted nature had rallied. The unavoidable scarcity of food will account for all this, in addition to the length and severity of the marches in the hottest part of Europe, and over the most execrable roads.

To reach and to secure the bridge of Almaraz was, however, of such vast importance, that if only fifty men of the division had strength to accomplish it, push on they must. In reality, we were not certain whether on our arrival we should not find Marshal Soult's army in possession of it; in which case, the situation, not only of our own division but of the whole British army, would have been far from enviable. At the end of fifteen hours' march we had the satisfaction to find two Spanish battalions encamped near the bridge, one arch of which they had destroyed, and thereby secured themselves and us from any force passing from the opposite bank. Below the bridge is a ford, but it cannot be deemed exactly practicable for infantry, even at the driest season of the year. Two companies of our battalion were immediately sent on picket at the ford, and the remainder bivouacked near at hand, to support the pickets if attacked. Not a Frenchman was at this time visible on the opposite bank.

It will not be denied that the British army had been in a state of jeopardy for a considerable time ; nor was the danger entirely removed until it had reached the left bank of the Tagus by the bridge of Arzobispo, and until the passage of Soult's army, or any strong detachment of it, was rendered impracticable, by the destruction of the bridge of Almaraz, and by the arrival of our division to guard the passage of the river at that point. From the 6th of August to the 20th we were stationed there for that purpose.

The main body of the division encamped near the village of Las Casas del Puerto, in the formidable pass through which runs the road from Badajoz to Madrid, by the bridge of Almaraz. A more extensive and magnificent prospect than that which one looks down on from this pass it is difficult to imagine. Our battalion was kept in advance during our stay in this position, and was encamped in an olive-wood near the village of Ramon Gordo, in readiness to support the two companies which were always on picket near the ford. Every evening at sunset we left the olive-grove, and lay down by our arms on the bank of the river near the pickets, returning to our camp-ground at sunrise.

The time which we passed at this spot, although sufficiently monotonous, was such as one is not likely to forget. To the best of my belief, not one issue of bread was made to the troops during the fortnight; but an exceedingly coarse kind of flour, mixed with bran and chopped straw, and in very small quantities, was distributed by the commissariat. This, moistened with water, and made into a sort of pan-cake, was baked on a camp-kettle lid, and speedily devoured. The only regret was that the quantity was so very small. If any person who belonged to the troops stationed at Almaraz at that period can say that his appetite was satisfied on *any one day of the fourteen spent there*, I can only remark, that he was infinitely more fortunate than his neighbours.

Now and then half-a-dozen antiquated goats, which the commissary contrived to take by surprise in the mountains, found their way into the camp-kettles. A small slice of one of those quadrupeds, without salt, a very limited allowance of bran-cake, and an *unlimited* quantity of spring-water, constituted our chief food. One day we were so fortunate as to stumble on some bee-hives in the gum cistus, with which the mountains abound; and in a shorter time than I have taken to relate the capture, the honey and the comb were consumed. Wine or spirits money could not procure. Perhaps the want of salt to help us through with the goat's flesh, was as much felt as any thing. In short, if any corpulent person despairs of reducing his weight by the means usually adopted, I strongly recommend a few weeks' change of air and scene at Almaraz; taking especial good care to observe the same rules and regulations for diet; and to roast himself throughout the day at the foot of a shadeless olive-tree, in the dog days. If that fails to have the desired effect, I give him up, and can prescribe nothing further.

On the evening of the 12th, a picket of French infantry first appeared on the heights opposite the bridge and ford, between whom and the Spaniards at the bridge some shots were exchanged. The Spaniards, as usual, were the aggressors in this unprofitable and ungentlemanly warfare, of popping at sentries on the advanced posts. During the eight following days after the arrival of the French opposite the ford, which post two hundred of our battalion always held, so far from a single shot being exchanged, our men and the French had the best possible understanding; and it frequently happened that the officers of both parties took off their hats and saluted each other across the river.

During the whole of the war in the Peninsula, the Spaniards could never be made to comprehend the meaning of this system; nor did they ever let slip any opportunity of shooting an unfortunate sentry on his post. Much as such a practice is to be deprecated between the armies of civilised nations, it cannot be denied that the Spanish soldiers had a thousand causes of irritation and of hatred toward their invaders which the British soldier had not.

Before we left Almaraz, the effects of the late harassing marches, bad provisions, the heat of the climate, &c. &c. began to be severely felt, and to shew themselves in fevers, agues, and dysenteries, which placed numbers on the sick-list. Some English newspapers were sent to us from headquarters of the army at Delatosa, in which were accounts of active preparations going forward for a secret expedition about to leave England. Its probable destination served us to speculate on in our mountain-camp; although not one of our politicians dreamt at the time that so fine and numerous an army was doomed to waste its strength in the pestilential marshes of Walcheren.

At midnight of the 20th, leaving two Spanish battalions at the bridge and ford of Almaraz, our division commenced its march towards the southern frontier of Portugal; and rejoiced we were to turn our backs on this land of starvation. We reached the town of Delatosa the following day, and found several brigades of our army encamped there. We had not long taken up our ground for the bivouac, when the thick brushwood by which we were surrounded, being as dry as touch-paper, was soon in one general blaze, occasioned by the carelessness of the soldiers in kindling fires in the midst of it. This was an occurrence by no means unfrequent, and the baggage, horses, mules, and asses, were often in imminent danger of being roasted.

On the 21st, the whole army, except our division, was in full march towards Truxillo, (the birth-place of Pizarro,) from whence it was to proceed by Merida to Badajoz. The same evening we left Delatosa, and marched until midnight, when we lay down by our arms on the road-side four hours; and at day-break of the 22d, instead of following the track of the army, our march was directed towards Carceres, where we arrived on the 23d. Carceres is a town of considerable size, standing in the midst of an extensive plain, with nothing remarkable either in or about it, except a white monastery, perched on the summit of a desolate-looking detached rock, at no great distance from the town.

The 24th, 25th, and 26th, were spent in a similar manner to the three preceding days, viz. marching during half the night and several hours of the day.

Those who have passed over the line of country from Almaraz to Valencia d'Alcantara, need not be told, that on its parched plains and barren mountains any thing like herbage, in the summer months, is rarely to be met with: it will not, therefore, be wondered at that our baggage-animals died daily by dozens. An issue of corn for them from the commissariat was utterly hopeless. I do not believe that I was more unfortunate in this respect than my neighbours; but I do know that I started from Lisbon with the light brigade on the 3d of July, and by the 26th of August I had only a donkey remaining out of my original stud, which had consisted of two horses, a mule, and the said donkey. Two died of starvation and fatigue, and the other was lost at Talavera, as before related.

If, during the retrograde movement towards Portugal, our quadrupeds had a bad time of it, the troops could boast but little better fare, as any thing like a regular issue of provisions was unknown; nor, until we reached Valencia d'Alcantara, on the 26th, was a loaf of bread to be procured, and there only with much difficulty.

On the 27th and part of the 28th we halted near Valencia d'Alcantara, an ancient walled town; but I do not remember having seen any cannon on the ramparts. From the gardens in the neighbourhood we regaled ourselves with vegetables and mulberries, the first luxury of the kind we had tasted for some weeks.

On the 29th, having marched the greater part of the preceding night, we entered Portugal once more, which is here divided from Spain by a rivulet. One of the most striking objects I ever beheld is the small fortified town of Maravao, a short distance within the Portuguese frontier, perched on the summit of a dark isolated mountain, which frowns over the road at its base. The only approach to it is by an exceedingly narrow zig-zag road, which a handful of men might defend for ever; and, as there is no ground within reach from whence it can be bombarded, I conceive that its reduction would prove an arduous undertaking, unless water and provisions failed the garrison. A march of several miles through a valley finely watered, and abounding with the largest and most luxuriant chestnut-trees, brought us to Castello de Vide, near which we encamped. In this town, the first time for many weeks, we had an opportunity of purchasing bread, rice, chocolate, and capital wine; and it is scarcely necessary to add, that little else went on in camp this day but eating and drinking the good things from which we had so long been estranged. If the whole truth must be told, such good use was made of a certain fluid called "confession wine," with which the cellars in Castello de Vide abounded, that not a thoroughly sober individual could have been found in the whole division by nine o'clock that night. Having nothing to apprehend in the way of a surprise, not a Frenchman being within several marches of us, the penance which we had done for some weeks on spring water, the most rigid stiff-laced person existing will admit to have been a sufficient apology for our jollification amongst the chestnut groves.

In its narrow and dirty streets, Castello de Vide resembles nine-tenths of the towns of its country. From the castle, or citadel, the eye ranges over a vast tract of sun-burnt country, mountain, and plain. Here we remained about a week, without any occurrence taking place worthy of a place in my journal.

On the 1st of September I considered it a point of duty to keep up the good old custom of waging war against the partridges, and started for the purpose at day-break, with one lazy old Spanish pointer, whose average pace was about three miles an hour. Between red-legged partridges, hares, and quails, the day's sport was not despicable. On this occasion I was very nearly minus a friend, and the king a good officer; for I made a double shot, killing my partridge, and throwing several grains of shot into my friend's regimental cap, which, for want of a more sportsmanlike head-dress, he wore on the occasion.

We moved from Castello de Vide on the 7th, and reached Portalegre the same evening, where we halted two days. It is amongst the best towns in Portugal; and we saw some tolerably fair specimens of Portuguese beauty in the convents. There is a fine church or cathedral here also.

General Catline Crawford's brigade was in Portalegre during our stay in it. These troops had arrived at Lisbon from England or Ireland, shortly after the light brigade, and were on their march to join the army at Talavera, when Marshal Soult crossing the mountains from Leon into Estremadura, obliged them to re-enter Portugal.

The 10th brought us to Aronches, an old walled town, but incapable of much defence. Another blazing hot march on the following day placed our division at its destination in Campo Maior. The whole British army arrived about this period near the Guadiana (which river divides

DISPOSITION OF THE ARMY.

the two countries), and was put into cantonments. Head-quarters with one division of infantry was at Badajoz; our own division at Campo Maior; others at Villa Vicoza, Estremoz, Albuquerque, and different towns and villages near the Guadiana. In the open country in our front, at or near Merida, were our advanced posts of cavalry and horse artillery.

CHAPTER VII.

The country near Campo Maior, and the climate of Alemtejo. The army becomes very sickly. Fate of General Cuestas' army after we parted company with it at Talavera. Various descriptions of field-sports near Campo Maior. How to keep off fevers, agues, &c. Shooting excursions in the forest of Albuquerque. Wild boars, wolves, and red deer. Bathing excursions of our battalion, and its march to and from the Caya. Destruction of hares, rabbits, and partridges. Riding down red-legged partridges. Lieut.-Colonel Sidney Beckwith's system contrasted with that of many commanding officers of regiments. Rumours of the army being about to return to England. The army continues sickly. The army leaves its cantonments on the Guadiana, and proceeds to the northern frontier of Portugal. Our march to that point. Students and young padres at the University of Coimbra uselessly employed. Sketch of the country between Coimbra and Pinhel, and our march through it. The 95th Rifle Corps and 1st German Hussars cross the Coa, and take up the outposts. The manner in which we passed our time in the outlandish regions between the Coa and Agueda, until the campaign of 1810 opened. Various amusements for the soldiers encouraged by Lieut.-Colonel Beckwith.

As the army remained stationary in this position three months, I shall touch slightly on what occurred under my own observation in General Crawford's division.

Campo Maior is a walled town, commanded by higher ground, and consequently incapable of standing a siege of any length. It is three leagues from Badajoz, and about the same distance from Elvas. The country in its vicinity abounds with olives, vines, corn, figs, pomegranates, and other fruits; and there are many *quintas*, or country-houses, near it, which have excellent gardens well supplied with water. Indeed, the Portuguese evince much industry and ingenuity in conducting water to their gardens from a long distance, and irrigating them. Without this precaution, all vegetation must cease in the summer months, the heat being so intense in this province of Alemtejo as to burn every plant to a cinder. The whole of Alemtejo, and more particularly that part which approaches the sluggish and muddy waters of the Guadiana, is proverbially unhealthy, especially in summer and autumn. The natives of the northern provinces dread it as a West Indies or Sierra Leone; and they have a proverb to this effect, "Once in Alemtejo, never out of it again alive." There proved to be too much truth in the adage; for during the three months our army was cantoned there, the mortality was frightful; and I am confident that I speak within bounds when I say, that one-third of the army was in hospital, from fevers, agues, and dysenteries.

The natives of Alemtejo may be distinguished at once from those of the north of Portugal, fever and ague being legibly imprinted on their cadaverous faces and emaciated figures. It is not, then, a matter of surprise, that the British army, which for months before its arrival on the Guadiana had been unavoidably subjected to long and harassing marches, constantly exposed to the heavy dews at night without tents, and subsisting on a very scanty allowance of food of the worst kind, should feel severely the effects of this unhealthy province.

A word or two now respecting the Spanish army of General Cuesta since our parting company with it at Talavera on the 3d of August. It reached the left bank of the Tagus, I believe, in safety; but was shortly afterwards attacked by Marshal Victor or General Sebastiani, or by both, and completely defeated and dispersed, with the loss of a great part of its artillery, and many men. Where and when this discomfited army rallied, and what benefit Spain in afterdays reaped from its services, I leave to the historian to relate. As a mere keeper of a daily log-book, it is unnecessary that I should dive into these matters.

Such amongst us as were addicted to fieldsports, had an excellent opportunity of gratifying our propensities in that way during our sojourn at Campo Maior, although the heat was so great until the end of October as to prove a damper to those who were not keen sportsmen. Except when a field-day occurred to prevent it, I was amongst the number of those who lived in the open air with gun or greyhound; and to the constant exercise I attribute having enjoyed good health, at a time when hundreds of our division were suffering from agues and fevers, and very many taken to their long homes. Doctors differed as to the mode of living most likely to retain health and to prevent sickness.

The water-beverage system found but very few supporters in our corps; and, as far as my own experience enables me to speak, I should recommend, *per diem*, under similar circumstances, and on the same spot, a fair allowance of generous wine, several cigars (to prevent infectious disease), the persecution of red-legged partridges, quails, &c. &c., or a gallop with the wire-haired greyhounds of the country across the plains after the hares, which occasionally give rare sport. To put in practice the latter part of the prescription was found exceedingly difficult, in consequence of the starved state of our Rosinantes rendering even a canter next to impossible. With some good English pointers and greyhounds, in few countries could better sport be had than in this neighbourhood. There are abundance of partridges, quails, hares, rabbits, (woodcocks and snipes in winter,) bustards on the plains, and florikins also in large flocks, plovers of various sorts; also a bird of the grouse kind, which the natives call *tarambola;* ducks, teal, and other wild fowl in the Guadiana and the Caya.

In the forest of Albuquerque, a few leagues distant, are red deer, wild boars, wolves, and foxes. To that forest we made several excursions, taking with us some of our best marksmen, and sleeping the night before in the small walled town of Ouguila, which is on the borders of the forest. Several fine red deer were killed, one of which, a very large stag, I was so fortunate as to bring down with a ball. Although neither wolves nor wild boars were brought to bag, we nevertheless had some shots at them. I look back on those excursions as amongst the happiest days of my life.

General Crawford directed that the regiments of his division should frequently be marched to the river Caya, about four miles distant, to bathe. This was done independently by battalions. Trifling occurrences sometimes make lasting impressions; and the animated scene which our visit to the river produced I have never forgotten. Not only do I cherish the recollection of days long gone by, which were full of excitement, but

I derive indescribable pleasure from placing before me, in battle array, some of those " trifles light as air;" one of which, relative to our bathing excursions in the Caya, shall be detailed in as small a compass as possible.

Whether the intention of General Crawford was, that the regiments should march to the river to bathe as fully armed and accoutred as if they were about to mount guard in some stiff-starched garrison, I cannot say; but I know that every corps did harness and march forth to the river in that form, except our own. Colonel Beckwith, on the contrary, always ordered our men, on these occasions, to take with them neither arms, accoutrements, knapsacks, nor any one thing except their light fatigue dress, foraging-caps, and a stick, for a purpose which shall immediately be explained. The officers were desired to take with them their fowling-pieces and greyhounds; and, in this light, easy attire, we marched to the river. As soon as we were clear of the walls of Campo Maior, the whole battalion was extended in one long line in skirmishing order, bringing rather forward the wings, and proceeding in this manner straight across the great plain to the river. Hares, rabbits, and partridges were soon started at all points; when such shooting, coursing, and knocking down with sticks and stones, and such *mobbing* of quadrupeds and birds commenced, that a game-preserving John Bull would undoubtedly have stigmatised us as a most nefarious corps of poachers. The process of bathing having been duly performed, the same scene took place on our return to the town; and the spirit and glee with which all hands entered into the sport may easily be conceived.

Those who know nothing of the habits of the red-legged partridge, would be surprised to be told that we frequently made parties to *ride them down.* I can fancy the incredulous stare of some of my countrymen, if they heard any person bold enough to make such an assertion. But that it is not more strange than true, there are many living witnesses to prove. If a red-legged partridge be pursued by a person on horseback whilst on the wing, and a great noise and shouting is made, he will not rise a second time, but will continue running, and at last crouch, and allow himself to be taken up. I have but rarely known them to rise and take a second flight.

As I am inclined to believe my most bitter enemies will acknowledge that adulation and flattery are not amongst my besetting sins, I may declare, without any apprehension of being taxed with the appellation of *toad-eater*, that I have ever considered Lieutenant-Colonel Sidney Beckwith to have been better calculated for the command of a regiment of light troops than most men who are to be found. In the common acceptation of the word, "*a capital commanding officer of a regiment,*" too often implies a good barrack-square drill—a man whose military ideas soar but little beyond the orderly room, the exact fit of the soldier's coat, and the proper allowance of pipe-clay wherewith to plaster his belts twice every twenty-four hours. Such a man does not discover, until the moment he actually finds himself in the field in good earnest, with his regiment placed in the teeth of an enterprising and experienced enemy at the out-posts, and constantly liable to be attacked, that he is little better than a novice in his profession (the practical part of it at least), and that commanding a battalion at Dublin or Portsmouth is one thing, and in the field another. It is also no less true, that the sentiments which I have ventured to express on this subject, many men of a certain school would be perfectly horror-struck at, as sapping the foundation of what they deem the essentials of the service. Be it so: Doctors differ. I speak not at hap-hazard, but from some little experience in those matters; and I must confess that the marching and counter-marching in a barrack-yard have but few charms for me.

Colonel Beckwith was, indeed, the very reverse of such commanding-officers as I have just described; and I may safely say, that he held those matters very cheap when compared with other things of so much greater importance, which daily presented themselves. Far be it from me to insinuate that Colonel Beckwith did not feel the vast and imperious necessity of discipline, or that any one iota of regimental detail was not performed to the letter; but he was always averse to tease and torment the old soldier with more than a certain *quantum* of drill, particularly at a time like that in question, when the army was reposing from its late fatigues and starvation. Whether the general system adopted by him rendered his battalion efficient in the field, and able to perform its duties at the out-posts of the army, to the satisfaction of the different general officers under whom it served many years in succession, I leave impartial judges to determine.

Rumours and reports of all kinds were circulated during our stay at Campo Maior. Amongst others, it was declared that transports had arrived at Lisbon to take the army to England, the cause of the Peninsula being considered hopeless. The sickness continued even after the cool weather in November appeared; and our loss of men was very severe. Many of our officers went to England for the recovery of their health, which some of them never succeeded in thoroughly regaining.

A strong corps of the French army having concentrated at or near Salamanca in the end of the autumn, by which the fortress of Ciudad Rodrigo and the north of Portugal were menaced, the British army broke up from the Guadiana early in December, on the 12th of which month the head of General Crawford's division, consisting of our own regiment, marched to Aronches, on its route to the north of Portugal. General Hill was left with his division and some cavalry in Alemtejo.

At this time, Marshal Beresford, ably seconded by other British officers attached to the Portuguese service, was actively employed in organising the new Portuguese levies; and in some few months after this date, enabled them to contend successfully with the veterans of France, as will be seen by and by.

Passing through Portalegre, Crato, Ponte de Sor, and Abrantes, without meeting any adventure worth relating, we reached Punheite on the 22d; which town I mentioned in our march from Lisbon to Talavera in July. We patronised in the evening what was dignified with the name of an opera; a very indifferent exhibition of bolero and fandango dancing.

Thomar, a good town, in which we found

Marshal Beresford's head-quarters, and many of the new levies, brought us up for the night on the 23d. The light brigade was put into a large, cold, cheerless convent; and as the weather was frosty, we had some trouble to counteract the effects of the easterly wind rushing through the long galleries, by a liberal allowance of mulled wine, brought up in camp-kettles, and drank out of half-pint tin cups, vulgarly denominated *black jacks*.

Two days' march more through a country not particularly enchanting, brought us to Lyria, a large town situated in a fertile valley. On a hill above it is an old castle, in all probability Moorish. I slightly mentioned Lyria last year, on the march of the army towards Roleia and Vimeira.

On the 27th we reached Pombal, by an excellent road. It is a town of no great size, with the usual accompaniment of a Moorish castle overlooking it. The one in question is a fine bold object, and imparts an air of some consequence to Pombal.

We arrived on the day following at Condeixa, one of the cleanest and neatest towns in Portugal. Our battalion was packed up for the night in one large house, the property of a man who had taken flight with his family to the Brazils, in the fear of a third invasion from the

French. It is probable that this mansion never contained so much company before, nor of so noisy a kind.

The road from Condeixa to Coimbra is capital; which latter place we entered on the 29th, and halted in on the 30th. Coimbra is considered the third city in Portugal, Lisbon and Oporto ranking before it. Possibly no city in Europe is more beautifully situated. It stands on high ground overlooking the Mondego, as it winds its course through a beautiful valley, cultivated with Indian corn, vines, &c. &c., and whose banks are not deficient in boldness. Across the river is a handsome bridge leading to the city, in which are many churches, convents, good shops, and the largest university (I believe) in the kingdom.

We could not but observe, that the crowds of students with which the streets swarmed, and the legions of idle young vagabonds coming under the head of *clericos,* with the crowns of their heads shaved, running all over the city after the host, might have been better employed at that moment in training themselves to the use of arms, to resist the numerous legions of France, which threatened for the third time to invade their country. Leaving our benedictions with these worthies, we prosecuted our march on the 31st over a mountainous tract of country, and by infamously bad roads, to Ponte de Marcella, a miserable village on the river Alva. I was one of eight officers for whose *particular* accommodation on that night was appropriated a little, dirty, dark den of a room, with an earthen floor. Having masticated some lean, tough, ration beef, and swallowed some sour wine, we contrived to whiff away care and sorrow with our cigars, and reposed in our cloaks on some Indian corn straw.

1*st January*, 1810.—Crawling out of our hovel as soon as daylight appeared, and having wished each other " a happy new year," our best legs were put foremost, and we quartered for the night at Venda and Gallices, two villages on the road leading towards Celerico, at the foot of the Sierra d'Estrella, a lofty and extensive chain of mountains, the tops of which were covered with snow.

Every yard of this road must afford pleasure to those who take the slightest interest in fine scenery; for here you have the boldest mountains on the right, from the sides of which may be seen villages and convents jutting out amongst the woods of pine in the most picturesque manner imaginable; whilst on the left of the road the country assumes a softer aspect, being diversified with valleys cultivated with the vine and Indian corn, and not wanting in villages, although of a poor description.

This sketch of the country which we marched

through on new year's day, 1810, must suffice for the general features of the line of march to Celerico, where we arrived on the evening of the 3d of January. It is an ancient town, with the old story of the Moorish castle, by way of citadel, overhanging it, and is perched in some rough rocky ground not far from the Mondego.

In passing through a village on the 3d, where there was a convent, we were welcomed by the nuns with reiterated *vivas*, and wavings of white handkerchiefs from the windows, coupled with curses and execrations on the French, who were hovering on the frontiers of their country, and would soon probably oblige them to decamp from their prison. I have already alluded to the pallid sickly appearance of the natives of Alemtejo, when contrasted with those of the north. The Portuguese are an ugly race at best; but those of the northern provinces are perfect angels of light compared with the southern.

Colonel Donkins' brigade, consisting of the 45th, fifth battalion of the 60th, and the 88th, which had been placed under General Crawford's orders, on the retreat from Talavera last summer, was now removed from his command, and he retained only his original light brigade, viz. the 43d, 52d, and our own 1st battalion. In the course of a few months from this period, two Portuguese Cacadore regiments (light infantry), Nos. 1 and 3, were sent to General Crawford, which, together with the three British corps just mentioned, formed the light division, by which name it was known during the remainder of the Peninsular campaigns. The 45th, 88th, and part of the 60th, were subsequently in the division commanded by Major-general Picton, who first arrived from England to join this army in the spring of 1810.

The 4th of January brought us to Pinhel, an old Moorish town, similar to Celerico, standing amongst rugged rocks, and having in it a palace belonging to the Bishop of Pinhel. In the castle are some curious and very ancient pieces of artillery, composed of a number of broad iron hoops bound together, thus forming a tube. The whole British army, except General Hill's division, which remained in Alemtejo, reached the north of Portugal about this period. Head-quarters with the Guards were at Vizeu; other brigades and divisions at Pinhel, Tranquosa, Celerico, and various towns on the left bank of the river Coa; General Crawford, with the 43d and 52d regiments, remained at Pinhel; and our battalion, with some of the 1st German Hussars, were the only troops pushed across the Coa to observe the enemy's outposts on the Agueda, the most advanced of which were at St. Felices, a Spanish town opposite the formidable pass of Barba del Puerco.

Crossing the Coa on the 6th of January,

1810, our regiment marched to Villar Torpim, Regada, and Cinco Villas, three poor villages; and we were frequently moved during the months of January, February, and March, (in consequence of various rumours and reports of intended attempts on the part of the French to surprise the outposts,) to other villages lying between the two rivers, well known to old light division men of that day, viz. Figuera, Mata de Lobos, Escallion, Escarigo, &c. &c. Deep snow fell soon after we had taken up our new quarters, which rendered the otherwise miserable desolate villages still more forlorn. Coursing and shooting were our chief employments by day, and at night we either whiffed away cigars over some Douro wine, and speculated on the campaign which was soon expected to commence, or danced boleros, fandangos, and waltzes, with the good-looking daughters of an Israelite, in whose house I was billeted, in Villar Torpim.

To detail the manner in which we killed time every day during the dreary winter months, some weeks of which we were nearly snowed up in our hovels, and in the poorest villages in the Peninsula, would be nearly a repetition of what I have just stated. Until, therefore, we began to feel for the enemy in the month of March, towards Barba del Puerco, my tale is quickly told.

It is not my intention to enter minutely into

the history of Padre Joan's pigeon-house near Mata de Lobos! There are but few, very few, of the good fellows now living who understand this inuendo. Stewed pigeons and pigeon-pies were esteemed great delicacies, and a most useful accompaniment to tough, lean, ration beef, at the outposts; but the less said the better as to the mode by which we procured them.

In the said village of Mata de Lobos I passed many happy but bandit-like days in February, sitting at night over a brass pan of charcoal, and, with my three jolly subalterns, reposing in the same diminutive den, rolled up in our cloaks, on some straw. Amongst our other amusements, whilst thus detached far in front of the army, we frequently got up foot-races (our horses being in but poor trim for such feats), played matches at foot-ball, and rackets against the tower of the church, had duck-hunting with dogs in a piece of water, and sometimes turned a pig loose, with his tail greased, when he was pursued by the soldiers, and became the lawful prize of the man who could catch and hold him, which was no easy matter. Our gallant commander, Colonel Beckwith, was ever amongst the first to encourage those meetings, considering, no doubt, and very justly, that to divert and to amuse his men, and to allow them every possible indulgence compatible with the discipline of the battalion, whilst an interval of quiet permitted it, was the surest way to make the soldiers follow him cheerfully through fire and water, when the day of trial came; for they well knew that he was the last man on earth who would give them unnecessary trouble, or, on the other hand, would spare either man or officer, when the good of the service demanded their utmost exertions. I venture further to assert, without fear of contradiction, that he was never deceived or disappointed in the liberal view which he took of those matters.

If any are inclined to accuse us, whilst thus isolated in those wild regions, in the depth of a dreary winter, of having passed our time in irrational and fruitless pursuits, let me remind them at once, and without beating about the bush, that although Malta, Gibraltar, Halifax, Quebec, Portsmouth, Plymouth, and various other garrisons, at home and abroad, can boast of excellent libraries, billiard-tables, whist clubs, and dinner clubs, independent of garrison balls and garrison concerts, &c. &c., the rascally villages between the Coa and Agueda, growing out, as it were, from amongst the huge blocks of granite, and peopled by the most wretched, dirty, idle, ignorant, priest-ridden peasantry any where to be found, afforded none of these resources.

Such brigades of the army as were in Alemtejo with General Hill, or behind the Coa, in Vizeu,

Tranquosa, and other towns, where one, two, or more regiments were quartered together, had resources by no possibility attainable by his Majesty's first battalion 95th Rifle Corps at that moment. In spite of which, however, I believe that few, if any members of the battalion, would have exchanged, on any terms, their situation with those rearward.

In the first place, we were neither pestered nor tormented with the formal process of mounting guard every morning, with band, bugles, drums, or trumpets; but in each village of our cantonments a small guard of a corporal and three or four men was mounted quietly, to ensure regularity. In the next place, we ranged free and unrestrained, with horse, gun, or greyhound, when and where we thought proper.

When the month of March arrived, matters of far greater moment claimed our attention than such pastimes as I have recently described. The sooner, therefore, I jump to the period when, for the first time during the campaign of 1810, we came in contact with the French, the better.

CHAPTER VIII.

A skirmish with the French near Barba del Puerco. The whole of our battalion moves up to the Agueda, and occupies an extended line of posts. Massacre of a French soldier by some Spanish shepherds, near Almofala. Night attack made on four companies of our battalion at the pass of Barba del Puerco. The enemy is repulsed with loss. Observations. Letter from Lord Wellington to Colonel Beckwith, expressing his approbation of the conduct of his corps on the occasion. General Crawford also thanks the regiment in orders. The French force at San Felices reinforced from Salamanca. Character of General Loison. General Crawford withdraws the troops from Barba del Puerco. We occupy Villa de Ciervo. Our ten companies reduced to eight, and some officers sent to England to recruit. Fine specimens of crystal found near Villa de Ciervo. My establishment is augmented by a young wolf. Two Portuguese light battalions join General Crawford. We are reinforced also by a troop of horse artillery, the 14th and 16th Light Dragoons. Extensive line of posts guarded by General Crawford's corps. A large army under Marshal Massena assembles near Ciudad Rodrigo, intended to invade Portugal. The three different corps which composed it. By whom commanded. Massena's proclamation to the Portuguese. He lays siege to Rodrigo. The light division watch him closely, and are constantly getting under arms from various causes. Invidious feeling of certain persons in the army towards the light division. The French batteries open on Rodrigo. Their cavalry drive our pickets over the Azarva.

OCCUPY BARBA DEL PUERCO.

Prognostications of some wiseacres in the army that the siege of Rodrigo would be raised by Lord Wellington. General Junot crosses the Azarva to reconnoitre our force. Captain Krauchenberg, of the 1st German Hussars, distinguishes himself. General Crawford retires across the Duas Casas, and takes up a position behind the Touron. General Junot's cautious manner of advancing. Query: Why did Massena never attempt to cut off the light division from the Coa with his numerous cavalry? Rodrigo surrenders to the French. General Crawford surprises a French detachment. Colonel Talbot, of the 14th Light Dragoons, killed. Gallantry of his regiment. Exemplary conduct of the French infantry in square. Observations.

On the 27th of February the first company of the battalion for detachment (Captain Creagh's) was ordered to march from Escarigo, to reconnoitre the village of Barba del Puerco, in which he found a strong detachment of French cavalry and infantry, with whom he had a skirmish, and fell back, agreeable to his orders, to Escarigo, where I joined him with my company; and a third company was pushed forward from Villar Torpim to Vermiosa, to support us.

The following day I was ordered to reconnoitre Barba del Puerco again, which, finding that the French had vacated, I occupied as a picket-post, sending a small party to the bridge at the foot of the pass; opposite to which was a picket of infantry and cavalry, detached from the French force at St. Felices.

By information collected at Barba del Puerco, from the padre of the village (who afterwards proved himself a vile traitor to his country), the French force at St. Felices consisted of 3000 men, infantry, cavalry, and artillery, under the command of Baron Ferez, a German in the French service, and a general of brigade belonging to General Loison's division. Our whole battalion was about this time ordered to close up to the Agueda, and, in conjunction with the 1st German Hussars, we held Villa de Ciervo, with four companies; Barba del Puerco, with four companies; Almofala and Escalhao, each with one;—thus watching all the fords on the river, from Villa de Ciervo on the right, to beyond Escalhao on the left, at the junction of the Agueda and Douro;—a long line of country for so small a force, and at such a distance from support.

With a view of keeping us on the *qui vive*, and of enabling every officer in the battalion to make himself acquainted, in the event of being driven back, with the line of the river, the roads leading from it towards the Coa, and the general features of the district entrusted to our charge, our companies frequently exchanged posts.

Being stationed at Almofala early in March, I witnessed a disgusting and cruel sight. Having gone with another officer to the mountainous bank which overhangs the river not far from the village, to visit the picket, we perceived a French soldier, *unarmed*, running down the mountain on the opposite side of the river, no doubt with the intention of trying to cross over and desert to us. Three Spanish shepherds who were tending their sheep on the same side of the river, intercepted him, and beat him to death with their clubs in less time than it has taken me to write an account of the sickening sight. We called out, and made signals to them to desist, and to spare him, but in vain. We fired several shots over their heads to intimidate them, but it had no effect, and the butchery went on without our being able to interfere, or to interrupt those savages in what they considered, no doubt, a most patriotic and meritorious exploit. A deluge of rain had so swollen the river, which roared at the foot of the mountain, that to pass it was impossible; and, indeed, could we have effected it, the blood-thirsty shepherds would have escaped, before we could by possibility have reached them. To have inflicted the summary punishment on them with a rifle ball, which we all felt well inclined to do, would have been only an act of justice; but it was a step, nevertheless, which the higher authorities would have visited with a heavy punishment.

If the number of men which the French army lost by assassinations of a similar kind, during the whole of the war in the Peninsula, could be ascertained, it would be an interesting and extraordinary document. Much as every man possessing the slightest degree of humanity must abhor the inhuman system of killing stragglers, adopted by the Spaniards, great allowance must, nevertheless, be made for them, who thus retaliated for the countless acts of cruelty committed by their invaders.

NIGHT ATTACK ON OUR POST AT BARBA DEL PUERCO.

The French general, Ferrez, who commanded at St. Felices, made a strenuous effort at midnight of the 19th of March to surprise the post at Barba del Puerco, which four companies of our battalion under Colonel Beckwith occupied. At the head of six hundred chosen men, grenadiers and light infantry, this general placed himself; and having concealed his force as near the bridge as possible, unheard by our double sentry on the other side of it, (for the roaring of this mountain-river, swollen by the late rains, was such, that no other sound but the rushing of its waters amongst the rocks could be heard,) dashed across, and driving before him a sergeant's piquet posted near the bridge, up the face of the pass, pressed on rapidly until met by our companies; when a conflict took place of the most extraordinary kind, both from the nature of the terrific mountain-pass in which the combatants met, and the unusual hour which the French general had selected for the attack.

One blaze of fire on the head of their column, as soon as it could be distinguished, followed instantly by a cheer and a charge, sent the enemy headlong down the side of the mountain in the utmost confusion, and across the bridge, to which they were pursued by our men, pouring in a constant fire, and with good effect.

On the opposite bank, lining the broken ground near the bridge, General Ferrez had placed the reserve of his infantry, stated to have been fifteen hundred men, to cover the retreat of the attacking party. Those men kept up a random fire across the river as soon as their routed countrymen had rejoined them, which did but little execution. It soon ceased; and thus terminated this nocturnal affray.

If a man be permitted to speak of his own corps in terms of approbation, I most assuredly feel myself entitled to do so on this occasion. Of the four companies stationed at Barba del Puerco for the defence of the pass, one was detached to a path far to the right of the village, to check any body of the enemy which might advance in that direction; and meeting no enemy there, of course it was not engaged; consequently, *three* companies, suddenly roused out of their sleep at midnight, beat back, in a short space of time, *six hundred* chosen veterans on their reserve of fifteen hundred men, and inflicted on them no trifling loss. Two French officers were found dead in the pass, with many of their soldiers killed and wounded; some prisoners were also taken. We lost one officer killed (Mr. Mercer), and from fifteen to twenty sergeants and privates killed and wounded. Colonel Beckwith received a shot through his cap, whilst in the act of rolling a huge piece of rock down on the fugitives, by way of accelerating their retreat. Lord Wellington sent a handsome letter of thanks to Colonel Beckwith, expressive of his approbation of the conduct of the regiment; and General Crawford, never lavish of praise, issued an order complimentary to the corps.

A few days after this affair, the post at Barba del Puerco was reinforced by one company of the 43d and two of the 52d, which regiments had recently been sent across the Coa from Pinhel; but the day after their arrival, the whole of the troops were withdrawn from the pass to Villa de Ciervo, and a small party of the German Hussars left as a picket.

Intelligence reached us on the 25th of March, that the French force at San Felices had been augmented by the arrival of the remainder of

General Loison's division from Salamanca. The name of Loison will not be forgotten by the Portuguese of the present generation; for he was one of the most cruel of their invaders, and at the time he commanded a division in Junot's army, in 1808, previous to the convention of Cintra, permitted such atrocities to be perpetrated by the troops under his command, as would have disgraced a band of untutored savages.

Early in April, orders reached us from England that the ten companies of which our battalion was composed should be formed into eight, and that two captains and a proportion of subalterns, with a few sergeants and privates, should proceed home to recruit. This arrangement was carried into effect soon afterwards, and the eight companies numbered about one hundred men each. It will, therefore, be perceived, that in less than nine months after our arrival from England with nearly eleven hundred men, we were melted down to about eight hundred; and for this we were principally indebted to the Alemtejo fever during the previous autumn, having as yet sustained but a trifling loss from the enemy.

Near Villa de Ciervo our officers discovered some good specimens of crystal, which, when afterwards sent to England, polished, and set, made seals much resembling white cornelian. Soon after this discovery, another of the natural productions of the country came into my hands, in the shape of a young wolf, which I purchased from a peasant, but which could never, whilst he remained in my possession, be made to receive the same fine polish of which the crystals were susceptible; for he was such a savage and untameable brute at six months old, and, moreover, so ravenous, that I found it no easy matter to satisfy his appetite, and that of my greyhound puppy likewise, which was his foster-brother. I made a present of him, after being tormented five months with his society in camp, bivouac, or quarters; and he found his way to England, in the autumn of the year of which I am now treating, under the especial protection of a noble lord, at that time one of Lord Wellington's aides-du-camp.

Towards the end of April, the 1st and 3d regiments of Portuguese caçadores were added to General Crawford's command, and, with the three British light regiments, formed what was from that period ever afterwards termed the Light Division.

In addition to the 1st German Hussars and his division of infantry, the following troops were sent across the Coa during the spring, to reinforce Brigadier-General Crawford: a troop of horse artillery, commanded by Captain Ross; the 14th and the 16th Light Dragoons; the whole forming a command of which a lieutenant-general might have been ambitious. With this force, General Crawford observed a long line of country through which the Agueda flows; patroling with his cavalry as far to the right as the fords in the neighbourhood of Fuente Guinaldo, and even yet higher up the river; and to the left as far as the junction of the Agueda and Douro, near Escalhao. His artillery, infantry, and the greater part of his cavalry, were stationed behind the Azarva (a small river running into the Agueda) in Gallegos and Espeja. He had cavalry pickets at Carpio, Marialva, Moulina dos Flores, at the ford of Val d'Espina, in front of Villa de Ciervo, and at Barba del Puerco, which, as a glance at the map will shew, was an extensive line to guard. He supported the cavalry posts on the Azarva by pickets of infantry.

A powerful French army, destined to invade Portugal, began to assemble in the beginning of May, on the right bank of the Agueda, preparatory to its laying siege to the Spanish fortress of Ciudad Rodrigo, which is distant three or four leagues from Gallegos, the head-quarter village of General Crawford's corps. That active guerilla chief, Don Julian Sanchez, hovered about the French army, and lost no opportunity of annoying and incommoding it.

This army, styled by the French "the Army of Portugal," was commanded by Marshal Massena, the Prince of Esling, and was to be composed of three distinct corps: the 2d corps, commanded by General Regnier; the 6th corps, by Marshal Ney, Duke of Elchingen; and the 8th corps, by General Junot, Duke of Abrantes. The cavalry had for its chief General Montbrun.

Massena, in his proclamation to the Portuguese nation, previous to his entering their country, declared, that he came *not* to invade Portugal, but to rescue it from the English, whom he intended forthwith to " drive into the sea, and to plant the imperial eagles on the citadel of Lisbon," and some more trash of the same nature. He added, that he was at the head of one hundred and ten thousand Frenchmen for the express purpose, and that resistance to the imperial decree was useless. The 6th and 8th corps only had been collected on the Agueda at the period now alluded to, the 2d corps being employed elsewhere.

A minute and detailed account of every different movement made by the enemy, for the purpose either of covering their large foraging parties, of reconnoitering our line of posts, or of trying the various fords, &c. &c. from the time of the affair at Barba del Puerco, on the 19th March, up to the period of General Crawford's corps recrossing the Coa, on the 24th of July, would fill a volume, and, moreover, afford but little interest to any one now living, except an odd one or two remaining on this side the river Styx, who were actors in the scenes to which I allude. It is sufficient to observe, that from the beginning of March until the 24th of July, we were stationed so close to the outposts of the French, as to render it necessary for the soldiers to sleep fully accoutred, and the officers, consequently, with their clothes on, ready to get under arms in an instant; and we were, as a matter of course, always under arms one hour before break of day. In short, the French cavalry were eternally in motion, in large bodies, towards our chain of posts, and we as often under arms waiting for them.

Jealousy is a demon which rears its head in all communities and societies, and, I fear, is to be found in military as well as in civil life. Amongst a certain number (I hope a few only) of malecontents in the army, the very name of the " Light Division," or the " outposts," was sufficient to turn their ration wine into vinegar, and to spoil their appetite for that day's allowance of ration beef also. In good truth, general officers were to be found, whom I could name, that bore towards us no very good will; perhaps because it was not their lot to hold so prominent a command as that of our more fortunate and favoured brigadier. But, be that as it may, those invidious barkers and growlers, whether in the subaltern or in the higher

ranks, in whose mouths was ever uppermost,—
"Ah! the Light Division! what is the Light Division more than any other?"— should have been briefly answered thus—The Light Division never did affect to place itself on a pedestal, as being superior to its comrades in arms; nor, on the other hand, when the most honourable, dangerous, harassing, and responsible post was allotted to it, and it was pushed across the Coa in the very teeth of Massena's numerous legions, which it watched night and day, month after month, along a difficult and extensive line of country, whilst the other divisions of the army were in cantonments behind the Coa, as perfectly at their ease, and as safe from surprise, as if they had been in a garrison in England,—could it have calculated on having its prominent services called in question by men, many of whom scarcely ever saw the Light Division in their lives, and were ignorant of the manner in which it was constantly employed in every successive campaign. I feel that I am justified in touching on this subject, (insignificant as it may appear,) inasmuch as it concerns every Light Division-man of that day.

On the 24th of May, the French threw a pontoon bridge over the Agueda, not far from Ciudad Rodrigo; and in the latter end of the month commenced operations against that fortress. Their working parties were constantly cannonaded, by day and night; and at times very heavily.

The French batteries, being at length completed, opened, at daybreak of the 25th of June, a most tremendous fire on the town, which was returned with equal spirit. At the same moment a large body of their cavalry advanced, and drove back our hussar pickets across the Azarva, on those of the infantry. Along the right bank of that river the enemy established a strong chain of cavalry posts, which they held during the remainder of the siege. This movement brought the pickets of the opponents extremely close to each other at the bridge of Marialva.

Soon after the French batteries opened on the 25th, a tremendous explosion was heard, which, we soon learnt, was occasioned by a shell from the town having fallen into one of the enemy's magazines. To detail the daily progress of the siege is not in my power: all we knew was, that the fire from the besiegers and the besieged was tremendous, and was kept up night and day with unremitting fury. Some wiseacres asserted roundly that Lord Wellington would cross the Coa, and advance with his army to the relief of Ciudad Rodrigo. It required, however, but a small allowance of consideration and common sense to be convinced, that to have marched against an army so numerous and experienced as that of Massena, with a force far inferior in numbers, and half that force made up of raw Portuguese levies who had never smelt powder, was not a measure likely to be adopted by so able and talented a commander as ours. But in all regiments, brigades, and divisions of every army, there are some few tacticians to be found of the same calibre, who fancy that the commander-in-chief is a perfect ignoramus in such matters, when compared with themselves.

Lord Wellington and General Spencer visited the outposts the day after the French batteries opened on the town. We still occupied Gallegos by day; but every evening General Crawford marched his infantry to a wood on some heights behind the village, towards the river Duas Casas, where we bivouacked, and returned soon after daybreak to the village. This, I presume, was a precautionary measure, fearing the enemy might attempt a night attack on the village, which their extreme proximity rendered probable.

From some commanding ground in the French lines, the return of our division from the heights to the village could plainly be perceived; and possibly being deceived on that point, mistaking us for reinforcements sent across the Coa to join General Crawford, Massena ordered General Junot to cross the Azarva at Marialva Bridge on the 4th July, with, it was supposed, about fifteen thousand men; and, by a close reconnoissance, to ascertain how matters really stood.

4th July.—Being under arms, as usual, an hour before day-break, on the heights, some shots were heard from our cavalry pickets at Marialva, who shortly afterwards retired slowly and in excellent order, keeping up a continued skirmish. Captain Kraukenberg, of the 1st German Hussars, an officer of the highest merit, distinguished himself on this occasion. Forming his squadron on some eligible ground near a small narrow bridge over a rivulet which runs through Gallegos, he waited until as many of the French dragoons had crossed as he thought proper to permit, when he instantly charged and put them into confusion, killing and wounding many of them, and bringing some prisoners with him to the heights, where General Crawford had drawn out the Light Division in line. The horse artillery opened with effect on the head of Junot's troops, who advanced with caution; but General Crawford having ascertained their great superiority of numbers, decided on retiring across the Duas Casas. This movement was covered by some cavalry and our battalion, who skirmished with the advance of the French until we had passed the river, which was effected with a very trifling loss on our part. Two hundred riflemen and some cavalry were left on the heights of Fort Conception as a picket, the remainder being placed in a position near the Portuguese village of Val de la Mula, behind the rivulet called the Turon, which is here the boundary of the two countries.

It has ever been a matter of surprise to those amongst us who have given it a thought, that a general of so rash and ardent a temper as Junot has been represented, should have displayed so much caution on this occasion. Had he been aware that the only force in his front was about four thousand infantry, a troop of light artillery, and some squadrons of cavalry, and that it had no support within many leagues, it is to be presumed he would have pushed us with much more vigour in our retrograde movement to the heights of Fort Conception; and had he done so, he might have made General Crawford fully sensible that he had delayed his retreat across the Duas Casas too long, whereby the safety of his division was in some measure endangered, and for no possible purpose.

Why Massena permitted the Light Division to remain so long between the Azarva and the Duas Casas, it is not for me to question, as the Prince of Esling was most indisputably a man of first-rate military ability. With greater reason may we wonder that, near as we were to so large an army for some months, with extensive plains between us and the Coa, no attempt was made by the numerous French cavalry to surprise and cut us off from that river.

We remained for some days in the position near Val de la Mula, having cavalry pickets on the Duas Casas. Ciudad Rodrigo surrendered on the 10th of July, after having sustained a furious bombardment of sixteen days, during the greater part of which the cannonade on both sides was tremendous. There was a large and practicable breach in the walls, and a numerous French army, highly exasperated at the obstinate defence of the garrison, ready to storm and take it, cost what it might. Perfectly aware that he had no chance of being relieved by the army of Lord Wellington, or by any of the Spanish forces, the governor capitulated, and the garrison became prisoners of war.

On the night of the 10th of July, General Crawford marched from Val de la Mula with seven companies of our battalion, two of the 52d, two pieces of artillery, the 14th Light Dragoons, and a part or the whole of the 1st German Hussars, to surprise a post consisting of about two hundred French infantry and a troop of cavalry, at the Spanish village of Barkela. Before daybreak we reached our ground unperceived by the French. The two field-pieces and the nine companies of infantry were drawn up on some rising ground about half a mile, or thereabout, from the village.

As soon as day broke and shewed us the enemy, in search of whom we had been marching the whole night, General Crawford ordered a charge to be made on them, as they were seen moving out of Barkela towards the French camp, on the other side of the Agueda. Their troop of cavalry was soon sabred or made prisoners; but with their infantry it was otherwise. Instantly forming a small square, they retired, rapidly and in good order, in the direction of the ford. Colonel Talbot, at the head of the 14th Light Dragoons, rode gallantly at and charged the little phalanx with great impetuosity, but without being able to break it.

No troops on earth could have conducted themselves with greater gallantry than the old and often-tried 14th Light Dragoons; and in so determined a manner did this distinguished corps make their charge, that Colonel Talbot, whose body I saw a few minutes after he was killed, bore the marks not only of bullets but of bayonets: and it is equally true, that he and many of his brave followers who actually reached the square, met their death by the bayonets of this invincible little body of Frenchmen, who steadily resisted their charges, and, without leaving in our hands one of their brave band, succeeded in making good their retreat over the plain. Some hundreds of the finest cavalry of which the British army could boast continued hovering about, ready to pounce on and to break them, if the least disorder should be detected.

It was impossible not to respect and admire the exemplary conduct of the French infantry; and this affair may probably tend to open the eyes of many men who talk with great composure of riding down and sabring infantry on a plain with cavalry, as if it was the most simple and feasible operation imaginable. But it must be confessed that such opinions are generally advanced by theoretical, not practical, soldiers. If the simple little fact in question be not considered conclusive, I must refer all sceptics on the subject to encounters of a more recent date; and they will find that at Waterloo not one British square was broken by cavalry on that bloody day.

It will be naturally asked, where were General Crawford's nine companies of infantry and his two pieces of artillery all this time? It may be answered, that they were standing without orders on a hill about half a mile distant; but *why* they were not ordered to advance, is more than I can explain. It is to be presumed that, had the field-pieces been ordered to advance at a brisk pace, with the cavalry, a few discharges of grape-shot would either have annihilated the square in ten minutes, or caused it to surrender; and it is no great presumption on the part of any individual belonging to the nine companies of British infantry present to pronounce, that they would have proved rather an overmatch for two companies of Frenchmen. Our loss on this occasion was, Lieut.-Colonel Talbot and a quarter-master of the 14th Dragoons killed, and about twenty-five men and horses killed and wounded.

CHAPTER IX.

General Crawford falls back to Junsa, on the Coa. The French advance. Fort Conception is destroyed by mines. Action of the Coa, 24th July, 1810. Major M'Leod of the 43d regt. French grenadiers storm the bridge, and are destroyed. General Crawford retires at night to Valverde. Reflections on the events of the day. We march to Celerico, and make huts near the town. The Light Division is divided into two brigades. Massena besieges Almeida. The Light Division moves up to support the cavalry. The powder magazine in Almeida explodes and destroys the town. The garrison capitulates. Affair between our cavalry and the French near Freixadas. The army retires towards Coimbra. Excursion to the summit of a mountain to see a lake. Discussion with a padre as to the qualities attributed to its waters. We continue the retreat. The Light Division arrives at Mortagoa. Affair of cavalry. We fall back on Buzaco, engaged with the French advanced guard. Sketch of the position.

LEAVING his cavalry at Val de la Mula, General Crawford withdrew the Light Division, on the 16th of July, to Junsa, a poor village about half a league distant from the Portuguese fortress of Almeida, and on the same side of the Coa, situated amongst some rocks overlooking the river.

On the 19th, a trifling affair took place between the cavalry in front of Val de la Mula, in which we made a few prisoners.

At break of day on the 21st, the Light Division and the artillery were ordered out of their bivouac near Junsa. Our battalion, with the horse artillery, advanced on the road towards the Turon, to support the cavalry, who were falling back from Val de la Mula, before a superior force of infantry, cavalry, and artillery. The remainder of the division was placed amongst some rocks and walls near Almeida.

On the advance of the French towards Fort Conception, on the 21st, the mines which our engineers had formed there were fired, and the whole exploded with a tremendous noise, and rendered the works useless to the invading army.

On the 22d, General Crawford drew his whole force back near Almeida, observing with pickets of cavalry the different roads on the great plain in front.

On the 23d, I happened to be on picket with my company in front of Junsa, amongst some granite rocks, as a support to the hussars on the plain. A more tremendous night of thunder, lightning, and rain, I never remember before or since, from which our only shelter was the lee side of the rocks. This was merely a prelude to what occurred on the following day.

ACTION AT THE COA.

24th July.—Soon after daybreak, the whole of Marshal Ney's corps, consisting of troops of all arms, to the amount of about twenty-five thousand men, advanced for the purpose of investing and laying siege to Almeida, and of driving General Crawford's corps of observation over the Coa, should it be found on the same side of the river.

General Crawford placed his infantry in line amongst some rocky ground and stone walls, his left being within seven or eight hundred yards of the walls of Almeida, and his right thrown back in a convex form towards the Coa. Our cavalry posts in the plain were soon forced back on the infantry, and a brisk cannonade commenced. The advance of the French cavalry were brought to bay by our infantry in the intersected ground; but Marshal Ney having more than twenty thousand infantry at his back, was not long to be delayed in this manner. Although the left of our line was under the protection of the guns of the fortress, the French assailed it with great impetuosity; and the right and centre also soon found itself beset with a swarm of light troops, supported by heavy columns constantly advancing, and aided by their artillery, which cannonaded us warmly.

ACTION AT THE COA. 147

It is not improbable that at this moment our brigadier began to think it would have been more prudent, and equally beneficial to the cause for which the British army was contending in the Peninsula, had he implicitly obeyed the positive orders of the Commander-in-Chief, to withdraw his corps of observation behind the Coa, on the fall of Ciudad Rodrigo, or on the first symptom of Massena's advance on Almeida, and by no means to risk an action against the superior numbers with which the French would undoubtedly advance towards that fortress. I never heard it yet doubted or denied that such were the orders transmitted to General Crawford from head-quarters, long before the 24th of July.

The baggage, artillery, cavalry, and the two Portuguese light battalions, were directed to retire instantly to the bridge over the Coa, and to gain the opposite bank without delay. Those who have seen and know this narrow and difficult defile, need not be informed, that to keep at bay as many thousand infantry as Marshal Ney might think proper to send forward, whilst the road was choked with troops, baggage, and artillery, which it was absolutely necessary should be covered and protected, during a retreat of a mile or more, and until they had crossed the bridge in safety, was no easy matter.

The troops destined to cover the retreat consisted of our own battalion, and a considerable part, or the whole, of the 43d and 52d regiments. No further description of this rocky defile is necessary, than that the road is very narrow, and as bad as the generality of mountain-roads in the Peninsula are; and moreover, that it is overhung by huge rocks in many places, from which, had our pursuers been permitted to possess themselves of them, they might have annihilated the troops underneath, without their being able to retaliate; and thus, the only option left them would have been a walk to Verdun as prisoners of war, or an instantaneous passage across the Styx instead of the Coa.

By this time the fight had begun in good earnest; and, in order that my story may not be too long, it will be sufficient to say, that from the commencement of the action at the edge of the plain until we reached the river, every inch of ground admitting of defence was obstinately contested by the rear-guard, which was followed by fresh troops every instant arriving to support their comrades. The French artillery failed not to help us along, whenever they had an opportunity, with a nine-pound shot.

As the rear-guard approached the Coa, we perceived that a part only of our cavalry, infantry, and artillery, had yet crossed the bridge; it became, therefore, indispensably requisite for us to

ACTION AT THE COA. 149

keep possession of a small hill looking down on, and perfectly commanding the bridge, until every thing had passed over, cost what it might.

I trust I shall be pardoned for saying that the soldiers of the old and gallant 43d, and that part also of our own battalion whose lot it was to defend this important hill, against a vast superiority of numbers, proved themselves worthy of the trust.

In ascending the hill, a musket-shot grazed the left side of my head, and buried itself in the earth close by. Both my subalterns, who were brothers, were severely wounded in the defence of this hill; and we had but barely time to send them, with other wounded officers and men, across the river, ere we were obliged to retire, and to make a push in double-quick time to reach the bridge; the whole time exposed to such a fire from the hill which we had just abandoned, as might have satisfied the most determined fire-eater in existence.

If any are now living of those who defended the little hill above the bridge, they cannot fail to remember the gallantry displayed by Major M'Leod, of the 43d, who was the senior officer on the spot. How either he or his horse escaped being blown to atoms, when, in the most daring manner, he charged on horseback, at the head of a hundred or two skirmishers of the 43d and of our regiment mixed together, and headed them in making a dash at a wall lined with French infantry, which we soon dislodged, I am at a loss to imagine. It was one of those extraordinary escapes tending strongly to implant in the mind some faith in the doctrine of fatality. This gallant officer was killed afterwards whilst heading his regiment at the storming of Badajoz, and was sincerely regretted by all who knew him.

The whole of General Crawford's corps at length gained the opposite bank of the Coa, and was strongly posted near the bridge, behind walls, rocks, and broken ground. The torrents of rain which fell the night before had so swollen the river, that all the fords were at that moment impassable; a fortunate circumstance, as the only way by which we could now be attacked was over the narrow bridge, on which we could bring a destructive fire; and we likewise commanded the approach to it from the opposite side with musketry. An incessant fire was kept up across the river by both parties, and after it had continued some time, the French sent a party of grenadiers to storm the bridge, with the vain hope of driving us from our new position. They advanced most resolutely in double-quick time, and charged along the bridge; but few, if any, went back alive, and most of those who reached our side of it unhurt were killed afterwards. This experiment was repeated, and it is almost needless to add, that it met the same fate each time.

The French officer who directed those attacks on the bridge, might have known, before he caused the experiment to be made, that a few hundred French grenadiers, advancing to the tune of "Vive l'Empereur!" "En avant, mes enfans!" and so forth, were not likely to succeed in scaring away three British and two Portuguese regiments, supported by artillery. It was a piece of unpardonable and unjustifiable butchery on the part of the man who ordered those brave grenadiers to be thus wantonly sacrificed, without the most remote prospect of success. They deserved a better fate, for no men could have behaved with more intrepidity.

About five o'clock in the evening the firing ceased on each side, as if by mutual consent; partly because, having been engaged since six o'clock in the morning, both parties found themselves pretty much exhausted, to say nothing, perhaps, of the hopeless case which our antagonists found it to drive us from our tenable position. Floods of rain fell after mid-day, which continued for some hours.

We permitted a party of the enemy, unarmed, to come on the bridge, and on our side of it, to bring away their wounded. Two officers of grenadiers of their 66th regiment lay dead at the head of the bridge, which, as well as the ground on each side of it, was covered with killed and wounded. The loss of our regiment in this action was two officers killed and eight wounded, three of whom died a few days afterwards. We lost several sergeants, bugle-boys, and about one hundred and twenty rank and file. The total loss of the Light Division was from three to four hundred men. Thus ended the affair of the Coa; a day which will not easily be forgotten by those who were present; and I may also add, that although an overwhelming French force obliged the Light Division to retreat, and to contend with it under every possible disadvantage, until it had gained the opposite bank of the river, the retreat was so well covered and protected by the excellent disposition of the troops forming the rear-guard, that we may, without being accused either of vanity or bravado, look back on it as a day of glory, not of defeat.

Soon after dark, General Crawford retired with his whole force from the Coa to a wild rocky country, near the village of Valverde, where we bivouacked late that night amongst some granite rocks, drenched to the skin with the rains of the preceding day and night. We had here time to reflect on the events which the last twenty-four hours had produced, and were extremely puzzled to conjecture why General Crawford, if he was determined to give battle with the Light Division, consisting of four thousand men, to Marshal Ney's whole corps of twenty-five thousand, did not cross the Coa, without waiting to be forcibly driven over, and having taken up a position on the left bank, then and there challenge his opponent. The investment of Almeida was not retarded five minutes by our waiting under its walls for the approach of the besieging army.

At midnight of the 25th we fell back from Valverde in a deluge of rain, and bivouacked near Freixadas, into which village we were sent on the 26th, by Lord Wellington's orders, who left his head-quarters at Celerico, on hearing of the action on the Coa, and came to meet us. Here we had the luxury of a roof over our heads,— quite a novelty in those times; and we lost no time in making ourselves as comfortable as circumstances would admit. One night of sound sleep in an old uninhabited house, and dry clothes, put us in condition again for whatever might be forthcoming.

On the 28th, passing through several villages from which the inhabitants had all fled, in fear of the approach of the French, we arrived at Celerico, and made huts of the branches of trees, in some woods near the town, in which were Lord Wellington's head-quarters. Here the Commander-in-Chief directed that our division should be divided into two brigades, and be commanded as follows: the first brigade by Lieutenant-Colonel Beckwith, consisting of one half of his own battalion, the 43d regiment, and the 3d Portuguese Caçadores; the second brigade by Lieutenant-Colonel Barclay, of the 52d, consisting of his own regiment, the other wing of the 95th Rifle Corps, and the 1st Portuguese Caçadores.

Immediately after our retreat across the Coa, on the 24th of July, Massena commenced the siege of Almeida, the governor of which, Colonel Cox, was an English officer in the Portuguese service.

On the 5th of August we were again ordered to the front to support the cavalry; and during the ensuing fortnight were constantly on the move from bivouac to bivouac, according to the reports received of the enemy.

Although the villages in this part of Portugal are, in general, extremely poor and wretched, the valleys in which some are situated, with the Estrella mountains frowning over them, are equally beautiful with most that are to be found in the Peninsula; and, from the secluded situation of some, one would have thought that an invading army, in its march from the frontier to the capital, might have passed near them without discovering that they existed.

Notwithstanding that we were night and day on the *qui vive*, sleeping in our clothes, and liable

OUR CAVALRY DRIVEN BACK. 155

to be under arms at the shortest notice, some sportsmen amongst us contrived to slay many hares, partridges, quails, and rabbits, which proved a happy addition to the lean ration beef.

On the 26th, 27th, and 28th of August, the rains fell almost without intermission, accompanied by lightning and thunder. As we were at this time vegetating under some huts made of the branches of trees, which kept out about as much rain as a large sieve would have done, we had the full benefit of this shower-bath.

The French batteries opened on Almeida about this period; and a few hours after the bombardment commenced, most unfortunately a shell exploded in the great magazine, blew half the town about the ears of the garrison, and so injured the works, that the governor was under the necessity of capitulating. This was a most unexpected misfortune, as Massena was now able to prosecute his march on Lisbon some weeks earlier than Lord Wellington had calculated on.

On the 28th, the French drove back our cavalry from Freixadas, after a skirmish in which we lost a few men and horses, and the enemy some prisoners, belonging to their far-famed 32d regiment of light infantry, said to have been the corps which in Egypt was styled "Invincible." The same night we made a long march in dreadful rain towards Celerico.

Early in September the army began to retrograde slowly towards Coimbra, which many people affirmed was a prelude to its embarkation at Lisbon for England. The Light Division and the cavalry followed the main body a few marches in the rear; and we were not molested by the enemy's advanced guard, until a few days before we approached the position at Buzaco, on which Lord Wellington had determined to measure his strength with Massena.

Being halted one day in a village at the foot of the Sierra d'Estrella, I started on an expedition with a brother-officer, to see a lake on the summit of a mountain, having read the following account of it in an old Portuguese book belonging to the padre of the village: "This lake is bottomless; the properties of its waters are to turn wine into vinegar in a short space of time. It communicates with the sea, notwithstanding its vast distance from the ocean; for when the sea is rough, the waters of the lake are troubled also."

As we did not for a moment doubt that, from the padre's direction, we should easily find the object of our search without a guide, we were rightly served, after a tedious ascent on foot, which occupied three hours and a quarter, up the face of a mountain covered with rocks, and with heath of an incredible height and thickness, to learn, from a shepherd on its summit, that we were still some leagues from the lake.

The day was far advanced, and we were too much fatigued to prosecute the search; so we descended, and arrived late in the evening at the village, drenched with rain, and in no great good humour with the padre, on whom we threw the whole blame of the failure. Discussing some wine the same night with our clerical friend, we endeavoured to enlighten him as to the wonderful history of the lake, and the properties ascribed to it. It might or might not be bottomless, for any thing we knew to the contrary; but, as for its turning wine into vinegar, we assured him, that had we been wise enough to have transported to its banks a bottle of his good wine, we should have taken for granted one part of its wonderful properties, and, instead of committing the bottle to the deep, to be converted into vinegar, the contents should have been put to a far better use. As for the latter part of the story, we accounted for it by concluding that the self-same gale of wind which agitates the sea, will have a similar effect on a body of fresh water, if exposed to its fury on the very summit of one of the highest mountains to be found in the Peninsula. The padre shook his head at our logic, and, I have no doubt, concluded that we were a couple of sceptical and heretical rascals.

On the 20th September we commenced our daily labours before daybreak, and, by a movement to the right, we left the road leading from Celerico to Coimbra, crossed the Mondego by a ford, after having marched along its beautiful serpentine banks several miles, and found ourselves on the main road leading from Vizeu to Coimbra. General Pack's Portuguese brigade, and some cavalry, were likewise on this road, by which the mass of the French army was moving down on Coimbra. The four following days we were constantly getting under arms, owing to the incessant arrival of reports from our cavalry pickets in front. In short, we slept with one eye open the whole time, and the men were always accoutred.

Lord Wellington arrived at the outposts on the 23d, just as our cavalry were skirmishing with and retiring before the French advanced guard near Mortagoa; and he immediately ordered Generals Crawford and Pack, and the whole of the cavalry, except a few squadrons, to retire by the road leading towards the Sierra de Buzaco. We bivouacked that night on a bleak cold hill, covered with heath; and having no provisions, nor any fluid stronger than water to counteract the effect of the dews and piercing wind, we were not sorry when ordered to stand to arms as usual, an hour before daybreak on the 24th. We then moved a short distance to the rear, and took up our ground in some pine-woods; several of our companies being posted as pickets to support those of the cavalry in their front.

Soon after mid-day the French came on with a body of cavalry, on whom our dragoons made a spirited charge, and drove them back with some loss. The remainder of the day we were tolerably quiet.

On the 25th, the French again came on with such a numerous and combined force of cavalry, infantry, and artillery, that the Light Division, General Pack's brigade of Portuguese, and the small cavalry force with us, immediately commenced their retreat towards the Sierra de Buzaco, on which the whole of the allied army, including General Hill's division from Alemtejo, was now assembling in a position covering Coimbra.

The French adopted a very efficacious plan in their pursuit of our rear-guard, by sending forward light infantry and light cavalry to skirmish, intermixed, side by side; thus affording mutual support to each other, as the ground became either open or intersected. By those means, and aided by their flying artillery, the French pressed our rear-guard closely, which was formed by a squadron or two of the cavalry, and some companies of our battalion and of the 52d regiment.

We continued to be engaged until we reached the position at Buzaco. Nothing could exceed the regularity with which this retreat was conducted; and it was effected without much loss.

The French cannonaded Colonel Beckwith's brigade heavily in the village of Sula, which stands on the side of the Sierra de Buzaco; and they attacked at the same moment with infantry a village farther to the right, which our other brigade, under Colonel Barclay, defended. The French, after a sharp fire on both sides, were driven back, and sustained some loss. The light troops of General Picton's division were, about the same time, engaged with the advance of General Regnier's corps far to our right. The two armies remained pretty quiet the rest of the day, except an occasional shot from the pickets.

Long before day dawned on the 26th, the loud brass drums of the French roused both armies from their slumbers, and we stood to our arms as usual. The night had been as cold as nights usually are in the end of September on the tops of high mountains. The appearance of the numberless fires which both armies had kept up throughout the night, and which were still burning when we stood to our arms in the dark, was a sight indescribably grand, and far exceeding all the illuminations that were ever got up at Vauxhall, the Tivoli gardens, or elsewhere.

When day broke, the hostile armies, divided only by a wide valley, were drawn out, waiting for the orders which should bring them in contact. Massena's army was concentrated in one immense dark mass on the brow of the opposite mountain, and the allied army was formed in lines ready for its reception. The precise disposition of our army I cannot pretend accurately to describe; but I know that General Hill was on the extreme right; on his left, Generals Picton, Leith, and Pack; on the left of the latter some Portuguese; and still further to the left, was the Light Division, with another division of British and Portuguese infantry in continuation to the left. I believe the reserves were in column near the convent, which stands on the highest part of the Sierra de Buzaco. As the mountainous regions, in which the two armies had posted themselves, did not admit of the use of their cavalry, I cannot take upon myself to say how ours was disposed of; but I believe a brigade under General Fane observed the enemy's movements far to General Hill's right; and the remainder were either in reserve behind the centre, or detached at a distance to the left.

Along the base of the Sierra ran an extended chain of our infantry pickets; and in like manner at the foot of the French ridge of mountains their pickets were thrown out. The valley, therefore, which divided us, was considered neutral ground.

Early in the morning the French cannonaded our four companies again, which were advanced into the village of Sula, but could not dislodge us. Massena then sent out a cloud of light infantry, who engaged our pickets all along the line; and under cover of this fire he reconnoitered our position. This fire of the light troops lasted without intermission until night.

Massena, during the morning, closed up from his rear all his troops, cavalry, infantry, and artillery, and placed them in one vast solid mass opposite to us; no doubt with the hope of intimidating the allies at the mere sight of such legions. Their numbers I do not pretend to determine; but his whole army was now in view, except the garrisons left in Ciudad Rodrigo and Almeida, and perhaps some posts of communication with the frontier. He must have sustained no trifling loss in the sieges of the two fortresses, added to which, many hundreds were killed and wounded at the Coa on the 24th July; but nevertheless, out of the 110,000 men, which he boasted being at the head of a short time before, in his proclamation to the Portuguese nation, something considerable must have yet remained to him.

The fire of the light troops throughout the 26th having been kept up without intermission, we relieved our companies at this duty every hour or two. The situation of a light bob, or a rifleman, was found to be no sinecure. The blaze of musketry with which the mountains and valleys had rung for twelve hours, ceased with night; and every thing was as quiet as if the two armies had been in their own countries in profound peace.

CHAPTER X.

Battle of Buzaco. Flag of truce. General Simon's baggage brought in. Wounded of the two armies removed from the field. Terrible carnage in and near Sula. The light troops constantly engaged. Deserters come over to us. Their reports of Massena's intentions. The French army breaks up, and marches away to our left. Lord Wellington retires from Buzaco to the lines of Torres Vedras. Occurrences on the march. Stores destroyed at Pombal. King John's coffin in the cathedral at Battalha. Affair between our rear-guard and the French advanced guard. Our habitation takes fire, and we are nearly burnt out of it,—horses, mules, donkeys, and baggage. Affair of cavalry near Alcoentre. Speculations on Massena not having pursued us more vigorously in the retreat. The Light Division reaches Alemquer. The French turn us out of it without our dinners. We retire to Arruda in bad humour and in dreadful weather. An agreeable surprise. A word or two relative to the lines of Torres Vedras. Gun-boats on the Tagus. Jack Tar's zeal. Great sufferings of the Portuguese from the French invasion. Reconnoissances made by Massena, and skirmishes brought on by it. Sharp affair between Sir Brent Spencer's division and the enemy. Scarcity of provisions in the country in our front. Our employments whilst we remained in the lines. The French army falls back to a position behind the Rio Maior. Sentries of straw. We march in pursuit and take some prisoners. Dead Frenchmen, horses, mules, and donkeys, on the road-side. The Light Division comes up with the enemy near Cartaxo. We are preparing to attack, when Lord Wellington arrives and countermands it. Causes thereof. The French retire across the Rio Maior. Rough sketch of their position. General Hill crosses the Tagus. The Light Division bivouac in a pine-wood. Washed out of a water-course by the rain. Lord Wellington makes demonstrations against the French position. The Light Division engaged with the enemy's light troops on the left. The troops are withdrawn.

BATTLE OF BUZACO.

27th.—DAY had scarcely made its appearance when Massena inundated the valley with light troops, with whom we were soon warmly engaged; and, as their columns of attack moved forward to their support, we were driven gradually up the face of the mountain on our reserves. A considerable portion of the infantry of Marshal Ney's corps advanced steadily and in excellent order by the road leading to the crest of that part of the position where the Light Division was drawn out in line. General Loison's division, which led the attack, was allowed by General Crawford to reach nearly the summit of the ridge, when he ordered a volley from his division, and a charge with the bayonet. The effect was instantaneous and most decisive; and it is impossible to describe the confusion and carnage which instantly ensued in the enemy's ranks.

It can be readily conceived, that so large a

column, wedged close in a road of no great width, being once broken and forced back, those pressing on from the rear to support it were literally borne back down the mountain by the tide of fugitives, in spite of any exertions of theirs to retrieve matters.

The instant the attacking columns were turned back, they were exposed to the fire of our whole division; whilst our battalion and some caçadores were ordered to pursue, and to give them a flanking fire, and the horse artillery continued to pour on them a murderous fire of grape, as they were struggling through the narrow streets of Sula, and trampling each other to death in their great haste to escape. Men, muskets, knapsacks, and bayonets, rolled down the side of the mountain in such a confused mass, as it is impossible to convey a just idea of.

The village of Sula, and the ground on each side of it, as also the road by which the columns of attack advanced, were heaped with killed and wounded, all lying within a small space of ground. Whilst we were thus employed, General Regnier made an attack equally desperate on Generals Picton, Leith, and Pack, far to our right. Those troops served Regnier's corps with much the same description of sauce which the Light Division had administered to Marshal Ney's. We were at too great a distance to distinguish what passed between the troops of Picton, Leith, and Regnier; but we were near enough to witness the gallant manner in which General Pack's Portuguese brigade charged and drove back with the bayonet a formidable attack made on it by the enemy, covering the ground with their dead. This was the first trial made of the new Portuguese levies, organised by British officers, and it proved most satisfactory.

The 32d and 70th French regiments, both of high renown, were stated to have been nearly destroyed by Picton's division. The French general, Simon, whose brigade was at the head of the column which attacked the Light Division, was wounded and made prisoner, with three hundred of his men, near the summit of the Sierra. No further attack was made by Massena after these failures, except by his light troops, who, like swarms of bees, filled the valley, and kept us constantly employed until towards evening, when the firing ceased on both sides, and a flag of truce came in, bringing General Simon's baggage, and with it a pretty little Spanish woman, part of his establishment. The fair one was in tears, and appeared much agitated. During this cessation of hostilities, unarmed parties of both armies were employed in bringing away their wounded.

I went down into the village of Sula, and had some conversation with several French officers and soldiers. They acknowledged their loss to have been very severe; and one man assured me, that his company, which numbered one hundred men in the morning, could only muster twenty-two effective men after their repulse. Amongst the dead in the immediate front of the Light Division, I found men belonging to the following French regiments, and I cut some buttons off their coats:—the 6th, 26th, 66th, and 82d, the Legion du Midi, and a regiment of Germans.

The time agreed on for the cessation of hostilities having expired, and the French evincing a disposition to hold the village of Sula with a few men, Lord Wellington, who was with our division at the moment, ordered a company of the 95th to drive them from it, which was speedily accomplished, and we established strong pickets in it for the night.

Thus ended the battle of Buzaco, a day in which the Marshal Prince of Esling was completely foiled in all his attempts, and was defeated with severe loss.

28*th*.—The next morning we were in expectation of another attack, as several deserters, who had come over to us in the night, agreed in the report that General Junot, whose corps had not been engaged the day before, had volunteered to storm, with fifteen thousand grenadiers, that point of the position where the Light Division stood.

No general attack, however, was made on the 28th; but Massena let slip swarms of light troops, as heretofore, and kept us eternally at work with them, until night put an end to the contest. The French erected a half-moon battery on a hill immediately fronting us, and our artillery endeavoured to throw shells on their working parties, but the distance was rather too long. Being on picket with my company in Sula, seven deserters came in during different periods of the night, all agreeing in the same story, that the French army had broken up, and was marching away to turn our left.

When day dawned on the 29th, we found that the reports of the deserters were correct, and that the whole allied army, except the Light Division and a small force of light cavalry, which were left on the position as a rear-guard, was already retiring on Coimbra. About nine o'clock in the morning we followed the main body, and bivouacked at night in a wood some miles from Buzaco.

Despairing of forcing the allied army from its formidable position, Massena had recourse to a wide movement, by which he was enabled to outflank us, and to advance on Coimbra by a road far to our left. It was now pretty evident that, having given up the position at Buzaco, the next spot on which Lord Wellington would challenge his opponent would be in the lines of

Torres Vedras; nor were we deceived. At Pombal, near which we bivouacked on the night of the 3d of October, some provisions and stores which the commissariat could not remove in time, were ordered to be destroyed. The streets flowed with rum, many casks of which had been staved, and the contents spilt, that the French might not benefit by them. So inveterate is the propensity of drink in the soldier, that, in spite of every precaution, many of them contrived to get drunk by dipping the rum out of the streets, on our march through the town, in tin cups, or in any vessel nearest at hand.

The 5th brought us to Battalha, where there was a magnificent cathedral, which was in some measure destroyed the following year in Massena's retreat out of Portugal. In the cathedral were buried many of the royal family of Braganza, and amongst the number a King John, in whose reign, I think, the cathedral was built. I know not who the culprits were, nor to what division of the army they belonged; but in going into the cathedral, I saw the coffin of the said King John open, and the body, which was of course embalmed, exposed to view, wrapped in rich robes of crimson velvet and gold. By way of a relic, I cut off a button and some gold fringe from his majesty's robes; whilst others, more ambitious, could be satisfied with nothing less than a royal finger.

OUR LODGING CATCHES FIRE.

On the same day, our cavalry of the rear-guard had an affair with the enemy's advanced guard, which it drove back in a spirited manner, and took some prisoners.

On the 6th, 7th, and 8th, we continued the retreat in unceasing rains, and halted one night in an uninhabited cottage with only half a roof on it, in which four of us, besides our servants, horses, mules, and donkeys, were huddled together. In endeavouring, by dint of a fire, to dry our clothes, which were fairly rusted on us by constant exposure to the weather by day and night, the remnant of the cottage, as the devil would have it, caught fire; and with great difficulty we succeeded in dragging forth from the flames and smoke our miserable quadrupeds and the baggage, and depositing them in the street, under as tremendous a torrent of rain as would have satisfied old Noah himself. With the assistance of the soldiers, aided also by the continued rain, the flames were got under, and we re-entered our hut, where we passed the night, and started the following morning, in another delicious day of rain, to Alemquer.

Near Alcoentre our rear-guard was again attacked on the 8th, and beat back the French with loss. It has ever been a matter of surprise, that Massena did not press more closely on the rear-guard from Coimbra to the lines of Torres Vedras.

No doubt that able chief had sufficient reasons for not doing so; but that he might sometimes have come up with us, had he been determined to do so, there can be no doubt, as the allied army did not make any forced marches in its retreat.

Our division entered Alemquer on the 9th, a good town, commanding a pretty view of the Tagus. Here we enjoyed the supreme luxury of a roof over our heads, and made up for lost time by a good night's sleep. The town was deserted by the inhabitants, through fear of the invading army.

On the 10th, as we were anticipating with great glee an attack on a turkey, that by some extraordinary piece of good fortune had found its way into the camp-kettle of our company's mess, we were suddenly called to arms by sound of bugle; for, in spite of the rain, those miscreants of the French advanced guard would not remain quiet;—I suppose because they envied us the glorious feast which was nearly ready for use. A few shots from the pickets soon explained how matters stood; and in less than ten minutes the whole division was under arms, and some companies engaged with the French advanced guard at the outside of the town. We were forthwith put in march towards Arruda, where, after wading through oceans of mud and water, and with an incessant shower-bath from above, we arrived after nightfall. The raging of the elements rendered our retreat comparatively quiet and comfortable; as the French were glad enough, no doubt, to shelter themselves from the storm in our late quarters at Alemquer, and to allow us to proceed unmolested. We were, nevertheless, in an exceedingly bad humour at being obliged to vacate in their favour, and to lose our dinners into the bargain. I think there is an old saying about "might giving right;" and as the French were by far the stronger party, I do not blame them for turning us adrift in the manner they did.

It sometimes happens, when we are anticipating every sort of evil and mishap, that a bright gleam of sunshine appears when least expected. This was just the case when we reached Arruda, in a dark tempestuous night, soaked with rain, half-famished with hunger, bitterly cursing the fellows who had, a few hours before, turned us out of our comfortable quarters, and expecting neither more nor less than to bivouac in some snipe-marsh. Our joy may be conceived, at finding, not only a roof over our heads in Arruda, but a prospect of not going to bed supperless. We consoled ourselves for the loss of the turkey at Alemquer with some fowls, and a good allowance of capital wine, which we found in the house allotted to myself and my subalterns.

Never was a town more completely deserted than Arruda. The inhabitants, dreading the approach of the French, had taken flight to Lisbon, leaving their houses, many of which were magnificently furnished, without a human being in them. The chairs and tables were subsequently carried up to the camp, which was formed on the fortified ridge of hills running from the Tagus to the sea, so well known by the name of the lines of Torres Vedras, and they proved highly useful to us in our canvass habitations.

The army had now reached those far-famed lines, which have been already so often described. The right rested on the Tagus, at or near the village of Alhandra, and the left somewhere near Torres Vedras on the sea. Gun-boats, manned from our fleet at Lisbon, gave additional strength to the right; and Jack Tar never lost an opportunity of bombarding with great zeal any party of the French which happened to heave in sight. On one occasion, a French general officer, whose name I have forgotten, was killed by a round shot from the gun-boats.

At certain parts of the chain of hills which were not scarped by nature, and therefore accessible, works of different kinds had been constructed, to impede the enemy in his attack. Numerous redoubts and field-works, mounting heavy ship-guns, had also been formed along the summit of the position. In addition to these defences, immediately on the arrival of the army each division had some hundreds of men constantly employed throughout the day, fair or foul, to give additional strength to that part of the position allotted it to defend. It was therefore evident that every day Massena delayed the attack was much in our favour, as our position was increasing in strength hourly.

Thousands of the unfortunate inhabitants of the provinces through which our army had recently retreated, had abandoned their homes, and were endeavouring to exist between Lisbon and the lines. There was, therefore, an immense population hemmed up in a small space of country, hundreds of them without a house to cover them, or food to eat, except what was afforded by the bounty of the rich at Lisbon, and by the liberal subscriptions raised for them in England.

In the course of the winter, the number of Portuguese who actually died of want was quite dreadful. It was not unusual to see hordes of those poor wretches, old and young, male and female, in rags, the very pictures of death, seated in despair on the wet ground, round a miserable fire, on which was placed an earthen vessel, full of such herbs as could be gathered in the fields and hedges. Thousands contrived to drag on a miserable existence on this vile sustenance. Their death-like, emaciated faces were sufficient to have touched the heart of the most callous and unfeeling. The British soldiers assisted them by every means in their power; and in the Light Division (as well as, I conclude, in every other) soup was made from the heads and offal of the cattle killed for the troops, and distributed amongst the starving inhabitants.

I have a thousand times wished it were possible that every man, woman, and child, of all ranks, in England, could have been transported to this heart-rending scene only for five minutes; that by having had an insight into the various miseries to which the ill-fated inhabitants of the theatre of war are inevitably subjected, they might return satisfied, and bless their stars that an army of Frenchmen were not riding roughshod over old England, and inflicting on its people similar miseries to those which I have attempted to describe.

As soon as tents were sent up from Lisbon, we encamped in due form near the summit of the lines, daily expecting a general attack, and wondering why it was so long delayed.

From the period of our arrival in the lines, on the 10th of October, to the 15th of November, when Massena fell back behind the Rio Maior, the rains, which never ceased falling, soon found their way through the tents, so that we were seldom dry. Massena frequently made reconnoissances on the position, which brought on various affairs with the pickets; and, on the 13th of October, a sharp affair took place between the light troops of Sir Brent Spencer's division and those of the enemy, who were repulsed with loss. On this occasion a company of our 3d battalion, which had recently arrived from England, and was attached to Sir Brent Spencer's division, had its captain and a lieutenant severely wounded, and lost many men.

A wide open valley, which divided the pickets of the two armies, in the immediate front of the Light Division, the French frequently made foraging parties into; but after the first week, I do not believe as much provision could have been found for man or horse, in the whole valley, as would have rationed half a squadron of Lilliputian cuirassiers for twenty-four hours.

Deserters were constantly coming over to us from the French lines, bringing all sorts of reports, vague and contradictory, but which, nevertheless, served us to speculate on. Thus, between constantly strengthening our position; endeavouring to keep off agues by dint of cigars, and of such fluids as were sometimes attainable from the sutlers who paid us a visit from Lisbon; reconnoitering our French neighbours with telescopes; trying to keep our horses, mules, and donkeys alive during the inclement weather, with chopped straw, or what little herbage the hills afforded, with, now and then, a very diminutive allowance of barley or Indian corn; and the occasional arrival of letters and newspapers from England,— we passed some five or six weeks, wondering whether Massena would attack us, or walk away from our front.

The 15th of November put to rest all surmises on this point. I happened to be on picket in front of Arruda on the night of the 14th; and looking, as usual, with all our eyes, in the twilight of the following morning, towards our opponents, the French sentries, we thought, could be discovered as heretofore: but when day broke thoroughly, we found that the cunning rogues had played us an old trick of theirs, by placing figures of straw upright, with a soldier's cap on each, and a pole by their side to represent a musket. Their whole army had retired, during the night, in the direction of Santarem; and we were sent in pursuit some hours afterwards.

We now began to think that the "frightened leopard" would have a respite; and that the operation of "driving him into the sea," as Massena had promised the Portuguese a few months before, was likely to be postponed for a time. Our division did not come up with the French rear-guard this day, and at night we bivouacked on a heath near Alemquer. Sir Brent Spencer's column took seventy prisoners near Sobral.

On the 16th, the Light Division made a movement to the right, which brought it close to the Tagus. We pushed on through Villa Nova and Azimbuja; and although we could not reach their rear-guard, we took many prisoners, who, from sickness, fatigue, or in search of plunder, had straggled from their ranks. The road from Alemquer to Azimbuja was covered with horses, mules, and asses, belonging to the French, which had died from want of forage. We passed many French soldiers lying dead by the road-side, whose appearance indicated that disease and want of food had carried them off. Every house in every town or village which lay in their line of retreat was thoroughly ransacked. Desolation and devastation marked their track.

On the 17th, long before day dawned, we were on the move, and about mid-day came up with the enemy, posted on some rising ground near Cartaxo, having a large plain, covered with short heath, in their front. They shewed only a few squadrons of cavalry and about three battalions of infantry; concealing their main force, as it was afterwards ascertained, behind the brow of the hill. General Crawford, conceiving it to be only a small rear-guard, the whole of which was exposed to view, instantly made dispositions for the attack, by forming the Light Division into a single line, which, with the troop of Horse Artillery and one squadron of the 14th Light Dragoons, constituted his whole force.

We were just about to advance across the plain when Lord Wellington arrived on the ground, and instantly put a stop to our proceedings; as the force in our front consisted of one whole French corps, numbering, it was believed, eighteen thousand infantry, and from two to three thousand cavalry, with a due proportion of artillery. We could, undoubtedly, have given a good account of the troops which the French general thought proper to expose to our view; but that we could have also mastered the remainder which were in reserve behind the brow, I will not undertake to say. Had other divisions of our army been sufficiently advanced to have aided in the attack, it is more than probable that Lord Wellington would have tried his hand at them. We were stationed for the night with the 4th and 14th Dragoons, in Cartaxo, where General Cotton and the cavalry head-quarters were also. This town had shared the same fate as every other through which we marched.

Before daylight on the 18th, we groped our way forward, and shortly after came up with the French rear-guard near the Rio Maior, which it was about to cross by a bridge and causeway.

After some skirmishing, they passed the river, and we had then an opportunity of examining the formidable position on which Massena had fallen back, whereby he was brought nearer his communication with the frontier and his resources, and, moreover, was enabled to canton his army in an infinitely more secure position than that which he occupied whilst fronting us in the lines of Torres Vedras.

The outline of this new position, which he held nearly four months, may be given in a few words. The front was covered by the river Maior, which, during the winter months, is not fordable. The bridge and causeway, leading across it to the foot of the heights of Santarem, are exceedingly long and narrow; and a smaller hill, detached as if it had been placed there for the express purpose, looks down on the causeway, which the French artillery and musketry stationed there completely enfiladed. The French formed breast-works for their infantry in various places near the head of the causeway, and abattis on it.

Rising boldly, and somewhat abruptly, from their end of the causeway, is a high hill, on the top of which stands Santarem, already mentioned in my journal of 1809. In that town were Massena's head-quarters during the whole winter.

The extensive woods of olive which clothed the sides and summit of the hill the year before, when we passed through on our route to Talavera, were cut down in less than forty-eight hours by the French, who constructed with them a double row of most formidable abattis across the whole of the ridge.

The right extended towards a country difficult of approach in the winter months, from the wretched state of the roads in the neighbourhood. General Hill's division crossed the Tagus in boats at or near Azimbuja, and occupied Chamusca and other villages on the left bank of the river. The Light Division, on the night of the 18th, was pushed close to the bridge, at which we had strong pickets; and those who were not on that duty turned into some roofless hovels near at hand, drenched with the never-ceasing rain.

Lord Wellington was employed on the 19th in reconnoitering the French position. The same day the First Division closed up from the rear, and joined us at Vallé, a straggling sort of village near the causeway. At night our division was ordered into a large pine-wood, to make ourselves as comfortable as we could; but in which we passed as cheerless a night as one uninterrupted deluge of rain might be supposed to produce. Hoping to escape in some measure from the fury of the storm, many of us crept into an old water-course in the wood, in which, rolled up in our cloaks, and doubled up with wet and cold, we did contrive, nevertheless, to fall asleep. But it is impossible to forget being suddenly awoke, a short time afterwards, and feeling myself all at once buoyed up and floating down the little ravine, in the same plight as if I had been dragged under a ship from stem to stern. There was a general outcry from all the party who had sought refuge in this water-course, and a scramble to get on *terra firma* took place. Taking a few mouthsful of rum and a cigar, the remainder of the night was spent at the foot of a fir-tree, smoking, shivering, and cursing our stupidity for having taken up so injudicious a position.

Daylight was never more welcome than when it broke next morning, although the rain rather increased. We had, however, something in perspective, which was likely to call into exertion both body and mind, and that pretty quickly.

A general attack, as we then understood, was forthwith to be made on the French position. The First Division made demonstrations near the causeway, as in like manner did other troops further to their left. The Light Division and some cavalry at the same moment crossed the Rio Maior, by a narrow bridge behind Vallé, and advanced along the marshy plain towards the extreme left of the enemy's position, which rested on the Tagus. We were soon engaged with their pickets, with whom we kept up a skirmish for some hours, and in such rain as might be supposed to have rendered fire-arms useless. Numbers of their light troops were scattered along the base of the position, ready for our reception, if we should advance to the attack; but Massena concealed his masses behind the brow.

Towards evening we were ordered to fall back again towards Vallé; and it was generally understood, that the object of the demonstrations which Lord Wellington had made, was to ascertain whether the whole French army was really there, or only a rear-guard. Finding a strong force concentrated, and posted in a most formidable position, no attack was made.

CHAPTER XI.

The Light Division holds the outposts at the bridge of Santarem.
General Junot wounded near Rio Maior. The allied army
is put into cantonments. How we passed the winter.
Sufferings of the French army from want of provisions and
forage. They are harassed by the armed peasantry and
militia. Shooting and coursing parties close to the French
videttes. Their courteous conduct on those occasions towards us. Anecdote of a dragoon and his cloak. Burlesque
on horse-racing in the cantonments of the Light Division.
Flags of truce. Conversation with French officers at the
bridge of Santarem. Theatrical performances. The Marquis de la Romana dies. The Duke of Brunswick's corps
joins the Light Division. They desert by wholesale to the
French. Several are shot by sentence of a court-martial.
The corps is sent out of the Light Division. Lord Wellington
contemplates relieving the Light Division for a time at the
outposts, to give the men rest. This is not carried into
effect. Some regiments join the army from England. The
7th division of infantry is formed. I go with a brotherofficer on a frolic to Lisbon for five days. Return to our
old post at the bridge. Lieutenant Strenowitz, of the 1st
German Hussars, surprises a French cavalry post. Marshal
Mortier defeats a Spanish army near Badajoz, and lays
siege to the place. Massena commences his retreat out of
Portugal. State of Santarem. The 1st battalion 95th
Riflemen drives the French from a village. The Light Division
and cavalry come up with the French near Pombal. The

castle is attacked. Action near Redinha. Reach Condeixa. The Portuguese militia gain possession of Coimbra. Massena changes his line of retreat. Lord Wellington attacks Marshal Ney. He falls back to Miranda de Corvo. Conduct of the French army during the retreat. The French leave numbers of baggage-animals on the road much lacerated. The Light Division finds the enemy on the Ceira. Action near Foz d'Aroce. Remarks. The army out-marches the commissariat. Major Stewart of the 95th Rifle corps. His character. Lord Wellington crosses the Alva. Massena retreats towards Celerico. Affair near Freixadas. The 95th loses its adjutant. His character. The army marches on Guarda. Massena falls back behind the Coa. Action near Sabugal. Colonel Beckwith.

As the two armies remained here in a state of comparative inactivity more than three months, I propose giving a short sketch of what occurred during that period, and the manner we generally passed our time.

The Light Division had charge of the outposts at the causeway, three hundred men being always on picket at the head of the bridge, and several more on inlying picket near at hand. On the bridge (which was mined and charged) we constructed an abattis; and to render our post at the causeway more secure, we made covert ways and traverses.

The French were employed in the same manner on the opposite side, and in a few weeks they completed a very neat battery on the little hill, so as to enfilade the bridge. Here they kept about a brigade of infantry.

In various half-ruined hovels and stables near the bridge, our division was stowed away pretty close, sleeping fully accoutred throughout the winter; being so near the enemy, that a few minutes would have sufficed to bring us in contact. The sentries of the two armies were so near each other on the bridge, and the videttes of the cavalry so closely advanced on the marsh on the right, that they might have conversed without exalting their voices much.

Sir William Erskine and General Pack held the posts some distance to the left of the Light Division, near the town of Rio Maior; and in the course of the winter they had some sharp skirmishing with the French, who made forward movements, with the hope of obtaining provisions and forage, but were always disappointed and driven back. In an affray of this kind, which General Junot headed, with a view of procuring salt for his troops in Rio Maior, he was wounded in the face by Sir William Erskine's light troops.

Lord Wellington's head-quarters were at Cartaxo, where the Guards and the other troops composing the First Division were stationed. Other divisions were cantoned still further to the rear. Every day brought some rumour as to the intended movements of our adversaries, not one in fifty of which proved correct; for instance, "Massena would be reinforced immediately with thirty or forty thousand men from a distant part of Spain, and would instantly make a grand attack on our lines." Two days afterwards, "Massena and his legions were off in a canter out of Portugal."

But I believe that the real state of suffering which the French army experienced during the winter was not exaggerated; nor, perhaps, until it retreated out of Portugal, was the full extent of the privations and hardships to which it had been subjected for some months, known to any one, except the Commander-in-Chief and a few officers of his personal staff. The horses in Massena's army were kept alive latterly on the stalks of the vine, bruised and mixed with corn, when they were so fortunate as to procure any of the latter article. Many of the Portuguese peasantry, armed with fowling-pieces, pikes, &c. &c., aided by the militia and the *ordonenza*, continually harassed the French, cut off their supplies, killed stragglers without mercy, and in various other ways placed Massena's army in any thing but an enviable situation.

The sportsmen in our division constantly had recourse to gun, pointer, and greyhound; and in the marshy plain between the Rio Maior and the Tagus we contrived to amuse ourselves very well, and often with success; hares, quails, snipes, and golden plovers, being abundant. In these pastimes the French cavalry pickets, posted on the marsh, never interfered with us, nor interrupted our sport, although we frequently coursed hares, and shot quails, within half range of their carbines. On the contrary, their conduct was courteous, and, if I may use the expression, gentlemanly to a degree. One anecdote in particular deserves being mentioned. It was customary for our cavalry pickets to patrole every morning before daybreak, to ascertain if any change or movement had taken place in the French chain of cavalry posts. One morning, in a thick fog, a small patrole of ours suddenly found themselves close to a superior force of French cavalry, and instantly retired ; but, in the hurry, one of our dragoons dropped his cloak. Our patrole had ridden but a short distance to the rear, when it was called to by the French, one of whom riding up to within a short distance, dropped the captured cloak on the ground and rode away, making signals to the English dragoon who had lost it, to pick it up. This was carrying on the war as it should be; and it is but justice to add, that we rarely found them deficient on this point.

In addition to shooting and coursing, the sporting characters at the outposts went through the formal process of racing, near Vallé ; and I can never forget the first essay of the kind, where six or eight half-starved devils, whose diet had for some months consisted principally of chopped straw and winter-grass, started, with *gentlemen riders*, for a sweepstakes. Before they had gone one hundred yards, the horse which was ridden by my friend T. of the 43d regiment, came down heels over head, from sheer debility; and those in his wake, according to the nautical phrase, ran foul of him and his racer, who lay floundering on the earth. A greater burlesque on horse-racing never was witnessed: were I certain of seeing so amusing an exhibition at Newmarket, Epsom, or Doncaster, I verily believe I should seldom fail to attend their meetings.

Flags of truce frequently passed between the two armies, which afforded us many opportunities of conversing with the French officers who came with them to the bridge. One of Massena's aides-du-camp talked very big of the gaieties which were going on at Santarem, and of the theatre which the French officers had established there. It was intimated to this loquacious gentleman by the field-officer of our pickets, that the arrival at the French head-quarters of a large drove of cattle, some waggon-loads of flour or bread, and a few other necessaries of the sort, might, by possibility, be as acceptable, and rather more useful to them than all their dramatic works.

If, however, the French could get up theatrical

performances, we, on the other side of the causeway, were determined not to be outdone in that respect. Accordingly, the soldiers of a certain company in our battalion did make the attempt, having converted an old house, in which olive oil had formerly been made, into a theatre: the blankets and great-coats of the soldiers made capital side-scenes; and had not too much wine and grog found their way behind them, no doubt the piece would have gone off with great éclat. But, as the truth must be told, they all forgot their parts; and it was a toss-up whether our attempt at horse-racing or play-acting was the most perfectly ludicrous.

Whilst we remained here, the Marquis de la Romana, who resided at Lord Wellington's head-quarters, died; and, as a patriotic, zealous, and upright man, was a great loss to the Spanish nation. General Crawford went on leave of absence to England during the winter. When we arrived here from the lines of Torres Vedras, the Duke of Brunswick Oels' corps of infantry, which had recently reached Portugal, was sent to join the Light Division. They deserted to the French in such numbers, that we had a *lease* of them but for a few weeks. Lord Wellington caused several of them who had been taken in the attempt to desert to the enemy, to be tried and shot; and, immediately afterwards, he directed that the corps should be sent away from the Light Division.

After the Light Division had been about three months at the Lridge of Santarem, Lord Wellington ordered over to his head-quarters the commanding-officers of regiments of that division, to confer about giving the men some rest, and relieving them for a time at the advanced posts. The unanimous wish of the officers commanding regiments coincided with that of his lordship, that the Light Division, which was only in its proper place, should remain where it was, and so it did. It was whispered that the Fusileer Brigade, and the remainder of General Cole's division, would relieve us at the outposts; but this, like a thousand other *on dits*, proved without foundation.

Several regiments arrived at Lisbon from England or Ireland about this time; amongst others, the 51st and 68th Light Infantry; and the 7th division of infantry was now formed, or, more properly speaking, the 8th, there being previously six numbered divisions, independent of the Light.

During our stay at Vallé I obtained leave of absence for five days, to go to Lisbon with a brother-officer, merely for the sake of a frolic. We lost no time on the road, and found ourselves at Latour's hotel in as short a time as our horses could conveniently carry us thither. It is not less strange than true, that on our return from the opera, when I got into a regular-built bed, I could no more sleep than I could have taken wing and flown across the Tagus. Ever since the month of February 1810 (exactly one year), we had been constantly so near the enemy at the advanced posts, sleeping in our clothes, in bivouac, or in some hovel of a picket-house, rolled up in our cloaks on the ground, that I felt quite like a fish out of water, and was not reconciled to a bed. We spent our five days' leave of absence in Lisbon in the manner which may be supposed, after having been so long estranged from civilised life. In truth we made the most of our time, and lost no opportunity of amusing ourselves in the ways best suited to our taste. When we returned to our old post at the causeway, we found every thing *in statu quo.*

During this temporary inactivity of the hostile armies, ours remained generally healthy. Many, however, were afflicted with fevers, agues, and dysenteries; but when the nature and description of our winter-quarters are considered (of the troops at the outposts at least), and the number of men always on duty, and exposed to the weather during several winter months, it appears extraordinary that so little sickness existed. A sharp attack of fever and ague, which I experienced early in February, placed me for a little time *hors de combat*, and reduced me to a skeleton. To the log-books of my comrades, therefore, I am indebted for items of what occurred during my short illness.

Lieutenant Strenowitz, of the German Hussars, at the head of his picket of twenty men, surprised and made prisoners one of the French cavalry pickets near the town of Rio Maior. This took place in February. During that month, the French, under Soult or Mortier, attacked one of the Spanish armies in the vicinity of Badajoz. The Spaniards were completely defeated; and the French forthwith commenced the siege of that fortress.

The remainder of the winter passed away at the outposts, much in the same manner as I have already described. A thousand reports, vague and contradictory, were ever afloat as to Massena's intentions. The 5th of March put an end to all surmises.

1811.

MASSENA'S RETREAT OUT OF PORTUGAL.

It had been rumoured for some time, that Massena was removing his sick, heavy artillery, baggage, and other encumbrances, to the rear, and as his army was known to be rapidly decreasing, from sickness, want of provisions, medicine, &c. &c. we daily expected that they would decamp and retreat into Spain. Lord Wellington sent orders to our division at the outposts to keep a sharp look-out, and to report the instant they disappeared from our front.

On the night of the 5th of March they retreated, and had recourse to an old trick of theirs, already alluded to in this journal; that of manufacturing sentries of straw, and placing caps on them. When day-light thoroughly broke, on the 6th, the deception was explained, which during the twilight had created something like a doubt. The Light Division was immediately ordered in pursuit; and on entering Santarem, where Massena's head-quarters had been the whole winter, that ill-fated town presented such a picture of misery, filth, devastation, and dilapidation, as no pen can describe.

In the march of the Light Brigade from Lisbon to Talavera in 1809, we halted two days at Santarem, at which time its appearance was altogether extremely prepossessing. How utterly changed was it now! The extensive and valuable olive-groves which clothed the sides of the hill on which the town stands, had long since been cut down by the French to construct *abattis*, and for firewood. For this act no blame can be attached to them, as no one will deny their right to strengthen their position by whatever means were nearest at hand, nor to their making as good fires as they were able, to keep out cold and the devil from their winter-quarters. But what defence can possibly be set up for the wanton destruction of houses, furniture, churches, convents, and, in short, of every place and every thing in and about this unfortunate town, and that, also, under the immediate eye of Massena and his numerous staff? Here and there a wretched, half-starved, cadaverous Portuguese, with an appearance scarcely human, who had contrived to drag on a miserable existence during the winter, might be seen amongst the ruined habitations, thereby completing the sickening picture.

Of our fair friends the nuns, it was difficult to say what had been the fate; but it is to be presumed that they left Santarem before the French occupied it. The convents, of which they had been inmates in 1809, exhibited now nothing but piles of filth, disgusting beyond description.

The French rear-guard had left Santarem before the arrival of the Light Division, which pushed on after them on the road to Pernes, where it passed the night. The sketch given of Santarem will suffice for Pernes, which had fared equally bad, and presented objects of misery and disgust at every step, sufficient to raise feelings of the highest indignation against

THE CASTLE OF POMBAL ATTACKED. 197

Massena and his followers, to whose name indelible disgrace will be attached for their atrocious and wanton cruelties.

The Light Division and some cavalry, which formed the advanced guard, were followed and supported by other divisions brought up from the rear, as soon as it was known that the French were retreating.

On the 8th of March, the Light Division first came in contact with the enemy's rear-guard, at a small village, which our battalion was instantly ordered to attack, and from whence it soon dislodged them. On the 9th the advanced guard came up with the enemy, who, in considerable force, was drawn out on a plain in front of Pombal, and some skirmishing took place towards evening.

The castle, as also the walls near it, and the town itself, all of which were very defensible, the French held with a strong force of infantry, the main body of their army having fallen back, on the 10th, to a formidable position behind the town. On the 11th our battalion and the 3d Portuguese Caçadores attacked the castle, and, after a sharp conflict, drove the enemy from it with considerable loss. Had the other divisions of the army been at hand, there is but little doubt that Lord Wellington would have made a general attack on their position behind the town. A deluge of rain descended at night, which, with the extreme proximity to the French advanced posts, was well calculated to keep people on the *qui vive*.

During the night of the 11th, Massena withdrew his army from Pombal; and on the following day, the Light Division and cavalry came up with them near Redinha. The French set fire to Pombal, in the most wanton and barbarous manner, before they retreated from it. Lord Wellington made dispositions for attacking them immediately. The Light Division was soon warmly engaged, and, after a fierce struggle, forced the French through some thick and extensive woods. The rear-guard made a gallant attempt to check their pursuers near the town of Redinha, the bridge leading across the river being choked at the moment with disheartened fugitives, for whose safety the rear-guard appeared inclined to make great sacrifices; but their flanks being assailed simultaneously, whilst they were pressed warmly in front, they were obliged to give way, and were chased through the town, suffering severely in killed, wounded, and prisoners, in their attempt to cross the bridge, to which they were crowding in great confusion and dismay. No respite was allowed them; and the Light Division, with some cavalry, stuck close to their heels until night.

On reaching Condeixa the next day, it was found to have shared the same fate as Pombal and other towns which lay in Massena's line of retreat. It had been plundered and set on fire, and such enormities committed, as would have disgraced a band of Hottentots or North American Indians. During this day, although no serious engagement took place, there was some skirmishing, which terminated only by the approach of night. The French withdrew from Condeixa to a position further in their rear, in consequence of a movement made on their flank by General Picton's division.

On the 14th, Marshal Ney, who commanded the French rear-guard, halted in a position presenting many obstacles. Colonel Trant, with a body of Portuguese militia and irregular troops, had got possession of Coimbra, which frustrated Massena's plans, and prevented his retreating by that city to Vizeu. He therefore bent his steps towards the river Alva, so as to reach the road from Ponte de Marcella to Celerico. Lord Wellington attacked Marshal Ney in front with the Light Division, whilst with other divisions he turned his flanks; and, after a long and extremely hard day's work, throughout the whole of which the Light Division was sharply engaged in driving the enemy from one stronghold to another, Marshal Ney fell back to Miranda de Corvo, which town, like Pombal, Condeixa, and others, was in flames.

It would be a useless repetition to detail the pitiable state of every town and village which lay in Massena's line of retreat. Flames, ruin, murder, and devastation, marked their track. If any man is to be found bold enough to defend their conduct in this retreat, he is a fit subject to have been incorporated with that army, which disgraced the name of Europeans.

Being closely pursued, the French destroyed at and near Miranda de Corvo a quantity of baggage, ammunition, &c.; and that their baggage-animals might not prove useful to their pursuers, they cut the back-sinews of their legs, and left great numbers of them in this state of suffering on the road. It would have been more humane, would have answered the same purpose, and have occasioned less delay to the French on their retreat, if a musket-ball had been sent through the head of each unfortunate animal, instead of their being left to linger in such a lacerated state.

During the early part of the 15th, a thick mist from the mountains favoured the retreat of the enemy, and for some time prevented pursuit. When it cleared away, the advanced guard followed through Miranda de Corvo, which was still burning, and towards evening came up with the French in position behind the Ceira, a mountain river; but Marshal Ney's corps, which formed the rear-guard, had not crossed, and was near Foz d'Aroce, having at its back the rocky bed of the Ceira, which was passable only by a bridge; heavy rains having rendered the fords impracticable. Of this perilous situation of Marshal Ney's corps, Lord Wellington, ever alert, took immediate advantage.

The day was drawing to a close, and the troops were cooking their suppers, when a sudden order reached the bivouac for them to fall in, and to attack the French rear-guard. The enemy were not driven from their ground without a stout resistance and many broken heads on both sides. At length they were forced back, in utter confusion, on the narrow bridge, which their comrades on the opposite side blew up; thus leaving on the same side the river with the British, many of their countrymen, who were drowned in the Ceira, by attempting to flounder through its rapid stream. Some hundreds perished in this manner; and they threw two of their eagles into the river, to prevent their becoming trophies of the victors.

Between the killed, wounded, drowned, and prisoners, the loss of the French must necessarily have been severe in this action, which, like many other engagements before and since, between advanced and rear-guards, where the Light Division happened to be principally engaged, has been dignified with the appellation of an *affair*. An unfortunate and disastrous affair it proved for the French; and it may here be observed, that the numerous engagements of this description, which rarely find their way into the Gazette, except under the head of affairs of posts, are not so very trifling in their nature as some persons may be inclined to fancy, who have merely hearsay evidence of such matters. In this action the 3d Division and other troops also took an active part.

It is difficult to conjecture why Marshal Ney's corps was placed in a position so opposite to all rule, and so replete with peril. If Massena directed him to occupy for the night the ground on which Lord Wellington attacked him, he was the person to whom culpability must be attached. If Marshal Ney took up that position without orders, he clearly committed an error. Massena, however, who (it is to be presumed) was at hand, and fully aware of Ney's situation, might have withdrawn his rear-guard across the Ceira before it was attacked. In either case, then, Massena appears to have been the person responsible for that grand error. These ideas naturally suggest themselves to persons not in the grand secret; but it is possible that Marshal Massena had some cogent reason for thus exposing his rear-guard. The contest did not terminate until after dark;

and during the night, he retired from his position on the Ceira.

Having out-marched the commissariat, and the country being so thoroughly ransacked and plundered as to afford provisions of no kind, Lord Wellington was unable to proceed far in pursuit of the French on the 16th.

During the operations of the last few days, our corps had to regret the loss of many of its members. Amongst the number must not be omitted the name of Major Stewart, who commanded one wing of our 1st battalion, at the head of which he fell, whilst gallantly leading it to the attack. By his death the regiment was deprived of an officer who thoroughly understood the command of light troops, and was quite at home at outpost duty. He had a quick and accurate eye in taking advantage of ground, was devoted to the particular nature of our service, and his mind soared far above the uninteresting minutiæ of barrack-yard drill—the exact distance from button to button on the soldier's jacket, the width of his leather stock, and other matters of the kind, which in too many regiments are considered of vital importance.

On the 17th the French army took up a position behind the Alva, the banks of which are rugged and difficult of access in many places. By means of fords, and a temporary bridge, Lord

Wellington contrived to effect the passage of the river at different points, turned their flanks, and obliged them to give up that line of defence. Some prisoners were made by the advanced guard, which pursued the harassed enemy until night. Massena continued his retreat by the road at the foot of Sierra d'Estrella towards Celerico, and was followed by the British with as much haste as the want of provisions would permit, their rapid advance having left the commissariat far behind, and the country affording not a morsel of any thing for man or horse. From these unavoidable causes, more respite was granted to the retreating army than would otherwise have been their lot.

From Celerico, Massena bent his steps towards Guarda; and in following him, the advanced guard came up with, in the end of March, part of the French rear-guard near Freixadas. Colonel Beckwith directed an attack on them by a party of the 95th Riflemen, who soon drove them from a windmill where they were at work, and through the village. On this occasion our battalion sustained a loss by the death of its adjutant, Mr. Stewart. It is perhaps not too much to say, that no man in any corps ever filled the situation of adjutant better than he did, and very few half so well. He was open-hearted, manly, friendly, and independent, a most gallant and zealous officer, and much devoted to his own corps. He neither cringed to, nor worshipped any man, but did his duty manfully, and with impartiality,—two qualities inestimable in adjutants. By the soldiers he was idolised, and very justly. When his duties as adjutant did not interfere, he was amongst the first to enter into any frolic and fun; and a more jovial soul never existed.

The army was directed to march on Guarda, where Massena had concentrated his force, and appeared confident, in the apparently impregnable position which he had taken up. The unexpected advance, however, of the allied army on different points simultaneously, had the immediate effect of hurrying him from the mountainous region on which he was perched, and obliged him to seek safety behind the Coa, where the advanced guard found him on the 1st of April.

The rocky banks of the Coa the Light Division had reason to remember, as eight months had scarcely elapsed since its collision with Marshal Ney's corps near Almeida. The French marshal failed not to make the most of the position which the rugged, and in some places inaccessible, banks of the Coa afforded. His left, under General Regnier, extended considerably above Sabugal, and occupied the formidable heights which overlook the river, and are in some places studded with chestnut-trees of large size.

Towards the left of the French position, Lord Wellington turned his particular attention; and on the 2d of April made arrangements for attacking it the following day.

ACTION NEAR SABUGAL.

The outline of the plan was, that the Light Division and some cavalry should pass the river by a ford at some distance above Sabugal, whilst other divisions assailed the position by fords and the bridge near the town. The operations of the day commenced by the Light Division passing the Coa at a ford of considerable depth, under fire of Regnier's advanced posts, who were driven back on their supports by Colonel Beckwith's brigade, which first crossed the river.

In this, as in all other mountainous regions, thick fogs appear and disappear very suddenly; and such was the case on the present occasion. Its temporary dispersion discovered Colonel Beckwith's little brigade almost in contact with the whole of Regnier's corps, which, after a sharp fire, forced back, with overwhelming numbers, the four companies of the 95th (that composed Colonel Beckwith's advance) on the 43d regiment; and, aware that the number of his opponents was trifling, the French general made an impetuous attack with infantry, cavalry, and artillery, to crush and annihilate them before support should arrive. But the 43d, on which the Riflemen were driven back for support, was a corps not to be meddled with free of expense, as they very soon proved to their antagonists, by driving them back in most gallant style with the bayonet. Fearful as were the odds, Colonel Beckwith's brigade pursued the French into their own position, and inflicted on them a severe loss; but being reinforced, they again drove back this handful of men. They, however, possessed themselves of some stone walls and broken ground, by which they contrived to hold on until they once more obliged their enemy to retreat; and entering their position with them, charged and captured a howitzer. For the recapture of this, the French were making another grand effort, when the second brigade of the Light Division, with troops also of the 3d and other divisions, arrived near the scene of action, which obliged Regnier to make a rapid retreat. In less than forty-eight hours afterwards, the whole French army was over the Portuguese frontier, and sought shelter under the guns of Ciudad Rodrigo. A French garrison was left in Almeida.

Thus did Massena's invasion of Portugal terminate; and in this manner was his threat fulfilled of "driving the English into the sea."

In consequence of the hazy weather, the

movements of the different divisions did not take place precisely as Lord Wellington intended; for some of them lost their way in the fog, and, not reaching the point of attack chalked out for them at the exact moment, the Light Division was thus unavoidably left for a length of time engaged in a most unequal contest. That it held its ground stoutly, and made a gallant and successful struggle for victory, will scarcely be denied by those to whom the very name of "Light Division" has ever been like wormwood. In his public despatches Lord Wellington eulogised the conduct of the Light Division in the highest terms. Colonel Beckwith's forehead was grazed by a bullet, and his horse was shot under him. That cool courage which can look calmly at danger, and adopt measures to meet it at the instant, under the most critical and appalling circumstances, Colonel Beckwith possessed in an eminent degree. The number of dead bodies left on the field by the French, attested the nature of the conflict. The loss of Colonel Beckwith's brigade was also severe.

CHAPTER XII.

The French army re-enters Spain. They leave a garrison in Almeida, which is blockaded. The Light Division and 1st German Hussars take up their original line of posts. Skirmishes at Marialva bridge. Some companies of our corps are sent to shoot the cattle at Almeida. Massena assembles his army to relieve Almeida. The Light Division and 1st German Hussars fall back and join the army in position, near Fuentes d'Onoro. Battle of Fuentes d'Onoro. Flag of truce in the evening. The wounded removed. Conversation with some French officers. A sprig of nobility in the French army at the head of one of their Hussar regiments. Colonel Beckwith's brigade occupies Fuentes d'Onoro for the night. Precautions for its defence. The hostile armies remain close to each other for many days. Waggon-loads of wounded Frenchmen sent to Rodrigo. Marshal Marmont arrives from France. Assumes the command of the army in our front, and supersedes Massena. He inspects the infantry of the Imperial Guard within view of our position. The French army retires behind the Agueda. We resume our original line of outposts. Almeida is blown up, and the garrison escape. Marmont sends a cavalry force to reconnoiter Colonel Beckwith's brigade. We send them back faster than they advanced. Intelligence reaches us of the battle of Albuera. We celebrate the king's birth-day. Sudden order to march in the midst of our festivity. Affair between the 1st Royal Dragoons and the French cavalry. We march into Alemtejo. A few lines relative to the march thither. Encamp on the Caya. Gallant but unsuccessful attempts against Fort San Christoval. The army offers battle to the united armies of Soult and Marmont. They decline the challenge, and fall back to Seville and Placentia. Terrible sickness in our army. Action of cavalry near Campo Maior. Fort La Lippe. I receive a present from a Portuguese don. Starved state of our horses. The army marches back to the northern frontier of Portugal. A bee-hive captured. Staff characters.

The Light Division, with its old friends the First German Hussars, soon took up the same line of outposts on the Azarva which they held last summer, during the period that Massena was laying siege to Ciudad Rodrigo. One brigade was at Gallegos, the other at Espeja, having Hussar pickets across the Azarva at Carpio and Marialva, and on the Agueda, at Moulina dos Flores.

Several sharp skirmishes between the infantry pickets took place at Marialva bridge, in the month of April. The French were invariably the aggressors; but what good result they expected from it, was known only to themselves.

The French garrison in Almeida was blockaded by General Pack's Portuguese brigade, and some British battalions. Several companies of our regiment were also sent to shoot the cattle that were turned out to graze under cover of the guns of the fortress. This frequently brought a cannonade on our men. Towards the end of

April Massena concentrated his army near Ciudad Rodrigo, for the purpose of attacking the allies, and of raising the blockade of Almeida.

On the 2d of May he crossed the Azarva in great force, obliging the Light Division and the German Hussars to fall gradually back; and we bivouacked between Espeja and the Duas Casas, close to the enemy's advanced guard.

On the 3d, before daybreak, we were again in motion; and having crossed the Duas Casas at Fuentes d'Onoro, without molestation from the French, took up the ground allotted for us on the heights above that village. Here we found the 1st, 3d, 5th, 6th, and 7th Divisions in position; the 2d and 4th being employed before Badajoz, under Marshal Beresford. The 7th Division, under General Houston, was on the extreme right, near Navis d'Avair, the 1st and 3d to the right and rear of the village of Fuentes d'Onoro, the 5th and 6th on the left towards Fort Conception, and the Light Division near the centre, as a flying corps, ready to be despatched to any point of this extended position most menaced.

The village of Fuentes d'Onoro was occupied by troops detached from the 1st and 3d Divisions; the greater part of the cavalry were towards the right, where the ground was favourable for their operations. This was nearly the disposition of our army, although I cannot answer for trifling inaccuracies. If the general outline be correct, it is enough for my purpose.

On the evening of the 3d the French made a brisk attack on the village, but were beaten back in handsome style, and with considerable loss, by the light troops of General Picton's division, commanded by Colonel Williams, of the 60th regiment, and, I believe, by some light infantry of the 1st Division also. In the midst of this attack the Light Division was marched off in great haste to support General Erskine's division on the left, which was menaced by General Regnier's corps; but nothing further than an affair of light troops took place at that point. The whole of the following day, which Massena employed in reconnoitering, passed as quietly as possible, although the sentries of the two armies were within pistol-shot of each other in some parts of the line. About sunset the Light Division was ordered to move from the left to the centre of the position.

BATTLE OF FUENTES D'ONORO.

May 5th.—The moment daylight appeared Massena sent a powerful body of cavalry, supported by heavy masses of infantry, with artillery, under the command of General Junot, to attack our extreme right. The Light Division was instantly ordered to occupy a wood in front of and to the right of the 1st Division. The vast superiority in numbers of the French cavalry obliged the 7th Division to fall back from near Navis d'Avair; and in performing this movement, some of General Houston's regiments checked the enemy's dragoons by their steadiness, and by well-directed vollies, whilst the British cavalry, under the Hon. General Stewart, made a brilliant charge on that of the enemy, who were endeavouring to interrupt General Houston's movement.

The 7th Division was now taking up a new alignement, with its right thrown back towards the heights near Villa Formosa, and communicating by its left with the 1st Division. Whilst this was in progress, the French attacked, with many battalions of infantry, the wood into which the Light Division had been ordered, and a sharp fire was kept up for some time on both sides. The British right being turned at Navis d'Avair, the mass of French cavalry, with artillery, continued to advance along the plain, threatening to cut off the Light Division from the position on the heights. We were, therefore, directed to retire from the wood, to form squares of battalions, and to fall back over the plain on the 1st Division. The steadiness and regularity with which the troops performed this movement, the whole time exposed to a cannonade, and followed across a plain by a numerous cavalry, ready to pounce on the squares if the least disorder should be detected, has been acknowledged by hundreds of unprejudiced persons (unconnected with the Light Division), who witnessed it from the heights, to have been a masterpiece of military evolutions. We sustained a very trifling loss from the cannonade, and reached our station in the position near the 1st Division.

Massena now halted Junot's corps pretty well out of range of our artillery; and contented himself by keeping up a heavy cannonade, and sending out swarms of light troops to amuse us, as the term is. Four companies of our corps, under Major O'Hare, being sent into the rocky valley of the Turon, to check some of these gentry who were endeavouring to penetrate between the 1st and 7th Divisions, drove them out from amongst the rocks and stone walls which they endeavoured to occupy. Our old comrades, the 1st Germans, and 14th and 16th Light Dragoons, headed by General Stewart, supported the high character of their respective corps; and, although very inferior in numbers to the French cavalry, taught them a useful lesson on that day.

About this period several desperate attacks were made on the village of Fuentes d'Onoro, in each of which the brave troops stationed there for its defence drove back their antagonists with great slaughter. The village was defended by troops from the 1st and 3d Divisions. The

French were charged with the bayonet through the village again and again, in spite of all their strenuous and energetic attempts to carry it. Lord Wellington sent down regiment after regiment, in detail, for its defence, according to the numbers detached against it by the enemy; and towards evening, the 88th regiment, on arriving at the head of the village from the heights above, met a French column pressing boldly on, and in great force, which this distinguished Irish corps instantly charged with the bayonet, and drove through the village with great slaughter. Judging by the number of killed and wounded lying near the spot where they came in contact with their enemy, Pat made excellent use of powder, ball, and bayonet. The 71st, 79th, the 2d battalion of the 24th, and all the regiments employed in the defence of the village, rivalled each other in gallantry and good conduct. On the left no serious attack was made; but the light troops of the 5th Division were sharply engaged with those of General Regnier, near Fort Conception.

Thus did Massena utterly fail in every attempt, and left the village and the ground near it covered with killed and wounded. Shortly before dark, Colonel Beckwith's brigade of the Light Division was ordered into the village, to relieve the troops of the 1st and 3d, who rejoined their respective divisions on the heights.

We had been but a short time at Fuentes d'Onoro, when a flag of truce came in, requesting permission to send into the village unarmed parties to bring away their wounded, who filled the streets and houses. During this truce, several French officers came down to the little bridge over the Duas Casas, at the foot of the village, on which happened to be posted a file of men of my own company, whilst two French grenadiers were on sentry at the other end of it. On the centre of the bridge three French officers met and conversed á considerable time with the officers of my company, and were politeness itself. After offering us a pinch of snuff, by way of prelude, the events which had taken place during the day were discussed. They paid many compliments to the gallant conduct of our army, and declared that to-morrow would be a great and decisive day, and full of glory for one of the two armies.

The captain of the 9th Light Infantry was a remarkably smart, talkative, Frenchman-like, little fellow. He had two musket-shots through his cap, one of which had grazed his head, and the blood was trickling down his face at the moment. He treated it very lightly, saying it was a mere nothing—the fortune of war!

Our attention was just then called, by our little friend of the 9th Light Infantry, to a flashy young man, dressed in a gay hussar uniform, who came galloping along near the bridge: "Do you see that boy?" said he: "he is about twenty years of age only; has just arrived from France to commence his career in Spain, and commands one of our hussar regiments. But," added our friend (with a shrug of his shoulders), "he is the nephew of the war minister, which accounts for it."

It was now nearly dark, and the greater part of their wounded were carried into their own lines; so, having made profound bows to our new acquaintance on the bridge, we commenced preparations for the defence of the village from a night attack. One part of it was still in possession of the French; and I may therefore safely assert, that on no occasion during the war was extreme vigilance more necessary than at this moment. The sentries of the two armies were so near each other that they might easily have conversed. We blocked up with large stones the narrow streets and paths leading to our part of the village; and Lord Wellington caused trenches and field-works to be made during the night, on the open ground in front of his right, where it was favourable for the operations of the numerous cavalry of his adversary.

The morning of the 6th found the two armies precisely in the same positions as on the preceding day. There was a dead calm and perfect silence: not a shot was exchanged throughout the day. From the highest point of our position could be seen carts-load of wounded French moving in the direction of Rodrigo.

The 7th, 8th, and 9th, passed just in the same manner as the 6th: not a shot was fired by either party. The French still continued to remove their wounded towards Rodrigo.

At break of day on the 10th, the Light Division and cavalry followed the enemy, who retreated during the night of the 9th behind the Agueda, and we soon found ourselves once more in our old quarters at Gallegos and Espeja.

Marshal Marmont (the Duke of Ragusa) arrived from France, in the midst of these operations, to take command of the " army of Portugal," and to supersede Massena. Marmont drew out the Imperial Guards, in review order, one day between the 5th and 10th, whilst the two armies remained inactive near Fuentes d'Onoro; and we were able clearly to distinguish this fine body of infantry without the assistance of our telescopes.

On the night of the 10th May, the French garrison in Almeida contrived to effect its escape through the force employed to blockade it, and to reach San Felicis by the pass of Barba del Puerco. In this bold and well-conducted movement the French lost some hundred men. General Brenier, the French governor, spiked and destroyed all the cannon on the works; and having placed mines in various places, and left slow matches in them, a terrible explosion took place some time after the garrison had left it, which blew the town and ramparts to atoms.

On the 12th, Marshal Marmont sent from Ciudad Rodrigo three regiments of cavalry to reconnoiter our post at Espeja. Colonel Beckwith formed his three battalions into squares, near the village, and opened a fire on the French dragoons as soon as they came within reach, which instantly sent them back over the Azarva, with the loss of a few horses.

On the 22d of May, intelligence reached us of the sanguinary battle fought at Albuera, between the French, under Marshal Soult, and the little army under Marshal Beresford, consisting of the 2d and 4th British Divisions, Colonel Alten's German Light Brigade, and a corps of Spaniards. The particulars of this hardly contested day are well known; and as the Light Division, with the other five of Lord Wellington's army, were at that time employed in the neighbourhood of Fuentes d'Onoro, many marches from Albuera, I am unable to give any account of it. We know, however, that British valour never shone more conspicuously, nor has the steady and unflinching bravery displayed by the regiments on that bloody day ever been surpassed. To their invincible courage was the victory due.

In the middle of May, the 3d and 7th Divisions of infantry marched from the north to join Marshal Beresford on the Guadiana; and towards the end of the month, the Light Division received orders to move in the same direction. Marmont was, about this time, detaching troops into Spanish Estremadura, through the passes of the Sierra de Gata, to form a junction with Soult, and to raise the siege of Badajoz, which Marshal Beresford had now a second time commenced, after having defeated Soult at Albuera. In proportion, therefore, as Marmont detached to the southward, were the British divisions directed to move in a parallel direction, by way of Castello Branco and Villa Velha.

It was not until early in June that the Light Division marched towards that point; and on the 4th, whilst we were celebrating the birth-day of George the Third, in the village of Espeja, with wine, cigars, and a dance with the Spanish fair ones, an order reached us to march before break of day. I will be sworn that our fair partners would have been fully as well pleased, as we should also, if the order had arrived some twelve hours later, for it broke up a merry party, and obliged us to retire to our hovels, to order our baggage-mules to be saddled, and to march without a wink of sleep; no, not even enough to give us a chance of dreaming of our black-eyed signoras.

On the 6th June, the 1st Royal Dragoons had an affair in the open country near Espeja, in which that distinguished old corps repeatedly repulsed the French cavalry, and made some prisoners. On the 7th, the Light Division bivouacked near Sabugal; and as the day was favourable for fishing, I ardently longed for the necessary apparatus to wage war on the trout, which are remarkably fine in this part of the Coa; but I had neither rod, lines, nor flies. We were now on our route into Alemtejo, and prosecuted our march there, day after day, under a scorching sun, without meeting with any adventure on the road worthy of being noticed. We took the route by Memoa, Penamacor, San Miguel, Castello Branco, Villa Velha, Neza, &c.

On the 11th of June, many hundreds of men were left by the road-side, quite exhausted by the intense heat. This obliged us to make frequent halts in the day, and to proceed at night; and by some mishap we were without our baggage, and consequently without provisions for forty hours. Passing from Neza through Alpalhao, Portalegre, and Aronches, halting a day or two here and there, we bivouacked, on the 23d of June, in the hottest and most parched piece of ground in the Peninsula, lying between Aronches and Campo Maior, and on the left bank of the Caya. In this neighbourhood Lord Wellington had concentrated his whole army.

Marshals Soult and Marmont, one from the north and the other from the south, had united their forces, amounting, it was calculated, to eighty thousand men. This obliged Lord Wellington to raise the siege of Badajoz. Several gallant attempts had been made to storm Fort San Christoval, a strong place on the right bank of the Guadiana, connected with Badajoz; but all unfortunately failed, owing, I believe, to the impracticability of the breaches.

I ought to have observed, that during Massena's retreat out of Portugal, in the month of March, this fortress fell before Marshal Soult's army, after a trifling siege, and the very shadow of a defence, at a time when the Spanish governor was aware that Marshal Beresford was marching to his relief.

What a favourable opportunity now offered to the Spanish armies (if they had any bodies deserving that name) to make play in the different districts, drained of French troops by the junction of Soult and Marmont on the Guadiana! I never heard that they profited much by it.

Our army remained in position on the Caya about one month; when the two French marshals, not liking to attack us, broke up from the Guadiana, after having completely garrisoned and provisioned Badajoz, without accepting the challenge given by our chief. If our ranks were not thinned by the sword at this moment, they were most terribly so by fevers, agues, and dysenteries, so prevalent and destructive in Alemtejo, particularly in the hot months. In no part of the world have I experienced a more constant, sickening, deadly heat, than in the encampment on the Caya. I never enjoyed better health, nor ever exposed myself more to the sun, with gun and greyhound; and I bathed twice a day in the stagnant waters of the Caya, which abounded with water-snakes, leeches, and all manner of devils.

On the 22d of June there was a sharp affair between some of our cavalry (I think the 13th Light Dragoons and 2d German Hussars,) and a body of French dragoons, supported by infantry, near Campo Maior. We made many prisoners, and sustained a loss of about forty men. This was the report which reached us in camp. We frequently rode over to Elvas, the fort La Lippe, which commands the town, being well worth a morning's ride to see.

Whilst we remained in this furnace of a camp, I received a present from a Portuguese don, or some big-wig, who had a country house near us, of an exceedingly fine puppy of the breed of Spanish bull, or wild-boar dogs, of a blue slate colour, and as big, when full grown, as the largest and most powerful mastiff. I lost him about a year afterwards, which in reality I was not sorry for, his temper being much on a par with that of my young wolf, already mentioned in these pages.

Had Don Quixote lived at this time, he might have gone blindfold through our camp, quite certain to have found a Rosinante in any horse on which he first laid his hands. Chopped straw and stagnant water, with constant exposure to a broiling sun, and being picketed under a shadeless tree, reduced them to a pitiable state, and established the well-known furrows down the hind quarters, so strongly indicating poverty and starvation.

On the 20th of July the army marched in a northerly direction, retracing its steps by Portalegre, Neza, Villa Velha, &c., and in a few weeks General Hill's Division alone remained in Alemtejo, with a few regiments of cavalry. On our march back to the north, being encamped one day at Villa Velha, I made an excursion with a brother-officer to the summit of the mountain on the north bank of the Tagus, where a Moorish watch-tower stands: there, amongst the gum cistus, as good fortune would have it, we stumbled on some bee-hives, which the Spaniards and Portuguese make of the outer bark of the cork-tree. We laid an embargo on one of them, and marched triumphantly into camp, smothered the bees with gunpowder, and voted the honey a capital substitute for sugar, of which we had none in our canteens, nor money to purchase any. Is there an old Peninsula man who has not long since ascertained that tea with honey is more palatable than tea without sugar?

I cannot help here observing, (on this as well as on many other long marches, where, from scarcity of forage and hard work, the horses of infantry officers resembled scare-crows, and were fit subjects only for the fox-hound kennel,) the infinite amusement we often derived from witnessing the glance of sovereign contempt which some of the young aides-du-camp deigned to throw on us and on our Rosinantes, as they rode along the flanks of the columns on well fed, pampered chargers, following in the train of their generals. No one will suppose that I am so illiberal as to make this a sweeping clause. Far, very far from it. I have known, and still do know, many excellent fellows who were not spoiled by having held staff appointments; nor did they think themselves degraded at the termination of the war by returning to their regimental duty.

If there is one school worse than another for a youngster, on his first obtaining a commission, it is that of being placed, *instanter*, on the staff as an aide-du-camp, before he has done duty with his regiment for a year or two. If a sprig of aristocracy assumes any airs with his regimental companions, he pretty quickly learns a useful lesson, and finds *that* system will not do. But once placed on the staff, such foibles are not so likely to be there corrected as at a company's mess in a bivouac, with a set of merry, hungry, cigar-smoking subs, and a rough and ready captain at their head.

CHAPTER XIII.

The Light Division crosses the Agueda. Lord Wellington reconnoiters Rodrigo. Don Julian Sanchez. The French governor taken prisoner by Guerillas. A picket of our light cavalry made prisoners in the Sierra de Gata. The Light Division reinforced by the third battalion of the 95th Rifle Corps from Cadiz. Deaths by Alemtejo fever. I cross the mountains with my own company and one of Portuguese. Wild scenery. Goatherds. Their dress, language, and habitations. Rejoin the Light Division. Marmont advances to Rodrigo. The Light Division in position on the Vadillo. Gallant conduct of General Colville's brigade. The Light Division joins the 3d and 4th near Guinaldo. The army falls back to Aldea de Ponte. The Light Division engaged with the French cavalry and dismounted chasseurs. Brilliant charge of the Fusileer brigade. General Picton's light troops engaged. The army retires to Soita. Marmont follows the allied army no further, and falls back to Placentia. Our army goes into cantonments. Comparative merits of Spanish and English greyhounds. A new governor arrives at Rodrigo. Winter quarters in Spanish villages. Libraries not in vogue. An essay on cigars, and their utility in campaigning. A party made to shoot wild deer. General Hill surprises a French division. A shooting party in the mountains. Boleros, fandangos, and Irish jigs. Capital sport with the woodcocks. A good dancer and a particularly bad shot. Excursion to Robadillia. Just punishment inflicted on a demi-brigade of padres. The Light Division invests and lays siege to Ciudad Rodrigo. Redoubt of San Francisco stormed and taken. The siege and storming of Rodrigo. Death of Generals Crawford and M'Kinnon. Remarks on the defence made by the French governor. Contrast between the siege of 1810 and that of 1812. The army marches to the southward and besieges Badajoz. Difficulty of keeping our horses alive during the march. Siege of Badajoz. Storming of the place.

BUT I must take leave of staff men, and proceed across the Agueda once more. This was effected by the Light Division and some cavalry on the 10th of August, at a ford called Vado de Carros. We occupied Martiago and other villages near it. On the following day Lord Wellington ordered us to accompany him in a reconnoissance on Ciudad Rodrigo. On our approaching the town, the governor sent out a few hundred infantry and some field-pieces, which did not advance from under the protection of the heavy guns of the works. We returned to our villages late that night.

The whole army, except General Hill's corps in Alemtejo, was now cantoned on the northern frontier of Portugal; our division and the German Hussars being advanced across the Agueda. Marmont's head-quarters were at Placentia, and the French also occupied Salamanca with some thousand troops. Although Ciudad Rodrigo was not strictly blockaded, it could not be said to have been much otherwise, for the Light Division and some cavalry occupied villages near it, on the right bank of the Agueda. Cavalry also watched it in the direction of El Bodon, on the opposite bank; and the active Guerilla chief, Don Julian Sanchez, eternally hung about the walls, ready to pounce on any small party which might leave the town. One day a party of those Guerillas made the governor and his escort prisoners, almost under cover of the guns of Rodrigo. About this period an officer of one of our light dragoon regiments, who was on picket in one of the passes of the Sierra de Gata, was surprised and made prisoner, with all his party, by a strong patrole of French cavalry.

On the 21st the Light Division was reinforced by five companies of our third battalion, under the command of Lieutenant-Colonel Barnard. They arrived at Lisbon from Cadiz, and had been present at the memorable battle of Barossa, fought on the 5th of March. Two companies also of our second battalion had been sent from England to join the Light Division within the last six or eight months; those being the most effective men that could be collected from a battalion which went to Walcheren in 1809, upwards of a thousand strong. Many officers and soldiers died whilst we were in this neighbourhood, having undoubtedly brought the malignant fever with them from that unhealthy camp on the Caya, in Alemtejo. Amongst the number were Colonel Drummond of the 24th regiment, (who commanded a brigade in the Light Division during Colonel Beckwith's absence in England, from ill health,) Major Elers of the 43d, three officers of our own regiment, and a great number of soldiers.

On the 9th September I was detached with my own company, and one of Portuguese Caçadores, across the Sierra de Gata to Las Herrias and Aldea Juella, two villages of the worst possible description, buried in the heart of mountains, as awfully grand and terrific as I ever beheld in Spain, Switzerland, or elsewhere. The inhabitants of those wretched hovels, which I have dignified with the name of villages, were all dressed in the skins of goats, sheep, and wolves, looking more like demons than any thing human. Although no Patagonian in height, I was obliged to stoop double, in order to go in and out of the shed, which, as commandant, I took care should not be the worst in the colony. Some dried fern in a dark corner, which looked as if the devil should have been its inmate, where myriads of fleas had established themselves as " lords and masters," was my bed, and my pillow a knapsack.

Although only a few leagues distant from the villages of Martiago, &c. &c. on the north side of the mountains, from which we came, where the Spanish language is spoken with tolerable purity, it was quite a hopeless case to endeavour to understand those goatherds, or to make them comprehend us. Their lingo resembled Hebrew or Arabic quite as much as Castilian. I often wished that some one highly gifted with descriptive powers could have taken a peep at the magnificent scenery which surrounded us on all sides, and have done something like justice to it.

We were detached to those villages to observe some narrow roads, by which infantry or light cavalry might have approached from Marmont's outposts, between us and Placentia, and to collect such information as we were able relative to the movements of the enemy.

During the fortnight which was spent amongst those uncouth goatherds, we were constantly accoutred night and day, and ready to stand to our arms at a moment's notice. The days were passed in patrolling, reconnoitering, and endeavouring to collect information from the mountaineers, who either could not or would not enlighten us as to Marmont's movements. I believe our colonists were not a little nettled because we took possession, by General Crawford's orders, of such goats and sheep as were requisite to ration the troops. Bread and wine were sent to us from the head-quarters of the division every fourth day, across the mountains on mules.

Two deserters came over to us on the 11th, who reported that Marmont was detaching troops from Placentia to Salamanca. We were heartily rejoiced, at the expiration of a fortnight, to be recalled, and to join the Light Division in more Christian-like quarters at Martiago. On our march across the mountains we saw a large wolf, which had been rambling about near a village, and at which one of our men sent a rifle-ball, but it had merely the effect of quickening his pace, the distance being too great to give us a chance of killing him.

Marmont had assembled his whole army, and having crossed the mountains from Placentia, was advancing to raise the blockade of Rodrigo, and to throw into it a large convoy of provisions. His advanced guard was on the Agueda, and some of his cavalry watched the Light Division, which occupied a very extended line of country behind the Vadillo, a mountain-river flowing into the Agueda; which latter stream separated us from the remainder of the army, and rendered our position an extremely ticklish one. Here we remained three days, on the last of which (25th September) Marmont sent forward from Rodrigo a strong force of cavalry with artillery towards El Bodon, in which village a brigade

GALLANT CONDUCT OF GEN. COLVILLE'S BRIGADE. 233

belonging to the 3d Division was stationed, commanded by the Hon. General Colville. On the heights near it, this brigade, with a few troops of (I believe) the 11th and 12th Light Dragoons, and some Portuguese artillery, was attacked most furiously, and they held their ground with a steadiness and bravery which should immortalise them.

The Light Division being at the time on the Vadillo, some leagues off, we could only hear the distant cannonade, and were kept many hours in a state of uncertainty and anxiety, knowing, that unless the troops on the left bank of the Agueda were able to keep the French in check, we must necessarily be cut off from the main body of our army, and scramble into the mountains, at whose base we were in position. Three British battalions, weak in numbers, the 2d battalion of the 5th, the 77th, and the 2d battalion 83d, composed General Colville's brigade; and having formed a square, they resisted repeated charges of a numerous cavalry, and were for a length of time exposed to a destructive cannonade. The conduct of the squadrons of our cavalry was equally gallant, who charged and drove back, again and again, very superior numbers of French dragoons. Some Portuguese guns, of which the French cavalry had gained temporary possession, were retaken by the 5th regiment, which charged and fairly beat them away.

This is almost the first instance on record of a battalion of infantry in line, and on a plain, attacking a body of cavalry; yet that such was the case on this occasion, I believe is beyond all doubt. This gallant little brigade fell back in the course of the day towards Fuente Guinaldo, near which the remainder of the 3d and 4th Divisions were in position, and had hastily thrown up some field-works.

The same night the Light Division marched from the Vadillo, and on the 26th, crossing the Agueda by a ford near the mountains, joined the 3d and 4th Divisions in the position at Guinaldo. Sir Thomas Graham was on the Azarva, with some troops of cavalry and infantry.

The French employed the 26th in bringing forward heavy columns of infantry and cavalry from Ciudad Rodrigo towards our position. As soon as it was dark, all the troops at Guinaldo retired in the direction of Aldea de Ponte, except the Light Division and some of the 1st German Hussars, which were left as a rear-guard. About midnight we followed the main body, and, with the exception of a short halt, were marching until the evening of the 27th, when we joined some other divisions near Aldea de Ponte. So much time would not have been requisite to go that distance, had we not been interrupted in our retreat by the French cavalry, who came up about mid-day, charging and driving in on us our small body of German Hussars. On each side of the road the ground was rough and rocky, which enabled us to bring their cavalry to a standstill; but some of them dismounting, attacked us as light infantry, which brought on a sharp skirmish between some companies of our regiment and their dismounted chasseurs. After getting some broken heads, and possibly not liking to carry on a light infantry warfare, they thought fit to return to their horses, and to resume the shape of cavalry. The remainder of the day they were more cautious in approaching us.

Late in the evening the Fusileer brigade, composed of the 7th and 23d regiments, under the command of the Hon. General Pakenham, made a brilliant charge, and drove back, in gallant style, a superior body of French infantry near Aldea de Ponte, which Marmont had sent to take possession of a hill, from which Lord Wellington was reconnoitering. The light troops of General Picton's division were briskly engaged also. Until night put a stop to it, there was an animated cannonade; when Lord Wellington, leaving the Light Division and some cavalry as a rear-guard, withdrew his army towards Soita.

Our division followed at midnight, and about eight o'clock the next morning reached a position near Soita, on which the whole allied army, except General Hill's corps, was drawn out to give battle to the Duke of Ragusa, should he think proper to accept the challenge. But Marmont followed us no further than Aldea de Ponte, except with some cavalry; and in a few days he withdrew his whole army across the Agueda, and from thence to Salamanca and Placentia. He had been obliged to collect, at great inconvenience, a force vastly superior to that of the allies, particularly in cavalry, and to march a long distance, for the purpose of introducing a convoy of provisions into Ciudad Rodrigo; and by draining Placentia, Salamanca, and other districts, of French troops, he afforded an opportunity to the Spaniards of operating on his flanks and rear.

In declining to give Marmont battle between the Agueda and Aldea de Ponte, it is probable that Lord Wellington was influenced by two most potent reasons: 1st, Because the French infinitely outnumbered the British, particularly in cavalry, for the operation of which arm the country was favourable; and 2dly, Because the further he drew Marmont away after him from the Agueda, and from his resources, the fairer was the opportunity offered to the Spaniards of stirring themselves in the part of the country recently vacated by their invaders. These are my own ideas on the subject, which may, however, be erroneous.

The Light Division was once more in villages on the Agueda, and the remainder of the army were stationed nearly as before Marmont's advance.

On the 10th of October a large coursing party went out on the plains near Guinaldo, to set at rest a point long at issue amongst our sporting characters, as to the comparative merits of English and Spanish greyhounds. A capital hare was found, and she went away for a mile or two over as fine a country for coursing as is any where to be found, before two English greyhounds, which had lately been sent out to the 43d regiment, and a Spanish greyhound, considered excellent. The hare was killed by the English dogs, which were so exhausted by the heat of the day and the severity of the course, that one of them died immediately, and the other was saved with great difficulty by bleeding. The Spanish dog came up very contentedly a long while after the hare and greyhound were dead. The heat had not affected him, because he was accustomed to the climate; and, moreover, he took particular care not to distress himself by an over-display of zeal.

However well the cross between the English

and Spanish greyhound may answer, I would advise no sportsman, who does not wish to expose his own judgment and his dog's prowess, ever to think of running a greyhound of the pure Spanish breed, even if he be the best that Spain ever produced, against a moderately good English dog, at Newmarket or elsewhere.

Marmont sent, in the latter end of October, to Rodrigo, a new governor from Salamanca, to replace the one who had been surprised some time before, and made prisoner by the Guerillas, almost under the walls of the town. This new governor was escorted by a body of cavalry and infantry, to relieve the troops in the place, who returned, immediately on the arrival of the new garrison, to Salamanca. When the weather permitted, we amused ourselves as usual with coursing and shooting, and at night either collected the village fair ones, and, aided by some musicians of the band, danced the night half through, or sat round a brass pan of charcoal, whiffing away care with our cigars, and speculating on what the next campaign might produce. When the winter rains confined us to our wretched hovels, and prevented us from following our usual avocations in the field, it must be allowed that we were sometimes brought to a nonplus, and sadly troubled to kill time during the day.

It should be remembered that Spanish villages do not afford the same resources as are to be found in every insignificant place in England. Books were quite out of the question. Some few individuals of a corps might possibly possess a small pocket volume or two; but when it is considered that the first and most necessary point, and that which occupied our chief attention, was to procure, by some means or other, forage for our horses and mules, that the baggage which contained our few comforts and necessaries might be carried with us from place to place, it will readily be comprehended that a portable library was deemed less essential for our existence than a portmanteau containing a few changes of linen, boots, &c. &c., to say nothing of tea, sugar, chocolate, rice, bread, meat, a pig's-skin of wine, a keg of spirits, cigars, spare horse-shoes and nails, &c. &c.,—that is to say, when any of these good things could be procured for love or money, which very frequently was not the case.

Our half-starved animals had more than enough to do in scrambling along with such matters on their backs, without the additional weight of libraries, even had it been possible to have procured books. A good telescope and correct maps of the country were indispensable; next to which may be mentioned cigars, without which there was no getting on.

To be able fully to appreciate their utility and

comfort, it is necessary that a man should sleep in a camp or bivouac in a dreary night of rain or snow,—that he should know what a night march is, and be initiated into every sort and kind of vicissitude which campaigning brings in its train. If a man in England, after having eaten an alderman's dinner, and lounged on a sofa, with a Turkey carpet under his feet, a blazing fire before him, and a cigar in his mouth, fancies that he really knows the comfort of tobacco in that shape, he is very much mistaken; as is in like manner the equestrian or pedestrian dandy, with unshorn lip, who whiffs his cigar all over London, and through the Park, on a fine, bright, butterfly morning. He must rise, wet to the skin and numbed with cold, from the lee side of a tree or hedge, where he has been shivering all night under a flood of rain, — then let him light his cigar, and the warmth and comfort which it imparts is incredible. Or, let him march, night after night, until he is so overpowered with sleepiness as to tumble off his horse during his momentary doze, (sleeping as he rides along, and falling in amongst the column of soldiers, who are in a similar plight); or if he is marching on foot, rolling about in the ranks in a state between sleeping and waking,—let him then apply his cigar, and he is awake again.

Although I do not calculate on any of my

friends in England trying such experiments, in order to satisfy their curiosity, or to prove the correctness of my statement, there are still living witnesses enough to prove that the picture is not overdrawn.

On the 8th of November a large party of us set out to shoot wild deer in the mountains near Serradilia. We soon roused three fine ones; but our party were very noisy, and, as is invariably the case where all are talkers and no hearers, a regular plan was not adopted, as should have been the case, to out-manœuvre the game, by which means they were shot at too soon, and in too great a hurry; and one of the marksmen was much nearer killing a brother-officer than either of the deer.

About the middle of November we heard of General Hill's corps having surprised the French General Gerard's division near Carceres; taking their baggage, with some prisoners, and dispersing the remainder. The French had many killed and wounded in this brilliant affair, which was planned with secrecy and skill, and carried into effect with infinite spirit and gallantry. It was with the greatest difficulty that the commissariat could provide bread for the troops at the outposts at this period; and we were sometimes without any for days together.

On the 11th of December, having heard of

a flight of woodcocks, I went, with two of my brother-officers, to a solitary farm-house in the mountains beyond the Vadillo, where we slept. We took with us our servants, a mule laden with provisions, portmanteaus, &c. &c., and the Irish piper belonging to the band. In the evening we danced boleros, fandangos, and Irish jigs, with the farmers' daughters, and early the next morning attacked the woodcocks, which I never remember to have seen more numerous. We had capital sport, and returned late at night to our quarters at Atalaia. One of our party, who was a better performer at the dance than with a gun, fired thirty shots, at least, without killing a single bird; and towards evening, by way of putting a finishing stroke to the day's work, he let fly at an enormous wild cat, which was perched on a tree above his head, not twenty yards distant, and the animal escaped unhurt. This was a standing joke against him ever after.

New-year's day of 1812 brought with it snow and frost in abundance, which induced a party of us to obtain a few days' leave of absence, and, with gun in hand, to make an excursion, on the 3d of January, to Robadillia, a large village in one of the deepest and most secluded valleys of the Sierra de Gata, where a Spanish family resided with whom we had become acquainted on the other side of the mountains in the previous autumn. We sent on two servants with mules, on which we carried a change of clothes, tea, sugar, cigars, meat, &c. &c.; for, be it known, that in Spain, if you wish to fare moderately well whilst travelling, nothing of this kind should be left to chance.

The snow was so deep on the mountains, that we passed them with infinite difficulty; and, but for the honour of the thing, might as well have left our guns behind us, as the only living animal we saw was a wild boar, going at the rate of thirty miles an hour, many gun-shots distant.

The old don, his wife and daughters, received us kindly, and procured billets for us in the village. They beat up for volunteers, and having collected the village belles, and a fiddler or two, we danced with great glee; after which, we gave the fair ones a supper at our billets. This was followed by duets, trios, catches, and glees, and melodies of all sorts and kinds, both Spanish, Irish, Scotch, and English. Some young padres, with the crowns of their heads shaved, were amongst the party invited to accompany the ladies to our fête; and these lads were evidently much annoyed at the preference which the signoras evinced towards the heretical Englishmen; nor did they attempt to disguise their feelings. I am free to confess that I never had a great predilection for any of that idle, vagabond class;

and in this I was by no means singular, for I found my comrades quite ready to join in any frolic or fun which might be proposed as a just punishment for their uncourteous conduct.

When the amusements of the evening were over, and we had escorted our partners to their homes, we still found some of those *clericos* hanging about the street with lanterns in their hands. We suddenly opened a heavy fire of snow-balls on them, of the hardest and most terrific kind, which smashed their lanterns to atoms, and battered them from head to foot, to a degree beyond a joke. We heard their curses and execrations on Englishmen and heretics gradually die away as they ran from us and hid themselves in their respective habitations.

Thus ended our frolic in Robadillia, which was soon followed by matters of a far different nature. Intelligence reached us that the Light Division was instantly to invest and lay siege to Ciudad Rodrigo, and that it was moving to El Bodon, Pastores, and other villages nearer that fortress. Having said farewell to our friends in Robadillia (not including the padres), we passed the whole day in floundering across the snowy mountains, and joined our battalion late at night at El Bodon.

We found that the 1st, 3d, and 4th Divisions, which had been moved up to villages nearer the

Agueda, were, in conjunction with the Light Division, to carry on the siege of Rodrigo, and that a pontoon bridge had been thrown across the river some distance below the town. The divisions were to relieve each other every twenty-four hours in the trenches, as the frost was very severe.

On the 8th of January, the Light Division marched before break of day, and forded the Agueda above the knees, near the convent of Carredad. The weather being very sharp, the process was not a pleasant one. The necessary dispositions for the investment of the place were soon completed, under the immediate directions of Lord Wellington. There was some cannonading from the town as the regiments advanced to take up the different posts allotted to them. General Pack's Portuguese brigade invested the town on the left bank of the river, and was in a position on the heights above the bridge which leads into it.

On some rising ground stood the redoubt of San Francisco, which it was necessary to take before operations could be commenced against the town. At nine o'clock at night, three hundred men, belonging to the 43d, 52d, 95th, and the 3d Portuguese Caçadores, under the command of Lieutenant-Colonel Colbourne, of the 52d, stormed and carried it. Our loss was three officers and about twenty men. We lost a lieutenant of the Rifle corps, a most promising young man. All the French troops in the fort, amounting to about seventy men and three officers, were either made prisoners or bayoneted in the assault. Strong working parties immediately commenced the first parallel on the heights where the redoubt stood; and, as the garrison kept up an extremely heavy fire, both of shot and shells, without intermission, throughout the night, we worked like rabbits, and before daybreak were tolerably well covered in the trenches. Daylight enabled the French to direct their fire with greater accuracy, which was tremendous.

The 1st Division relieved ours on the 9th; and the French being enabled to overlook us from the top of the cathedral tower, and to see the troops as they arrived to relieve each other, always took that opportunity, when the trenches were crowded with double numbers, to open every gun and mortar which could possibly be brought to bear, and kept up as dreadful a fire of shot and shells as men were ever exposed to. General Crawford's horse was killed under him by a round shot. Having been relieved by the 1st Division, we went through the freezing operation of fording the Agueda, and returned to our villages late at night, they being some leagues distant from the fortress. No rocking was necessary to send us to sleep, after thirty-six hours spent in the manner I have related.

The siege was prosecuted the two following days by the 3d and 4th Divisions; and on the 12th the Light Division was again in the trenches. We were employed all day in completing some batteries, and at night in laying the platforms for the battering artillery. The garrison kept up, as usual, an eternal fire of shot, shells, and grape, by which we lost many men. Some companies of our regiment were sent out of the trenches, after it was dark, to get as near the town as possible, and to fire at the artillery-men through the embrasures. If this operation was a disagreeable one to the enemy, it was far from a delectable one for us: they threw fire-balls among us, which were composed of such combustible matter, that they could not easily be extinguished, and made every thing near them as visible as at broad day. The moment we were perceived, musketry and grape were served out with no sparing hand. When relieved by the 1st Division on the 13th, we went through the same fiery ordeal again, from every piece of ordnance which the garrison could make use of.

On the night of the 13th, a convent in the suburbs, in which the French had three pieces of artillery, which enfiladed the trenches, was stormed and carried with great intrepidity, by some troops of the German Legion, belonging to the 1st Division. On the following day, the 40th regiment assaulted most gallantly another convent in the suburbs; and at four o'clock the same afternoon our batteries opened on the town for the first time. The 3d Division was in the trenches on the 15th, and the firing from both parties was kept up with great fury. It was the turn of the Light Division in the trenches on the 16th, and we commenced at night a battery for seven guns very near the town. Every person who shewed his nose above the trench next morning was instantly saluted with grape and musketry, whilst shells were constantly dropping into the battery. A sortie was made one morning under cover of a thick fog, favoured by which the French approached unperceived near the trenches; but some men of the 2d battalions of the 24th and 42d regiments on duty there, immediately charged with the bayonet, and drove them back into the town. Two breaches in the walls having been reported practicable on the 18th, the 3d and Light Divisions were ordered to arrive on the ground on the 19th, and to storm the town that night.

STORMING OF CIUDAD RODRIGO.

The outline of the attack was as follows:—The 3d Division was to storm the large breach, and the Light Division the lesser one, whilst General

Pack's Portuguese brigade should make a false attack at a different point. At eight o'clock at night the assault was given, and in less than half an hour both the breaches were carried, after a severe struggle, during which the assailants were exposed to a most destructive fire of musketry and grape, hand-grenades, &c. &c.

Whilst the 3d Division was engaged at the large breach, one of the enemy's expense magazines exploded with a terrible crash, which blew up a great number of both parties, amongst whom was Major-General M'Kinnon, who commanded a brigade in the 3d Division. Captain Uniacke, of our battalion, who had been sent, before the storm commenced, to keep up the communication between the two divisions along the glacis, and to endeavour to keep down the fire of the French infantry from behind the ramparts, was blown up, with many men of his company. He was a remarkably fine young man, and greatly regretted. General Crawford received a mortal wound whilst bravely leading his division to the assault, and was buried near the spot where he fell. General Vandeleur, who commanded a brigade of the Light Division, was also severely wounded; as were also Lieut.-Colonel Colbourne, and Major George Napier of the 52d regiment: the latter lost an arm in command of the storming party of the Light Division, consisting of three hundred men of the 43d, 52d, and 95th regiments. The loss of the 3d and Light Divisions was very severe, although not more so than might have been expected.

When a town is stormed, it is inevitable that excesses will be, as they ever have been, committed by the assailants, more particularly if it takes place at night. It affords a favourable opportunity for the loose and dissolute characters, which are to be found in all armies, to indulge in every diabolical propensity. That this was the case to a certain extent, on the night in question, no one will deny; but, at the same time, I feel convinced that no town taken by assault ever did or ever will suffer less than Rodrigo. It is true that soldiers of all regiments got drunk, plundered, and made great noise and confusion in the streets and houses, in spite of every exertion on the part of the officers to prevent it; but bad and revolting as such scenes are, I never heard that either the French garrison, when it had once surrendered, nor any of the inhabitants, suffered personal indignities or cruelty from the troops. About midnight some houses in the main street caught fire, and the flames spread rapidly, the engines being out of repair and almost useless. By dint of great exertions, the fire was in some measure got under.

Daylight of the 20th presented a horrid sight,

and unfit to be contemplated in cold blood. Many objects, of both parties, lying near the spot where the magazine had exploded, were frightful to a degree. Bodies without limbs, and limbs without bodies, were scorched and scattered about in different directions; and the houses near the breaches were filled with such of the wounded as were able to crawl away from the ramparts, with a view to find shelter from the severe frost, which numbed their wounds. The French garrison were marched off as prisoners of war, either to Oporto or Lisbon, on the 20th.

I think it will have forcibly struck every man who was present at the siege and storm, that the governor directed much more of his attention to keeping up an unremitting fire of shot and shells at the working parties in the trenches, during the whole of the siege, than to a judicious defence of the breaches.

The 5th Division was ordered into Rodrigo to assist in the repair of the works and to garrison the place, and the 3d and Light Divisions, and General Pack's brigade, marched back to their respective villages. Twelve days only after the town was first invested, it was stormed and taken; and the operations against it were carried on in the dead of winter, during very severe frost. It is fair, therefore, to remark, that Massena, in 1810, besieged it with a numerous army, when it was defended only by Spaniards, whom he affected to despise; yet it occupied him three times as long to reduce the place as it did Lord Wellington, although it was defended against the British and Portuguese by imperial legions. If it is urged that the Spanish garrison in 1810 was very superior in numbers to the French garrison in 1812, let it not be forgotten that the besieging army and battering train brought against it in 1810 were proportionably numerous. Marshal Marmont was so completely taken by surprise, that the town had fallen almost as soon as intelligence reached him of the allies having laid siege to it. Any attempt, therefore, on his part, to relieve the garrison would have been hopeless.

We remained in cantonments, within a short distance of Rodrigo, about one month after the siege, and were then ordered to march to the southward, and to besiege Badajoz. The 3d, 4th, and Light Divisions, were selected for this duty, as it was considered they had learned something of their business in that way at the siege of Rodrigo; the breaches in which place were now in a tolerable state of repair, and a Spanish garrison ready to march in.

A few days before we moved towards the south, several deserters, who were taken in Rodrigo, were tried by a general court-martial, of which Major-General Kempt, who had just joined the army in the Peninsula, was the president. Some were shot and the remainder pardoned. The reason they alleged for deserting to the enemy was, that they had several months' pay due, which they saw no prospect of ever receiving. The excuse was a lame one, and the remedy which they adopted, in the hopes of bettering themselves, most unjustifiable.

On the 25th of February we were to commence the march towards the Guadiana; but the great consideration was, how we were to persuade our scarecrows of baggage-horses and mules to perform the journey in winter, when there was no green forage on the ground, nor any hay, straw, or corn to be procured in the line of country through which our route lay. I well remember purchasing, before we set out, a *fanega* of wheat (weighing about seventy pounds) for eleven Spanish dollars, and thought myself fortunate in being able to procure it at that price; so completely had every thing of the kind been consumed, or bought up by the commissariat for the staff, cavalry, and artillery. In addition to the wheat, we purchased for our quadrupeds, at an enormous price, small cakes of Indian corn-flour, which the Portuguese peasantry eat. With those, the wheat, and the straw, or rotten winter grass, which we were sometimes able to glean after our day's march, we contrived to reach Elvas on the 16th of March, our division having halted at

Castello de Vide from the 7th to the 13th of the month.

On the 17th of March, at break of day, the Light Division marched out of Elvas to the tune of St. Patrick's Day, in commemoration of that saint; and we joined the 3d and 4th Divisions before Badajoz, on the left bank of the Guadiana, which divisions had arrived there the day before. Some Portuguese troops invested the town on the opposite bank.

Detachments of the 3d, 4th, and Light Divisions, commenced operations, as soon as it was dark, against a strong redoubt called Fort Piccurina, from which vollies of musketry and shells were fired on the covering and working parties during the night. The rain descended in torrents, and the cold was extremely severe. No sooner had day broke, than a heavy fire from the town and the redoubt opened on us. At the expiration of fourteen hours, we were relieved by detachments of the three divisions, and returned to our camp, which was a short distance out of range of the guns of Badajoz, situated in a muddy marsh full of water. The other divisions of our army, not employed in the siege, were in a position in the neighbourhood of Albuera, to protect the besieging army from any attempt which Marshal Soult might make from the south to relieve the garrison.

A sortie was made on the 19th, with about 1500 infantry and some cavalry, who were driven back with considerable loss. Just before the sortie was made, and for some time after it was repulsed, every gun on the works was kept in play on the troops in the trenches, in the most furious manner; and it occasioned us a heavy loss. The siege was prosecuted with the utmost vigour, in spite of the rains, which descended almost without intermission during the first ten days, and filled the trenches with water. So many men were required to carry on the operations, that nearly one half of our time was spent in the trenches.

On the 22d, some riflemen were ordered to approach as near as possible to the Guadiana, and to endeavour, by shooting the artillerymen across the river, to silence some field-pieces brought out by the French from Fort San Christoval, which enfiladed the trenches. This had the desired effect; and the field-pieces were withdrawn into the fort, after some of the gunners had bitten the dust.

On the 25th, our batteries opened their fire on the town, which was returned with equal spirit. The same night Fort Piccurina was stormed and carried by detachments from the 3d and Light Divisions, after considerable resistance, and with the loss of many men. Immediately on its fall, another parallel was commenced. From the ravelin of San Roque, and from the walls of the town, the covering parties were exceedingly galled by a constant fire of musketry.

In the end of March and the beginning of April our batteries were in full play on the town, which being breached in several places, orders were given that it should be stormed on the night of the 6th of April.

STORMING OF BADAJOZ.

Two breaches were to be stormed by the 4th and Light Divisions, the former assaulting that on the right, and the latter that on the left. The 3d Division was to escalade the castle, whilst the 5th Division, which had not taken a part in the siege, and had recently arrived in the neighbourhood, was directed to attack the town and the fort of Pardaleras to the left of the Light Division. Some Portuguese troops threatened Fort San Christoval and the works on the right of the Guadiana.

Soon after dark, the columns moved out of the trenches to the different points allotted them to attack. Major O'Hare, of the 1st battalion 95th, commanded the storming party which headed the Light Division; and some companies of our corps lined the *glacis*, to keep down the fire of the enemy from the ramparts. The discharge of grape-shot and musketry, with buck shot in addition to bullets, the hand-grenades, rafters of wood, and various weapons of destruction hurled from the ramparts on the heads of the assailants in the ditch, in their desperate and reiterated attempts to force their way through the breaches, and to mount the ladders for the escalade of the castle and town, was of so dreadful and destructive a nature, as to beggar all description, and to render it a hopeless undertaking for the most gifted person to depict in true colours.

The enemy had dug deep trenches between the top of the breaches and the town, and had fixed sword-blades and pikes in the trench. From some houses near the top of the breach a terrible fire of musketry was poured on such as contrived to reach its summit. Those obstacles alone were insurmountable, without the addition of a continued and most deadly fire of grape and musketry from the ramparts, and from the summits of the breaches; in the repeated and fruitless attempts to carry which, the assailants were falling in vast numbers every moment. The 3d Division having at length, after sustaining a dreadful loss, gained possession of the castle by escalade, and the 5th Division having penetrated into the town by the same means, and also possessed themselves of Fort Pardalleras, the French were forced to retire from the breaches, by which the 4th and Light Divisions, with difficulty, entered the town. The French governor retired to Fort San Christoval, with some hundreds of his men; but finding that the town and castle were in possession of the allies, he surrendered.

In this manner fell Badajoz, after perhaps as desperate and destructive a struggle as the annals of history afford, considering the numbers employed in the attack and defence. Never were troops exposed to a more terrible fire, or placed in a situation where their sterling qualities were put more to the test. Every regiment employed suffered exceedingly, both in the storm and in the arduous duties of the siege. Amongst the many whom our regiment had to lament, was Major O'Hare, who fell in the breach. The service boasted not a more truly gallant soldier.

Marshal Soult was marching from the south to the relief of Badajoz, but his movements were too slow; and he retired towards Seville, on receiving intelligence of its fall.

The Dukes of Dalmatia and Ragusa were most completely outwitted, deceived, and disappointed, — one by losing Ciudad Rodrigo, and the other Badajoz. Two frontier fortresses of vast importance were laid siege to in winter, in the teeth of the French armies, and wrested from them in a most skilful manner.

CHAPTER XIV.

Marmont penetrates into Portugal during the siege. Lord Wellington marches back to the north. General Alten appointed to command the Light Division. The army advances to Salamanca. Takes up a position. Marmont's army opposite. A fortified convent in Salamanca is besieged by the 6th Division. It is set fire to, and the garrison capitulates. Marmont retreats behind the Douro. We follow him. A dance at Navis del Rey. Arrive at Rueda. Wine vaults. French soldiers assassinated by the Spaniards. Marmont is reinforced. The Light Division falls back to Castrejon. The French cross the Douro. Attack the troops at Castrejon. We fall back behind the Guarena, closely followed by Marmont. Beautiful evolutions of the two armies. The 27th and 40th regiments repulse the French with loss. Deaths from want of water and excessive heat. British six-pounders and French nines, with their respective advanced guards. Observations on the fire-arms of French and British dragoons. The two armies march within cannon-shot of each other for several days in succession. The Light Division crosses the Tormes, by a ford at night, in a tremendous thunder-storm. Battle of Salamanca. Marmont's promises to the Spaniards of destroying Lord Wellington's army not fulfilled. Opinions of certain British officers in the Portuguese army, as to the comparative merits of Portuguese, British, and French soldiers. Gallant attack of General Bock's cavalry brigade on the French rear-guard. We pursue the French many days. Various reports of

MARMONT ENTERS PORTUGAL. 261

Marmont's death. Corpse of the French General Ferez dug up and exposed to view by the Spaniards. We cross the Douro. Valladolid. Mode adopted of raising the wind to purchase bread, &c. The army marches on Madrid. Segovia. A beautiful Castilian. Palaces of El Rio Frio and San Ildefonso. Pass the Guadaramma mountains. Encamp in the park of the Escurial. The palace. Affair between some Portuguese and French cavalry. The army enters Madrid. Its reception. French garrison in the Retiro capitulates. A word or two about the capital. Its palace, streets, public walks, Castilian women, &c. Pheasant-shooting in Joseph Bonaparte's park. A grand ball. A bull-fight. Extravagant fondness of the Spaniards of both sexes for this amusement. Four divisions march to Burgos, and lay siege to the castle. Soult raises the siege of Cadiz and marches on Madrid. General Hill and Colonel Skerrit join the troops at Madrid. Colonel Skerrit repulses Soult's advanced guard at the bridge of Aranjuez. The Light Division marches to the front from Madrid. Soult passes the Tagus. We bid adieu, with great regret, to Madrid.

MARSHAL MARMONT had entered Portugal during the latter end of the siege, and penetrated towards Castello Branco, dispersing the Portuguese militia and irregulars. This movement caused Lord Wellington to march from Badajoz a few days after its fall, towards the north. Marmont fell back behind the Agueda on his approach, and subsequently to Salamanca. With the exception of a corps under General Hill, which was left in Alemtejo, the whole army was cantoned on the northern frontier of Portugal, with the Light

Division and some cavalry on the Agueda; and in the month of June it advanced towards Salamanca.

About this time, Major-General Baron Charles Alten, of the German Legion, was appointed to command the Light Division, vacant by the death of General Crawford. During the siege and storming of Badajoz, the command of it had devolved on Lieutenant-Colonel Barnard, of the 95th Rifle corps, who conducted it most ably and gallantly through all its arduous duties. If a thorough knowledge of their profession, calm, cool courage, great presence of mind in action, frank and gentlemanly manners, and the total absence of what may be termed teazing those under their command, are qualities to be appreciated, I do say (and in so saying utterly disclaim all adulation or flattery) that both Baron Alten and Colonel Barnard merited the high estimation in which they were held.

On arriving at Salamanca, the army was obliged to cross the Tormes by fords, as the bridge was commanded by a convent, which the French had long since converted into a fort, mounted with heavy guns, and having a garrison within its walls of many hundred men. The 6th Division was left to besiege the fort, and the other divisions took up a position on some heights, about a league in front of Salamanca, with the right resting on the Tormes. Marmont was in position on a line of hills opposite, about two miles distant; a wide, open valley dividing the two armies.

On the night of the 24th of June, a party of the 6th Division assaulted the fortified convent, but unfortunately did not succeed, and sustained some loss in the attempt. On the 27th they stormed an outwork near the convent, and carried it in fine style. Our batteries having plied the fort with shells and red-hot shot, and set it on fire, the garrison, consisting of eight hundred men, capitulated, and were made prisoners of war. The same night Marmont, having learned the fate of the garrison, withdrew his army from our front, and in a few days crossed the Douro, at Tordesillas, taking up a position behind that river, and occupying Zamora and Toro. There were several sharp skirmishes, and much manœuvering on the part of Marmont, whilst the two armies were in front of Salamanca, but it led to no serious result.

We followed the French rear-guard on the 28th, 29th, and 30th of June, without coming up with it; and on the 1st of July the Light Division and some cavalry entered Navis del Rey, where we made a few prisoners. In spite of fatigue, we contrived to get up a dance at night, which many of the signoras honoured with their presence. Having snatched a couple of hours' sleep, we were again on the road before day dawned; and, after a burning march, reached Rueda, a decent kind of town, a few miles distant from the Douro. Our cavalry made some prisoners from the French rear-guard.

The whole country from Salamanca to Rueda is one vast sun-burnt plain, with scarcely a tree, but abounding with corn, and, near the Douro, with vines. All the towns and villages in this part of the country may literally be called so many wine vaults. Every house and street is excavated, and filled with white wine of tolerably good quality.

Descending, after a long day's march under a roasting sun, into those deep cellars, where the air and wine were both like ice, was no trifling luxury; the transition being nearly as great as from the equator to the pole. This, however pleasant, might be supposed to have been an unsafe experiment. The only inconvenience, however, complained of was, that the wine was so cool and delicious, as to render it no easy matter to ascend the long flight of steps, and to regain our billets above ground. Several stragglers who were found in the wine-cellars by the Spaniards, after the French rear-guard had left Rueda, and before we arrived, were put to death; and we saw several others in the churchyard, cut and lacerated in a shocking manner. The system of warfare carried on between the Spaniards and French was revolting to the greatest possible degree.

We remained at Rueda with the head-quarters of the army some days, watching Marmont, who remained tolerably quiet in his position behind the Douro, until reinforced by General Bonnet with troops from some of the northern provinces.

About the 15th he began manœuvering, and made many feints to cross at various points, which caused corresponding movements on our part.

On the night of the 16th, the Light Division marched from Rueda, and the next day we took up our ground near the village of Castrejon, with the 4th Division, General Pack's brigade, and some cavalry. After marching and counter-marching his army for a day or two, with a view of deceiving Lord Wellington, Marmont passed the Douro at Tordesillas, on the night of the 17th, with the whole or greater part of his army, and on the morning of the 18th bore straight down on the troops at Castrejon. A furious cannonade soon commenced; and as the country was quite open, and every way favourable for cavalry, the infantry were ordered to form close columns or squares of battalions: in this manner we remained stationary for a length of time, under a heavy fire of artillery, whilst the cavalry, and some companies which had been thrown out in front, were engaged in a sharp skirmish.

Lord Wellington now ordered the infantry to retire in columns, covered by the cavalry and horse artillery. No man who was present can possibly have forgotten that magnificent sight, nor the steadiness and extreme regularity with which the columns fell back over this extensive plain, followed and assailed in flanks and rear by overwhelming numbers of cavalry and artillery.

During this retreat we were exposed to a constant cannonade, and threatened by heavy masses of infantry, ready to close with us if our pace was relaxed for a minute. Nor was the steadiness and gallantry displayed by the cavalry and horse-artillery less worthy of admiration. A halt of two or three minutes would have enabled the French infantry to reach us. Thus we marched some miles over a country as level as a chessboard, in columns of battalions, ready to engage the French infantry if they should overtake us, and equally so to receive their cavalry, in square or close column, if they attempted to charge. The beautiful series of evolutions of the two armies on this day, and on the three following, were such as a man may never witness again if he lives for ages.

The heat was suffocating, and there being no water on this sun-burnt plain, numbers of men dropped on the road, and, of course, fell into the hands of the enemy, as we could not stop to bring them along. Many soldiers, particularly of the Portuguese, died on the road, from the heat and want of water. At length we arrived at the edge of this elevated plain, which looks down on the Guarena, a small river in the hot months; and when we reached it, man and horse made a rush to quench their thirst. I have never quite forgiven our pursuers for pounding us with round shot from the heights above, and not allowing us time to swallow a mouthful of the lukewarm, muddy beverage, without the accompaniment of a nine-pound shot.

Soon after we had got into a position, on some high ground not far from the river, a column of infantry endeavoured to turn our left. The 27th and 40th regiments were posted there, and, by a volley, a cheer, and a resistless charge with the bayonet, instantly drove back the French, taking a general officer and upwards of two hundred men prisoners, killing and wounding many more. During the remainder of the day we were tolerably quiet. A hot wind with a thick suffocating atmosphere set in and lasted a day or two.

It is worthy of remark, that the horse artillery which accompanied our advanced and rear-guards, consisted of light six-pounders only, whereas the artillery attached to the French advanced and rear-guards were usually eight-pounders, equal to British nines. It is obvious, therefore, that our people always laboured under a great disadvantage in this respect, as the French could batter and pound us at such a distance as it was not in the power of our light six-pounders to return with effect. I have heard officers of our artillery complain of this, and have frequently witnessed the fact myself. Surely, if the cats of horses in the French army could drag along, at a pace sufficient to keep up with their cavalry, nine-pounders, the beautiful and powerful English horses belonging to our horse artillery were equally capable of drawing guns of the same weight of metal, and at a much more rapid rate, if required.

It is to be hoped that those who have the direction of affairs at Woolwich, have already considered those matters, and that they will adopt measures accordingly. It is equally desirable that those at the head of the British cavalry should bear in mind, that the French dragoons and chasseurs à cheval were armed during the Peninsular war with a long fusée, which could throw a ball as far as the musket of an infantry soldier, and that our dragoons, on the contrary, both light and heavy, were armed with a little pop-gun of a carbine. The consequence of this was, that when bodies of cavalry met at a distance from their infantry, the French dragoons often dismounted where the country was intersected and woody, and shot at our dragoons at a distance which rendered our short carbines almost useless. I appeal to old Peninsula cavalry men and officers for the accuracy of my statement.

As we should never be too proud to fight our enemy with his own weapons, nor to take a leaf out of his book, I think it would be advisable that our cavalry, both light and heavy, should not only be furnished with longer fire-arms, but be perfectly instructed also how to dismount and to skirmish as light infantry. That they will be required sometimes to oppose their enemy in that manner, if a continental war ever again takes place, they will most assuredly find. In the French army, one man was left in charge of three or four horses, out of reach of fire, whilst the dismounted dragoons or chasseurs became efficient light infantry, and acted as such if their own infantry were not up.*

On the 19th of July the two armies remained in a state of perfect tranquillity until the cool of the evening, when Marmont, instead of attacking the position in which we had offered him battle on the 18th and 19th, put his whole army in motion along the Guarena, threatening our com-

* Since writing the above, a better carbine has been given to our light dragoons, and the men are instructed to dismount, and to act as light infantry.

munications with Salamanca. Lord Wellington instantly made corresponding movements, by marching the 1st and Light Divisions and cavalry to the right, followed by the remainder of his army, in a direction parallel with that of the French. We advanced in columns with the same exactness and regularity as at a field-day in England, ready at a moment to halt, and to form either lines or squares, as might be necessary. The French marched within cannon-shot of us, with apparently the same exactness, each army eyeing the other as two game-cocks do before coming to close combat. Round shot and shells were sent every minute across the valley which divided us; and the cavalry skirmishers, who covered the flanks of their respective armies, were frequently engaged. Night put a stop to the marching and firing, and we laid down by our arms as near to our enemy as it was possible to do, without treading on the toes of each other.

The manœuvering of hostile armies in presence of each other has often been compared to a game of chess; and if ever that simile held good, most assuredly it did on the 20th of July, as well as on the preceding days. Daylight put the two armies again in motion, each marching towards the same point, with precisely the same regularity as on the 18th and 19th. The country being open, the cavalry on both sides covered the march, aided by light artillery, which frequently opened where a bend in the roads happened to bring the hostile columns a trifle nearer to each other. The infantry preserved the same order of march as on the preceding days, and were often so near that a few minutes would have been sufficient to bring on a general engagement.

Many hours were passed in this manner, when a sudden turn of the road by which the French columns were marching, drew them away from us for a time. We made a short halt in the afternoon, the troops being much exhausted with the heat, want of water, and continual marching in such exact order. We soon resumed our march, which was prosecuted during the greater part of the night of the 20th, and on the morning of the 21st we halted on the right bank of the Tormes. The same evening we passed the river by a ford, in one of the most violent storms of rain, thunder, and lightning, I ever remember, and bivouacked on its left bank. The thunder and lightning so terrified the cavalry horses, that many of them broke away from their picketings and galloped into the French camp.

BATTLE OF SALAMANCA.

22d July.—An hour before daybreak we, as usual, were under arms; shortly after which Lord

Wellington dislodged, with the 7th Division, some French infantry from a hill, and reconnoitered his antagonist from that point.

The hostile armies were now once more opposite each other, that of Marmont occupying some heights called the Arapiles, threatening with his left to outflank the British right. Many hours were spent by him in various evolutions, and by a continued fire of light troops.

I presume not to detail minutely the disposition of our army; but I know that the 3d Division, commanded by General Pakenham, in the absence of General Picton, who was sick, was withdrawn from the heights on the right bank of the Tormes, and suddenly directed to march to the extreme right of our line. On the left was the Light Division, with the 1st near it, and in the centre were the 4th, 5th, 6th, and 7th, General Pack's Portuguese Brigade, the reserve artillery, cavalry, &c. &c. General Hill's division was in Alemtejo.

In the afternoon, Marmont recommenced the system which he had adopted ever since he crossed the Douro, of endeavouring to turn our right flank, and to cut off our communications with Ciudad Rodrigo, instead of making a general attack on the position. Whilst he was in the act of so doing, the 3d Division, supported by some cavalry, was directed to attack the French left. This distinguished division, led by the brave General

Pakenham, bore down all opposition, and upset with the bayonet every thing which crossed its path, in spite of the destructive fire of artillery and musketry to which it was exposed. It was bravely seconded and supported by several regiments of cavalry, who sabred and made prisoners a great number of the enemy. This was followed by various desperate and successful attacks, made by the 4th, 5th, and 6th Divisions, and General Pack's brigade, with some cavalry; all of which conducted themselves with an intrepidity and resolution which nothing could withstand; and that army which had for many days before followed the British from the Douro to the Tormes, confident of victory, found itself, on the night of the 22d of July, most completely defeated, with the loss of many thousands killed, wounded, and prisoners. They lost a considerable portion of their artillery also.

The 1st and Light Divisions took but little share in this glorious battle; nor am I aware that the 7th Division was seriously engaged. Half of our army, therefore, inflicted so severe a loss on the French, that they would have been destroyed or taken, if we had been favoured with two hours more of daylight. Under cover of the night, the enemy retreated rapidly, and recrossed the Tormes, which they might have found no easy matter, if a corps of Spaniards had defended some of the passages across the river, as desired by Lord Wellington. Just before dark the Light Division was ordered to advance, and attack the 1st French Division, commanded by General Foy, which had been in our front the whole day; but as they offered no serious resistance, and were already in the act of retrograding, nothing more than a sharp fire of light troops took place, in which our general, Baron Alten, was wounded, with some other officers and men.

Marshal Marmont was severely wounded by the bursting of a shell in the middle of the action, and the command of his army devolved on General Clausel. The French lost several general officers killed and wounded; amongst the latter were Generals Ferez, Bonnet, and others.

On our part, General Le Marchant was killed, whilst gallantly leading a brilliant charge of cavalry. Generals Beresford, Cotton, Alten, Cole, and Leith, were wounded. The army bivouacked near the ground from which the enemy had been driven; and thus terminated the glorious 22d of July.

Marshal Marmont had often assured the Spaniards, that although Lord Wellington knew how to defend himself in the mountain fastnesses of Portugal, he would make a severe example of him and of his army if ever they ventured into the plains of Leon. It requires but little logic to prove that our chief *did* venture into the plains of Leon, far away from his mountain fastnesses, and that for many days he manœuvred within cannon-shot of the Duke of Ragusa's army, and offered him battle more than once on those plains, and that he finally gained a glorious and decisive victory over an army of veterans, led by experienced generals. Nor should it be forgotten, that the French army was numerically stronger than the allies, many thousands of whom were Portuguese, who, although they had been embodied upwards of two years, and had conducted themselves remarkably well, could not be considered equal to the veterans of France.

Some few British officers in the Portuguese service have been bold enough to declare, that they would rather command a Portuguese regiment than a British, and that they were in every respect equal, and in some respects superior, to the British, and decidedly so to the French troops. Those, however, who advanced such doctrines, must have been well aware of their absurdity.

The moment daylight appeared on the 23d, the cavalry, with the 1st and Light Divisions, were sent in pursuit of the retreating army. General Bock's brigade of heavy dragoons of the German Legion, supported by a regiment or two of light cavalry, found the French rear-guard of infantry and cavalry on a height, near the road leading to Peneranda. The infantry formed a square, which their cavalry shamefully abandoned to its fate.

General Bock forthwith attacked their square with his heavy dragoons, and succeeded, after losing many men and horses, in breaking it. Nothing could be more daring than this charge, or more worthy of admiration and imitation. About 1700 prisoners were taken, consisting of two or three battalions of the French 69th regiment. Some horse grenadiers were also taken about half an hour before.

My faith in the capability of a well-formed square of infantry to resist cavalry, will not be shaken by this single instance to the contrary; for it is the only one that has ever come within my knowledge in the Peninsular war; and I am confident that forty-nine times out of fifty, if the square is well formed, and artillery out of the question, the infantry will have the best of the fight. This was also the first instance that came under our eye of the French cavalry having shewn a want of spirit. Their general conduct was such as to draw forth the admiration of their enemies.

This square being disposed of, we followed in pursuit, and soon afterwards found a strong rear-guard of cavalry, infantry, and artillery, formed on an eminence near a village; and Lord Wellington, who was with us, made dispositions as quick as lightning to attack them. The first and Light Divisions, with the cavalry and horse artillery, advanced across the plain in beautiful order; but the French melted away and disappeared before we could reach them. Our cavalry took some prisoners in the course of the day.

General Clausel conducted the retreat of the French army with considerable ability and rapidity; and although his rear-guard was seen at a distance moving over those extensive plains, day after day, we could not overtake it. We followed him by Peneranda, Flores d'Avila, Aldea Secca, Arevalo, Olmedo, &c. &c.; and after many long and tiresome marches over those parched plains, in weather intensely hot, the first and Light Divisions, and some cavalry, crossed the Douro on the 30th of July, and bivouacked on its right bank, a few miles distant from Valladolid. In every town and village through which we marched, from the Tormes to the Douro, Marmont's death was reported as certain. He positively died at Peneranda, so he did also at Arevalo; and he was buried in half a dozen different towns.

The French General Ferez, who died of wounds received at Salamanca, was buried outside the town of Olmedo; and the Spaniards, in a most savage and brutal manner, had dug up the body, and exposed it to view by the road-side. I went, with some others, to see the corpse, which was that of an amazingly athletic man, apparently of the middle age. We caused the body to be re-interred, but I have no doubt that the Spaniards dug it up a second time. This was the same general who commanded the night attack on four companies of our battalion, in the pass of Barba del Puerco, in the month of March 1810.

We halted on the Douro about twenty-four hours, which was a great god-send, as, from the 16th of July to the evening of the 30th, the army had been constantly marching or fighting. A day's rest on the bank of a large river, where we could bathe and get our linen washed, was a luxury which we well knew how to appreciate and to make the most of.

Valladolid was soon filled with officers and soldiers, endeavouring to purchase bread, wine, and other things—those at least in the army who could muster a few dollars, which were rare articles, there being seven months' pay now due to us. For my own part, I sold some silver spoons and a watch to raise the wind, considering a loaf of bread, some chocolate, and a few other things of the kind, far more necessary than plate, after the scanty allowance of provisions which we had been on for some weeks. We found in Valladolid about a thousand sick and wounded French, which they had not time to remove. It is a city of great antiquity, full of churches and convents, has a large plaza or square, a Scotch college, and some good shops.

The French army continuing its retreat on Burgos, Lord Wellington left the 6th Division of infantry as a corps of observation near the Douro, and with the remainder of his force marched towards the capital, which we were all on the tiptoe of impatience to behold.

On the 8th of August we halted, after a long march, on the banks of the Eresma; and being only twelve miles from Segovia, which we thought could not be seen too soon, a small party of us stole away from camp on horseback, and did not relax our pace until we had reached that far-famed city. We met, on the promenade near the town, one of the most lovely women I ever beheld in any part of the world, attired in the most bewitching manner. Years have not erased from my memory her countless charms, which assertion may appear ridiculous and incredible, as we had not the felicity even of exchanging words with her. Her elegant but simple costume of black silk with slashed sleeves, and the numerous *et cetera* of the Castilian female dress, which are perfection itself, her beautiful figure, sparkling intelligent eyes, her small feet and ancles, her easy and graceful walk, and an infinity of female graces happily blended, formed a whole which I have never seen surpassed. If the fatigue occasioned by continual marching was likely to send us into the arms of Morpheus, the image of this enchantress had a contrary effect, for that night at least. But, alas! we never saw her after, although we patrolled the next day all over Segovia, the public walks, squares, convents, &c. &c.

The cathedral, the aqueduct, and the castle of Segovia, are all objects of interest, particularly the latter, which at once reminds one of Gil Blas. The French had fortified the castle, and converted it into a citadel to overawe the town. The square is large and handsome, and a good market was held in it. The promenades under avenues of trees, on the banks of the Eresma, are exceedingly pretty. This place is famed for leather and leather-curriers, one whole street being inhabited solely by them, and by some legions of cobblers.

On the 9th we were obliged to take our departure, and to join our division, which we found encamped near an ancient palace of the kings of Spain, called El Palazio del Rio Frio. The French had stripped it of every kind of furniture and ornament. About two leagues distant from it is the palace of San Ildefonso, which I regretted not being able to see. Lord Wellington's head-quarters were there on the 9th. Both those palaces are situated on the north side of the Guadarrama mountains, which divide Old from New Castile, and are cool retreats in summer from the intolerable heat, which roasts every thing to a cinder in the plains below.

We crossed the Sierra de Guadarrama on the 11th, by an excellent winding road, and encamped on the southern side, in the park of the Escurial. We soon mounted our horses, and went off, pell-mell, to the palace of the Escurial, which was a few miles from the camp, counting the moments until we reached it. This, like the Palazio del Rio Frio, had nothing left but the bare walls; the French having carried away all the paintings and valuables. The building is very extensive, but I was altogether much disappointed. Some paintings on the walls, intended to represent battles between the Moors and Spaniards, were much defaced. The only thing which I remember worth seeing, was the sepulchre in which the royal family of Spain are interred. The whole of the dome, as well as the entrance to it, is composed of the finest marble, highly ornamented with gold. The gardens, which are extensive and full of fountains, were entirely neglected, and overgrown with weeds.

It was now ascertained that Joseph Bonaparte had left Madrid with the whole of the garrison, and taken a southerly direction.

On the 10th or 11th there was an affair, on the road from the Guadarrama mountains to Madrid, between General d'Urban's Portuguese cavalry brigade and some French dragoons, in which the Portuguese were driven back, and abandoned two or three field-pieces that were attached to them. The arrival of a regiment or two of British cavalry set all right again, by their driving back the enemy and retaking the artillery.

On the 12th the army entered Madrid. It would be labour in vain to attempt to describe the enthusiasm and delight evinced by all classes of the inhabitants on our arrival. Old and young, men, women, and children, in tens of thousands, filled the streets, embracing the officers and soldiers, kissing the colours of the regiments, and the happy ensigns who carried them. They cried, laughed, sung, and danced with joy, so that it was impossible to doubt their sincerity. Few of us were ever so caressed before, and most undoubtedly never will be again. The windows and balconies were crowded with elegantly dressed females, all joining in the enthusiasm of the moment. The French had been four years in possession of Madrid, and at length they witnessed their departure.

In the Retiro, a royal edifice, which is situated on commanding ground near the city, the

French had left a garrison of two thousand men. This Lord Wellington instantly invested. On the 14th the governor capitulated, and the garrison became prisoners of war. Many thousand stand of arms, a great number of cannon, stores, ammunition, provisions, &c. &c. were also taken in the Retiro.

Madrid has been described a thousand times by a thousand different people, which renders it unnecessary for me to attempt it. The regularity of the buildings, and the general cleanliness of the streets, were so unlike what we had been accustomed to for some years, that we were quite enchanted. The street of Alcala would be admired in any capital in Europe, as would also the far-famed promenade at its foot, which has ever been remarkable for its beauty and regularity, and ought to be still more prized on account of the crowds of lovely women who are to be seen there in the cool of the evenings, dressed inimitably well, in their elegant and most becoming national attire. Many of my countrymen were most desperately smitten during our stay in this delightful quarter, or thought they were so. The palace contained, in addition to its own finery, every thing that was worth transporting from the Escurial and other palaces. The walls were consequently studded with paintings and ornaments of all kinds.

Near the walls of the city is a royal cottage, called the Casa del Campo, the favourite retreat of Joseph Bonaparte, with his court. In an extensive enclosure or park he had established a good sprinkling of pheasants, which were brought from France; and thinking them fair game, we employed many of our leisure hours in the grounds very successfully with our guns.

On the 15th a grand and crowded ball was given to Lord Wellington and the army by the inhabitants, and we here had a glorious opportunity of feasting our eyes on Castilian beauty, which shone most resplendently.

On the 31st of August a grand bull-fight was given, in a large amphitheatre called the Plaza de Toro, which is capable of containing many thousand spectators. Tickets of admission were sent to all the regiments, and in we went, all curiosity, to witness this barbarous and ancient national amusement. The countless numbers of Spanish females, of all ages, belonging to the higher class of society, dressed as if for a grand ball, and taking intense interest in this cruel amusement, did certainly puzzle us Englishmen not a little, and was a convincing proof of what early habit will effect. If an opinion of the general character of Spanish females is to be formed from seeing them once only, and that at a bull-fight, one would naturally conclude them to be utterly devoid of feeling, and a most inhuman set of devils in the garb of angels. But when it is remembered, that from their earliest infancy they are taught to look forward to a bull-fight as the first, the greatest, and most delightful of all amusements, in the same manner as our young misses in England contemplate going to a masked ball or an opera, our wonder will cease in a great measure. I should, nevertheless, be much better satisfied, on account of the admiration which I feel for the fascinating Castilians, if they abhorred the diabolical process of torturing the noble animal to death, and turned from it with the same disgust as the females of other parts of Europe naturally would do.

Eight extraordinary fine bulls, in the highest possible condition, with coats like silk, were killed on this occasion; and the instant each unfortunate animal was slain, several mules, of immense size, ornamented with ribands and flowers on their trappings, were brought into the amphitheatre; and the dead bull being made fast to the traces, he was drawn round the scene of action in triumph; whilst the flourish of trumpets, bands of martial music, and the deafening exclamations of "bravo!" from thousands of all ages and of both sexes, concluded this affair of blood. Lord Wellington gave a grand ball the same evening.

The 1st, 5th, 6th, and 7th Divisions, with all

the cavalry, except the 1st German Hussars and 14th Light Dragoons, marched from Madrid on their route to Burgos, which was forthwith to be laid siege to. Lord Wellington soon afterwards left Madrid, and followed this part of his army. The 4th Division remained at the Escurial, and the 3d and Light, with the German Hussars and 14th Dragoons, in and near Madrid.

The months of September and October passed much to our satisfaction in this delightful quarter; during which we had frequent accounts of the operations before Burgos. Marshal Soult, on hearing of Marmont's defeat at Salamanca, and the occupation of the capital by the allies, raised the siege of Cadiz, which had employed his army nearly three years; and evacuating Andalusia and the southern provinces, marched on Madrid in October, with every man he could muster.

On the siege of Cadiz being raised, the British garrison in that place, as well as General Hill's corps from Alemtejo, marched on the capital, and reached Aranjuez, on the Tagus, during the month of October. General Hill now assumed the command of all the troops in and near Madrid; and in the latter end of October, Marshal Soult having arrived opposite Aranjuez, and threatened to cross the Tagus, the 3d and Light Divisions were marched out of the city, and made a forward movement towards that river.

Our division marched to Alcala on the 25th, a good town, five leagues from the capital; and on the following day to Arganda: but, in consequence of some movement of the enemy, we had no sooner settled in our quarters for the night, after a long march, than we were ordered to retrace our steps to Alcala; thus marching and countermarching the whole twenty-four hours. On the 30th we returned to Madrid, and all the troops encamped on the heights near it.

Soult had effected the passage of the Tagus with a force so numerous, that it was certain we must abandon Madrid, and form a junction with the other wing of our army, which was about this time retreating from before Burgos; having unfortunately failed, in spite of many desperate efforts, and after having lost a number of brave men, in attempting to reduce the castle. General Skerret's division had a sharp affair, at the bridge of Aranjuez, with Soult's advanced guard, in the end of October, and repulsed it with great spirit.

I went into the capital to take a last farewell of it, and of my Spanish friends. There was a gloom and sadness depicted on the countenances of all the inhabitants, and a death-like silence in the streets, which, when contrasted with the unfeigned joy evinced, on our entry three months before, was very disheartening. Their new friends were about to leave them, and their old oppressors advancing, with rapid strides, to re-occupy their city, and perhaps to wreak vengeance on them for the kind reception which they had given to the British. Many a curse did we bestow on the Spanish general, Ballasteros, for not having thrown every impediment in the way of Marshal Soult's army, during its advance from before Cadiz to Madrid. Envy and jealousy of our great chief actuated him, without doubt.

The moment of our departure had now arrived: the rear-guard of cavalry was gradually falling back towards the heights; and, in a dark, gloomy afternoon, on the 31st of October, we bade farewell to that city, in which I passed some of the happiest days of my life, and shall ever look back on with mixed sensations of pleasure and regret. The rains of winter had already commenced; the prospect of a long and dreary retreat, of wet camps and bivouacs, and the long train of privations and vicissitudes which winter campaigning more especially brings with it, stared us in the face. Ample employment for mind and body was in perspective, which left us but little time to muse on our friends in Madrid, or to think of any thing but the active business in which we were forthwith to be employed.

CHAPTER XV.

Commence the retreat to Salamanca. A wild boar killed. The armies from Burgos and Madrid unite near Salamanca. The army retreats to the Agueda. Sketch of the retreat. Rations of acorns and oak-leaves for man and horse. The Light Division engaged at San Munos. General Paget taken prisoner. We arrive at Rodrigo. The campaign of 1812 concludes. A few lines relative to it. We go into winter-quarters. Establish a regimental mess in an old barn. A supply of Douro wine. Vocal performers. Circular letter to officers commanding regiments, relative to the late retreat. The Light Division establish theatrical performances. Lydia Languish and Julia drink punch and smoke cigars behind the scenes. Coursing, woodcock-shooting, and Lord Wellington's fox-hounds. Boleros, fandangos, waltzes, &c. &c. in our village. Hot punch by no means disapproved of by our fair partners. Lord Wellington proceeds to Cadiz for a short time. The French general Foy makes an attempt to surprise General Hill's advanced post at Bejar, and is repulsed. General Kempt is appointed to command a brigade in the Light Division. Preparations for the campaign of 1813. Lord Wellington reviews the Light Division and 1st German Hussars. The Hussar Brigade, the Life Guards, and Blues, join the army, from England. The eight divisions of infantry, and by whom commanded.

WE encamped on the 2d of November at the foot of the Guadarrama mountains, and had scarcely taken up our ground for the evening, when two wild boars were roused out of the brushwood. An instantaneous attack was made on them with swords and bayonets: one of them was killed and the other escaped, fortunately for him, or he would have shared the fate of his associate, who was cut up into fifty pieces in a few minutes, and grilled on camp-kettle lids, with the hair on.

We crossed the Sierra de Guadarrama on the 3d, and on the 7th reached Alba de Tormes, having met with no particular adventures during those five days' march; nor did the French advanced guard overtake us. The rains had set in with great violence. We were here joined by the four divisions which had fallen back from Burgos. They had been much harassed in their retreat, and were now in a position on the heights of San Christoval, in front of Salamanca. The 2d, 3d, 4th, and Light Divisions, crossed the river at Alba de Tormes, and bivouacked, in tremendous rains, for a few days, in some woods near it.

On the 11th, the enemy made an attempt to drive General Hill's division out of Alba de Tormes, but were repulsed with some loss. The armies of Marshal Soult and General Clausel, the former from the south and the latter from the north, had now formed a junction in our front, their united forces being reckoned at eighty thousand men.

On the 14th, the whole allied army was on the left of the Tormes, and took up a position nearly on the same ground where it had gained so signal a victory on the 22d of July. Soult crossed the river also above Alba de Tormes, and General Hill's corps drove back his advanced guard towards evening.

On the 15th, Soult had recourse to a wide flank movement, threatening our communications with Rodrigo. Finding himself vastly outnumbered, Lord Wellington commenced his retreat, by two or more roads, towards the Agueda. The Light Division formed the rear-guard to that column commanded by the Hon. General Edward Paget, consisting of several divisions. The rains descended in floods, and our division did not arrive on the ground allotted for it until long after the other troops had bivouacked for the night. We had no provisions; and had we been so fortunate as to possess some, the weather was so inclement as to prevent the possibility of kindling fires with the green wood of the swampy forest in which we passed the night, under the lee of the largest trees we could find.

The 16th was a repetition of the 15th: we were ploughing through mud and water to the knees, from before break of day until long after dark, and over as bad roads as are to be found in Christendom. No provisions were forthcoming for man or horse, except the acorns of the Spanish oak, that abounded in the gloomy forests through which our route lay. The rains never intermitted, and lighting fires was consequently an undertaking of great difficulty.

On the 17th, we were again on our legs long before daybreak, and ready for another start. What I have related as to roads, weather, fatigue, and want of food, on the 15th and 16th, applied in every respect to the 17th. But we had this day, in addition to other troubles, the cavalry of the French advanced guard to deal with, which, coming up with the Light Division early in the day, employed us to keep them at bay from our flanks and rear, in their frequent attempts to molest us from the more open parts of the forest. Nothing of consequence, however, took place until afternoon. The enemy had by this time brought forward a large force of infantry and artillery so close to the heels of the Light Division, as enabled them to attack us at the moment we were passing the Huebra, by a deep ford near San Munos. They cannonaded us heavily at this unfavourable moment, and at the same instant assailed us with a swarm of light troops, which some companies of ours and of the 52d were thrown out to oppose. No troops at a field-day in England ever manœuvered, or marched with greater steadiness and regularity, than did the Light

Division in its retreat from the heights to the river and across it, although exposed to a heavy fire of round shot, which constantly plunged into the columns, and was kept up long after we had reached the opposite bank. Here we formed lines ready for the reception of the French infantry, if they thought fit to follow us. Their light troops, who galled our rear and flanks, received, nevertheless, a useful lesson from those by whom they were opposed; and the difficult and perilous operation of retiring in columns over a river by a deep ford, in close contact with a superior force, and under manifold disadvantages, was accomplished without serious loss. It was believed that Marshal Soult in person directed the operations of his advanced guard.

Whilst we were passing the river, he sent a number of light troops to endeavour to ford it at another point, and to attack our left flank. In this attempt he was foiled by some companies of the 52d and 95th regiments. Not a Frenchman passed the Huebra that night, and the pickets of the two armies were divided only by this narrow stream.

After dark, the commissaries brought some bullocks for the troops, which were instantly knocked on the head; but it was next to impossible to cook the meat, in consequence of the continued rains and sleet, and the green wood not igniting. By dint of perseverance, we at last did kindle a spark of fire, and were busily engaged in toasting, on the points of our swords, our scanty rations, which had been alive and walking about the forest half an hour before. I never shall forget the dismay and disappointment of some half dozen of us, when, crowded round an apology for a fire, in a state of starvation, and ready to bolt the beef before it was half toasted, down came the drops of rain from the trees above, shaken violently by the storm, and in an instant extinguished the fire, and with it our hopes of a supper. In a fit of despair, we commenced groping about under the trees for acorns, of which consisted our repast; whilst our unfortunate horses plucked away at the leaves, which, in reality, was the only food they had for four days.

The numerous carcasses of animals belonging to the army which covered the road from Salamanca to Ciudad Rodrigo, were the strongest proofs I can adduce of having neither caricatured nor exaggerated. It is equally true that acorns were the food of nine-tenths of us for several days. Our division sustained considerable loss on the 17th, chiefly from the French artillery; but when it is considered that we were obliged to engage them under such extremely unfavourable circumstances, the only wonder is that our loss was not more severe.

A few minutes before we commenced our retreat across the Huebra, Sir Edward Paget was taken prisoner by a party of French cavalry, which stole in from the forest between the interval of the 7th and some other division, and carried him off with his orderly dragoon.

When day broke on the 18th, and allowed us to look about and see what part of the play was next to be performed, we found ourselves (I mean the Light Division) all alone on the heights above the Huebra, and made up our minds to a serious attack from Soult's advanced guard, which was separated from us only by the river. Most fortunately for us the French felt themselves so weary of the pursuit, and, probably, (like ourselves) so nearly famished with hunger and cold, without the power of bettering themselves, unless by turning their backs on those inhospitable forests, and retracing their steps to Salamanca, that they did not attempt to cross the river, or to molest us during the remainder of the retreat. Had Soult known what we knew, most assuredly it would have been otherwise; for the 7th and some other divisions were floundering through a muddy defile not a mile from us. This would have necessarily obliged our division to wait on the heights above the Huebra, and to protect the retreat of the other divisions, cost what it might. Fate ordered it otherwise, and after another day of swimming, rather than marching, through this endless, swampy forest, in sleet, snow, and rain, we bivouacked near Santa Espirita, cold, wet, and supperless, as on the three preceding nights. The quartermaster of the 52d regiment administered a mouthful or two of rum to me on the 18th, which I firmly believe was the most beneficial cordial ever imbibed by man.

The 19th brought us under the walls of Rodrigo, from whence bags of biscuit were instantly sent out to meet us, around which it was found necessary to post sentries with bayonets fixed, to prevent the soldiers from rushing in and helping themselves before a regular distribution could be made. We encamped on the banks of the Agueda some days, whilst arrangements were making for quartering the troops during the winter. Thus ended the retreat of the army from Burgos and Madrid, and with it the campaign of 1812.

If Lord Wellington failed in his attempt against Burgos, he took during that campaign, by storm, the fortresses of Rodrigo and Badajoz; and he gained the glorious battle of Salamanca, which obliged Marshal Soult to raise the siege of Cadiz, and to evacuate the southern provinces of Spain, which were thereby free; and thus gave an opportunity to the Spaniards of exerting themselves in the cause of their country, by the formation of armies for the ensuing campaign. By the end of November, the army was settled in winter quarters. General Hill's division was stationed at Coria, the Light Division and the 1st German Hussars in villages near the Agueda, and the remainder of the cavalry, infantry, and artillery, within the Portuguese frontier.

A few days after we got into houses, and indulged in sitting over charcoal fires, there was a pretty general complaint amongst men and officers of a sensation in the limbs not unlike being frost-bitten. Our *medicos* pronounced it to be the effect of a transition from cold and wet bivouacs to more comfortable accommodations, rest, quiet, and something better by way of food than acorns.

This winter it was the good fortune of our battalion to be quartered together, for the first time during several campaigns, in the Spanish village of Alameda. We instantly, therefore, set to work to establish a regimental mess; and having ransacked the canteens of each company for knives, forks, spoons, &c., and purchased wine-glasses and tumblers at Almeida, nothing was now wanting but a mess-room and some good Douro wine. The first difficulty was soon obviated, by our taking possession of a barn, through the roof of which we built two large chimneys, rather uncouth as to size and shape; and making a long table with benches, equally rough, around it. A great quantity of excellent wine reached us from the Douro, far preferable, in my opinion, to the best bottled Port wine to be found in England; and it would be folly to deny, that we made excellent use of it during our temporary repose in winter quarters, or that its exhilarating qualities brought to light many vocal performers, of whose musical talents we had not until then been aware.

Soon after the army was put into winter quarters, the Commander-in-Chief sent a circular letter to the officers commanding regiments, expressing his highest disapprobation of the conduct of the army at large during the late retreat, which we found as difficult to digest as the acorns in the woods of San Munos. That many regiments were guilty of great irregularities, and did fall to pieces and lose their discipline during this disastrous retreat, was too true; but it was no less so, that many others, which I could name, maintained their order, good spirit, and discipline, throughout the retreat, and left no men behind who were not either too badly wounded on the 17th of November, at San Munos, to be brought on, or were actually expiring from sickness, excessive fatigue, cold, wet, and want of food. The charge was, therefore, thought by many people *too sweeping*.

The Light Division established a theatre during the winter at Gallegos, which might have vied with half the provincial ones in England, if we could but have procured female performers. Lord Wellington and his staff rode over from headquarters one dark night, (twelve miles through execrable roads,) to witness our performance. It is impossible to imagine any thing more truly ludicrous than to see *Lydia Languish* and *Julia* (which characters were performed by two young and good-looking men, dressed uncommonly well, and looking somewhat feminine on the stage,) drinking punch and smoking cigars behind the scenes, at a furious rate, between the acts.

There was good coursing and woodcock-shooting in the neighbourhood, which occupied much of our time and attention. Lord Wellington's fox-hounds often met within reach of our cantonments, but such was the miserable state of our horses, that the staff-men only could avail themselves of it. We now, as on former occasions, assembled the village fair ones, and frequently danced half through the long winter nights; nor were our fair partners at all averse to hot punch between the boleros and fandangos. Our nights were spent in the utmost conviviality and harmony, in the old barn where we messed. Here we also perused the English newspapers, which sometimes reached us.

Lord Wellington left the army for a short time, and proceeded to Cadiz, to consult with the

Spanish Cortes about the co-operation of their armies in the ensuing campaign.

In the month of March 1813, the French General Foy made an attempt at night to surprise General Hill's advanced post at Bejar, occupied by the 50th regiment and a regiment of Portuguese Caçadores. The French were repulsed with loss, and obliged to make a hasty retreat. In April, Major-General Kempt was appointed to command a brigade in the Light Division. We were now beginning to arrange pack-saddles for our baggage animals, and various other matters indispensable for opening the campaign.

Early in May, Lord Wellington reviewed the 1st German Hussars and the Light Division on the plains of Espeja. Many spectators, who neither belonged to the troops assembled, nor could have been particularly interested about the Light more than any other Division, pronounced their whole appearance, and the style in which they moved, to be as near perfection as possible.

About this period, the Life Guards and Horse Guards Blue, and the Hussar Brigade, joined the army from England, and looked as fair and beautiful as lilies, when contrasted with the sunburnt visages and battered appointments of the cavalry regiments which had been many years in the country.

The campaign of 1813 was about to open:

the army was in the highest health and condition, the losses sustained in the late campaign had been filled up by reinforcements from home, and every one anticipated a march to the Ebro, if not to the Pyrenees. The disastrous retreat of Bonaparte from Moscow had obliged him to recall from the Peninsula many thousands of his veteran troops, and with them Marshal Soult, to join him in the north of Europe.

The eight divisions of our infantry were thus composed and commanded. I cannot take on myself to state the names or stations of all the commandants of brigades. Each division had several Portuguese battalions attached to it, besides which there were some independent Portuguese brigades, not belonging to any division. Every division had a troop or brigade of artillery. How the cavalry were brigaded I know not, except that the newly arrived Hussars were together, and the Life Guards and Horse Guards Blue formed the household brigade. I may possibly err in the posting of one or two regiments of infantry, but I am certain that the following is tolerably correct.

DIVISION OF THE INFANTRY IN THE CAMPAIGN OF 1813.

The 1st Division was commanded by Lieutenant-General Sir Thomas Graham, and consisted of the Guards and troops of the German Legion.

DIVISION OF THE INFANTRY.

The 2d Division was commanded by the Honourable Lieutenant-General Stewart, and consisted of the 3d regiment or Buffs, 28th, second battalion 31st, second battalion 34th, 39th, 50th, 57th, second battalion 66th, 71st Light Infantry, and the 92d Highlanders.

The 3d Division, commanded by Sir Thomas Picton, consisted of the 5th, second battalion 24th, 45th, 74th, second battalion 83d, second battalion 87th, 88th, and 94th regiments.

The 4th Division, commanded by Sir Lowry Cole, consisted of the second or Queen's, 7th Fusileers, 20th, 23d Welsh Fusileers, the third battalion 27th, 48th, and second battalion 53d regiments.

The 5th Division, commanded by Sir J. Leith, was composed of the third battalion of the Royals, 4th or King's own, 9th, second battalion 30th, 38th, second battalion 44th, second battalion 47th, and second battalion 59th regiments.

The 6th Division, commanded by the Honourable Major-General Sir E. Pakenham, in the absence of Sir Henry Clinton, consisted of the 11th, 32d, 42d, 61st, 79th, and 91st regiments.

The 7th Division, commanded by the Earl of Dalhousie, was composed of the 6th, 51st, second battalion 58th, 68th, 82d, and a part of the Duke of Brunswick Oels' Light Infantry.

The Light Division, commanded by Major

General Baron Charles Alten, consisted of the 43d and 52d Light Infantry, the 1st, 2d, and 3d battalions of the 95th Rifle Corps, (in all eighteen rifle companies), the 1st and 3d Portuguese Caçadores, and the 17th Portuguese regiment of the line; which latter corps was appointed to the Light Division after the retreat from Burgos and Madrid.

Part of the 5th battalion of the 60th (German Riflemen) was distributed amongst the different divisions of the army, the head-quarters of the regiment being in the 3d Division. In speaking of Sir Rowland Hill's corps, the second division, with some regiments of cavalry and Portuguese brigades, are included. Sir Thomas Graham, properly speaking, commanded a corps consisting of the 1st and 5th Divisions; and subsequently other troops were added to his command.

Having attempted a description of our winter quarters, and the manner in which we passed our time; and, moreover, having drawn out on paper the eight divisions of infantry, the sooner I put them in motion the better.

CHAPTER XVI.

The campaign of 1813 opens. The 2d and Light Divisions march on Salamanca. Sir Thomas Graham, with the six other divisions, crosses the Douro. He advances to the Esla and crosses it. The Light Division encamps at San Munos. Contrast between our situation then with that of the 17th of November, 1812, on the same spot. We reach the Tormes. The French retire from Salamanca, and are pursued towards the Douro. They suffer from our horse artillery and cavalry. The Light Division crosses the Douro at Toro. Brilliant affair of cavalry, wherein the Hussar brigade distinguishes itself. We follow the French to Palencia, and from thence to Burgos. The French blow up the castle of Burgos, and retreat behind the Ebro. We pass the Ebro at Puente Arena. Magnificent scenery. Appearance of the troops descending the pass. Language, dress, and appearance of the people northward of the Ebro. Beautiful scenery at every step. The Light Division surprises a French division near St. Millan. The French army assembles near Vittoria. Sale by auction in the camp of the Light Division. Ladies' dresses, &c. &c.

On the 21st of May the Light Division broke up from its winter quarters, crossed the Agueda by the ford of Moulina dos Flores, and encamped near San Felices Chico. Salamanca was the point on which our march was to be directed.

SINGULAR CONTRAST OF SITUATION. 305

Our old friends, the 1st German Hussars, and the 14th Light Dragoons, accompanied us, as did also the brigade consisting of the Life Guards and Blues. Lord Wellington and head-quarters moved with us. Sir Rowland Hill's corps advanced on Salamanca, by a road parallel on our right. The 1st, 3d, 4th, 5th, 6th, and 7th Divisions of infantry, with the remainder of the cavalry, under the command of Sir Thomas Graham, crossed the Douro somewhere near (I think) Torre de Moncorvo, a day or two before the 2d and Light Divisions moved towards Salamanca. The passage of the Lower Douro was thus effected without difficulty or opposition; and whilst Sir Thomas Graham was advancing towards the Esla, the 2d and Light Divisions, with the cavalry regiments already mentioned, marched on Salamanca.

On the 23d our column encamped, after a tolerably long march, on the left bank of the Huebra, near San Munos; and we found ourselves on the identical spot where we had passed so dreary and miserable a night on the previous 17th of November. What a contrast did our situation now offer! When last there, we had bivouacked without fires, in a deluge of rain and sleet, without provisions for man or horse—cold, wet, half-famished, and nearly in rags. Now, on the contrary, the weather, the country, and every face, looked smiling and gay. A beautiful May morning, the valley abounding with grass for our animals, plenty of provisions in our canteens, the horses and mules quite renovated by rest, men and officers refitted in all the requisites for this their sixth campaign, and having the cheering prospect before them of driving the imperial legions nearer to their own country. We halted on the 24th on the same ground; and having nothing better to do, I went with my subalterns to the Huebra, in which we caught a number of dace, which soon found their way into the frying-pan.

On the 26th we reached the Tormes; and the advanced party of the French cavalry retired to Salamanca on our approach. The French garrison in Salamanca fell back towards Toro, and were followed some miles by the 1st German Hussars and the 14th Light Dragoons, with a troop of horse artillery, which cannonaded their squares and caused them some loss. We crossed the Tormes on the 28th, and encamped near Aldea Nueva de Figuiron, where Lord Wellington left us, under Sir Rowland Hill's command, and set off to join Sir Thomas Graham on the right bank of the Douro. Here we remained encamped until the 2d of June, when we advanced on Toro, where the enemy had destroyed some arches of the bridge over the Douro.

On the following day the Light Division crossed, after a tedious process, on planks, and by a small flying-bridge hastily constructed. Sir Thomas Graham had passed the Esla without any serious loss or opposition, and advanced on Toro, whilst the 2d and Light Divisions menaced it from the opposite bank. Those combined operations obliged Marshal Jourdan to abandon the line of the Douro almost without a shot, although it had been fortified with great labour. The French army retired in the direction of Palencia, leaving near Toro a strong rear-guard of cavalry, which was attacked with great spirit and gallantry by the newly arrived Hussar brigade, and defeated, with the loss of 200 prisoners, and many killed and wounded. This brilliant affair reflected the highest credit on the Hussar brigade.

Joseph Bonaparte had evacuated Madrid, and having formed a junction with Jourdan, their united forces were marching on Palencia, with the allies in their track. Various were the speculations and calculations as to the time and place where Joseph Bonaparte would offer us battle.

Passing over a sun-burnt, parched, brown, uninteresting country, affording scarcely any wood or water, and still less provisions, with a terrific sun over our heads, we reached, in four days from Toro, Palencia, where the greater part of the army assembled.

Near a small town called Ampudia, we saw immense heaps of a kind of crystal from which the Spaniards make lime. In England it is called *talc*. Its appearance is very beautiful, much resembling thin, yellow glass.

Joseph Bonaparte had reviewed a part of the French army near Palencia the day before we arrived, and then directed it to march on Burgos. Palencia is an ancient city, standing on the left bank of the Carrion, in a well-cultivated valley; and it has a canal which communicates, I fancy, with the Ebro. So many thousand troops were encamped near the city, that a great scramble was made to purchase provisions at any price.

On the 8th, 9th, 10th, and 11th, we continued marching over an open, uninteresting country, totally destitute of wood. The water which it afforded was often brackish. Heavy rains fell during the greater part of the time.

On the 12th, the Hussar brigade, General Ponsonby's Heavy Dragoon brigade, and the Light Division, having found the French in force near the villages of Isar and Ornelio, were directed to halt on the heights above, until a movement, made by General Victor Alten's light cavalry and Sir Rowland Hill's corps, obliged the enemy to abandon their position, and to retire towards Burgos. In this movement their squares of infantry received some damage from the fire of our horse artillery. Sir Rowland Hill's corps and the Light Division had prepared matters to attack the French infantry, but having the start of us by a mile or more, it was impossible to overtake them in their retreat to the river Urbel.

Soon after daybreak on the 13th, a heavy explosion was heard in our front, which was occasioned by the castle of Burgos being destroyed by mines. Marshal Jourdan was now in full retreat towards the Ebro, taking the great road by Miranda. The Light Division and some cavalry immediately marched towards the Ebro, by the road to Puente Arena, encamping that night near Tovar, and on the 14th near Quintana Juan; the country over which we passed affording but little to cheer the heart of man or beast. Sir Thomas Graham, with the 1st and 5th Divisions, and a corps of Spaniards, had been detached to the left, with directions to cross the Ebro near its source at Reynosa. Thus that line of defence, if Marshal Jourdan ever projected it, was, by a series of rapid and masterly movements, turned and rendered untenable; and the left wing of our army was actually across it as soon as, if not before, the French.

The 4th and Light Divisions, with the Hussar brigade and General Ponsonby's dragoons, marched on the 15th; and after traversing some leagues of the same uninteresting kind of country over which we had been moving for the last fortnight, a scene suddenly burst on our view, when we reached the head of a pass leading down to the Ebro, which it is impossible to forget as long as the powers of recollection remain. I have since passed the Alps and Appennines, and travelled over many parts of Switzerland; but nothing have I seen comparable to this magical and lovely spot, according to my own ideas of beauty.

From the Tormes to the Ebro our route had lain over one of the most monotonous and uninteresting countries I ever beheld,—without wood, feature, verdure, streams of water, picturesque villages, or any one recommendation whatever to the admirer of fine scenery. Scarcely any thing could be purchased, as we drew near the Ebro, to help out the homely fare of ship-biscuit, rum, and lean ration beef, which was alive and merry in the morning, and consumed before night. What, then, was our excessive delight on suddenly and unexpectedly beholding an extensive valley at our feet, through which flowed the rapid Ebro; and that valley, as well as the country for miles beyond, teeming with fresh woods, fruit-trees, beautiful villages, gardens, and every thing which could delight the sight! For hundreds of miles before, the eyes had dwelt constantly on rocks, brown stubble, and more frequently on uncultivated wilds, where a hare would have been put to its shifts to find sustenance, or a jack-snipe to procure one day's rations. The lofty mountains which overhang the Ebro near the Puente Arena are clothed to the summit with the most luxuriant woods of oak, beech, and birch. Here, also, the box-tree grows to an incredible size. Great numbers of young eagles and vultures were sitting on the ledges of the precipices, whilst the old birds soared far above them.

In this valley we encamped on the night of the 15th, and procured fresh bread, fruit, and vegetables,—luxuries of which we had known but little for many weeks. Our horses were, no doubt, equally rejoiced at the change of diet, from thistles and stubble, to fine fresh grass. The appearance of the allied army descending this pass—cavalry, infantry, and artillery, British, Hanoverians, and Portuguese, in red, blue, green, and brown—requires a pen much more able than my humble one to describe.

Proceeding on the 16th, by a mountainous road, along the right bank of the Ebro, for about a league, we suddenly turned our backs on the river, and saw its waters no more. We encamped in a beautiful valley near Medino del Pomo, where there was a large convent, but whose inmates we had not a sight of.

Why Marshal Jourdan did not attempt to stop us in the passage of the Ebro, at Puente Arena, it is not my business to inquire; nor why he did not leave a small party of cavalry to observe us at that point. The language, dress, and appearance of the inhabitants on the north of the Ebro are very dissimilar to those of Castile and Leon.

On the 17th, the Light Division was sent, by a difficult mountainous route, impracticable for artillery, through a continuation of the most bewitching scenery in the universe, — the valleys watered by the clearest streams, and producing abundance of wheat and Indian corn, and the mountains covered with the finest timber. We encamped near Rio de Loza.

AFFAIR NEAR ST. MILLAN.

The next morning, our battalion and a squadron of the 1st German Hussars were ordered to form the advanced guard of the Light Division; and as we were feeling our way through an intricate, thickly wooded country, we stumbled on a party of French Hussars, in front of the village of San Millan, with whom our German friends instantly had a brush, and took some prisoners. I know not where Lord Wellington's head-quarters had been the night before, nor from whence he came; but in an instant he appeared on the spot, and directed the 1st and 3d battalions of our corps, supported by the remainder of General Kempt's brigade, to attack a brigade of French infantry, which we had pretty nearly caught napping in San Millan. We engaged them briskly in front, whilst some of our companies assailed both their flanks simultaneously. This drove them in confusion from the village, with the loss of some baggage. On a rising ground behind it they formed a battalion in line, to cover the retreat of the remainder. A few minutes, however, sufficed to disperse it, and we pursued them closely for some miles, killing and wounding many, and making some prisoners. We lost many men in this affair, but fewer than the French.

Whilst General Kempt's brigade was thus employed, the second brigade of the Light Division, commanded by General Vandeleur, to our great surprise was heard engaged in our rear with another French brigade. General Vandeleur took all their baggage and some hundred prisoners, dispersing the remainder, and driving them into the mountains, whither a corps of Spaniards, who well knew the intricate country, were sent in pursuit, and, without doubt, shewed most tender mercy to such of the unfortunate fugitives as fell into their hands. The rapidity of Lord Wellington's movements had been such, that this

French division, which we surprised at mid-day, were not even aware of the allied army having crossed the Ebro; so at least many of the prisoners declared.

The 4th Division, which marched by a road parallel on our left, had a brush with the French light troops, who were retiring towards a position near Vittoria.

We halted on the 20th to allow other divisions to close up from the rear. From the summit of a mountain near our camp we had a splendid view of the country about Vittoria, where Joseph Bonaparte and Marshal Jourdan were assembling their forces. The horses, mules, and baggage, which had been captured from the enemy by the Light Division on the 18th, General Alten directed to be sold by auction in the camp this day, and the money produced by the sale to be divided amongst the troops, before any more heads were broken by a collision with our French neighbours. Portmanteaus and trunks were consequently forced open, and various articles exposed for sale; amongst others, a large assortment of female dresses. Silks, satins, muslins, cambrics, gauzes, lace, flounces, bobbinets, tabbinets, poplins, and all sorts of finery, were put up to the hammer, and sold, *without reserve*, to the highest bidder. That a universal feeling of regret for the fair females who had thus lost their wardrobes pervaded all minds, I am ready to declare; but as there was no remedy for their misfortunes, abundance of purchasers were found.

CHAPTER XVII.

Battle of Vittoria. The Light Division and some cavalry pursue the French rear-guard on the road to Pampeluna. Engaged with them several days. Two French ladies restored to their husbands. Baron Alten directs the movements of the advanced guard with great judgment and effect. We take the last piece of artillery but one in possession of the French rear-guard. The country between Salvaterra and Pampeluna favourable for a retreating army. Reflections on approaching the Pyrenees. Lord Wellington marches with the 3d, 4th, and Light Divisions against General Clausel. A Spanish priest apprises that general of our movements, and mars our plans. Our benedictions on the said padre. We return to Pampeluna, and assist in the blockade. March into the Pyrenees. Splendid scenery. Sir Rowland Hill's corps engaged in the passes. Vale of San Estevan. A week spent there. Dress, language, &c. of the Spanish Basques. Trout-fishing on the Bidassoa. The Light Division advances to Vera. Drives the French out of it into the pass. The first view of the ocean for four years. Cheers of the soldiers on seeing it. Rough sketch of the position of our army in the Pyrenees. Quadrilles danced by our French neighbours in their encampment opposite to us. Sir Thomas Graham besieges St. Sebastian. The French entrench themselves in our front. An attempt to storm St. Sebastian fails. Marshal Soult attacks our right wing. It falls back towards Pampeluna. Defeats the French, and drives them again into France, with great slaughter. The 7th and Light Divisions fall back from Vera and Echelar. Soult's proclamation to his army before he attacked the allies in the Pyrenees. The Light Division makes forced marches to reach the bridge of Yanci. The Riflemen inflict a severe loss on the retreating columns of the French. General Kempt's brigade drives the enemy from a high mountain into France. Gallant attack made by General Barnes' brigade. The hostile armies occupy their former positions.

BATTLE OF VITTORIA.

On the 21st Lord Wellington made a grand attack on the French position near Vittoria, and gained a splendid victory, which those who took a part in are vain enough to suppose will be remembered long after old Charon has crossed the Styx with them, unassisted by a pontoon bridge. A minute detail of the great struggle between two such large armies, on which the fate of Spain depended, I do not presume to give; but a rough sketch I shall attempt. The French right and centre were covered by the Zadora, and their left extended towards, and rested on, a mountainous ridge overlooking the less rugged ground on which the centre was posted.

The scene of action has been termed "the plains of Vittoria;" but although compared with the left of their position it was level, there was no lack of hill and dale, and, in some parts, of enclosures. Sir Rowland Hill's corps commenced the action by attacking the left of the French position, on which a perceptible impression was soon made, notwithstanding that the enemy offered a stout resistance, and occasioned our troops a heavy loss.

This success of the right wing was soon followed by a general attack with the 3d, 4th, 7th, and Light Divisions, directed by Lord Wellington in person. Those troops crossed the Zadora by different bridges opposite the French centre, against which they immediately advanced, under a tremendous cannonade, and in such beautiful and imposing style, as no one who was an eyewitness is likely to forget. Long before the centre of our army passed the Zadora, the 1st and 3d battalions of our corps were pushed forward to its banks, and warmly engaged with the French light troops posted on the opposite side amongst the rocks. The passage of the Zadora was effected, and some companies of our battalion had crowned the heights not many hundred yards from it, when a murderous fire of musketry was opened on us, from several battalions of infantry at its foot placed behind stone walls. This sudden blaze of fire checked the skirmishers, and prevented our descending the hill until the supporting columns arrived; which, with a part of the 3d Division, who opened a flanking fire, dislodged the French from the walls. We then followed them through a village near at hand, where our battalion took three pieces of artillery and some prisoners.

The French now opened a terrible fire of artillery on the village and the troops about it, under cover of which they re-entered it, and endeavoured to retake the guns. But our men had cut the traces; and as many of the gunners and artillery-drivers, with their horses, had been shot, the guns remained in our possession. Except in after-days, at Waterloo, I do not remember to have experienced a more furious cannonade than at this point. Whilst this was going forward, Sir Rowland Hill was driving the French left before him, and the British centre was fast closing with theirs. They soon, therefore, commenced a general retreat towards Vittoria, taking advantage of every favourable piece of ground to check us with their numerous artillery, and covered also by a swarm of light troops.

About this period of the day,—(as a regimentalist, and tied to my battalion, I do not pretend to accuracy as to moments or minutes,)—the troops under Sir Thomas Graham, consisting of the 1st and 5th Divisions, with some cavalry and Spaniards, attacked, in the most resolute and spirited style, the French right, and, after a succession of sanguinary contests, drove the enemy from their ground on the higher part of the Zadora; and thus completed one of the most brilliant victories ever gained. That the French lost all their artillery, baggage, stores, military chest, and the whole material of their army, is universally known. The greater part of the French army was obliged to retreat, without delay, by the Pampeluna road, into the "sacred territory of France."

It was a fine sight, shortly before dark, to behold the French cavalry formed in one dense mass, to cover the retreat of their discomfited army. I conclude, that if daylight had lasted a short time longer, we should have seen the cavalry of the two armies measure their strength. Such, however, was not the case. From the moment of crossing the Zadora, early in the day, until night put an end to the contest and pursuit, we had been constantly engaged.

We bivouacked about a league from the city of Vittoria, amidst waggon-loads of captured baggage of all kinds, consisting of boxes of gold and silver belonging to the military chest, clothes, trinkets, horses, mules, ammunition-waggons, guns, commissariat stores, and waggons belonging to French general officers, where we found fresh bread, Swiss cheese, wine, brandy, &c. &c., of which we made good use, having tasted nothing since daybreak. Two officers of my company were severely wounded in this battle, and were a great loss to our little mess in the bell tent. This signal victory was gained by seven divisions; one (the 6th) having been left near the Ebro, and consequently taking no share in the battle. Joseph Bonaparte narrowly escaped being made prisoner; and many fair ones, both French and Spanish, who could not contrive to escape with their husbands or lovers, were left in Vittoria, or amongst the baggage on the field. Men and officers were so occupied with discussing the events of the day over the camp fires, smoking cigars, and making free with the wines and other good things found amongst the spoils, that daylight arrived, and summoned us again to move, almost before we could take any repose.

On the 22d, the Light Division and the 4th, with some cavalry, followed by the remainder of the army, marched in pursuit of the enemy by the road to Pampeluna; and Sir James Graham's corps advanced in the direction of Tolosa. We did not reach the French rear-guard; and encamped at night near Salvaterra, a town with a wall round it.

Next morning, at daybreak, the Light Division, with the 1st German Hussars and 14th Light Dragoons, went in pursuit, and came up with their rear-guard early in the day, just after they had set fire to a wooden bridge over a small river. We found a ford, by which our battalion, forming the advance of the Light Division, passed, and immediately commenced an attack, supported by the cavalry and horse artillery. We continued a running fight until the afternoon, driving them through Lacanza, and taking many prisoners. It rained tremendously the whole day.

The French set fire to several villages in a wanton and cruel manner; and when we reached them, they were half consumed. With great difficulty we were able to get through the streets, as the burning rafters were falling into them every instant. For a moment it was a matter of doubt whether the horse artillery, with their ammunition, should venture to pass; but the ardour of pursuit overcame all other feelings, and they rattled through at a brisk pace, fortunately without any mischief occurring.

Late in the afternoon a carriage was seen coming up from the rear with two ladies. These proved to be the Countess Gazan, wife of the chief of the French staff, and the wife of some other French officer, who had fallen into our hands in the late battle. Lord Wellington lost no time in restoring them to their husbands, and they were handed over to their countrymen at the advanced posts.

On the 24th, the Light Division, with the German Hussars and the 14th Light Dragoons, started again at daybreak, and came up with a rear-guard of several thousand infantry, occupying a formidable position behind a mountain river called the Araquil. The banks being extremely rocky and difficult of approach, and the fords impracticable from the heavy rains, which still descended, they could not be attacked but by a narrow bridge. The only infantry advanced thus far were the 1st and 3d battalions of the 95th Riflemen, with which, however, General Alten immediately set to work, before the remainder of the division arrived. Our 3d battalion climbed a mountain on the left, which enabled them to throw a fire on the enemy's right, whilst the 1st battalion blazed at them in front across the river. This, with the appearance of the remainder of the Light Division approaching, caused the French gradually to melt away and to continue their retreat.

We lost many men in this desultory fight. Coming up with them again soon afterwards, in a more open country, the horse artillery cannonaded them with considerable effect, and the cavalry charged and sabred many men. At this moment there was a strange mixed fight of the three arms, cavalry, infantry, and artillery, all scuffling and pounding their adversaries simultaneously. Never did the commandant of an advanced guard bring into play more quickly, and with better judgment and effect, the different description of troops under his command than Baron Alten, and, moreover, without the least confusion or delay. He was always with the most advanced party, whether it happened to be cavalry or infantry; and in his quiet, cool manner, did the business to admiration. We stuck close to the heels of the enemy, and captured from them the last piece of artillery but one which remained out of the whole of their immense train before the battle of Vittoria. They took refuge under the guns of Pampeluna; and our advanced guard occupied for the night some farmhouses and villages within a few miles of it. The country from Salvaterra to Pampeluna is highly favourable for a retreating army, as it affords various positions amongst the defiles and woods, and behind the rivulets, to stop its pursuers, without the aid of artillery.

At an early hour on the 25th we advanced towards Pampeluna, and began to think it possible, nay, probable, that ere long we should not only behold from the Pyrenees " the great, the grand, the beautiful France," but tread its soil. Contrasting the present situation and position of our army with what it had been three years before, when shut up in the lines of Torres Vedras, it appeared like a dream. Then Marshal Massena threatened to kick us into our ships; whereas now, the " Leopard," having cleared the Peninsula of its invaders, was advancing with rapid strides to threaten in his turn. We threw out strong pickets towards the fortress, and occupied Villa Alba, and other small villages near it.

The appearance of Pampeluna, standing in a large plain not far from the base of the Pyrenees, and watered by the Arga, is very imposing. It is a place of considerable strength; but to the engineer department, or those better versed in fortification than myself, I leave the task of describing its weakest and strongest points.

Lord Wellington, taking with him, on the 26th June, the 3d, 4th, and Light Divisions, and some cavalry, marched in pursuit of General Clausel, who, with three French divisions, was endeavouring to reach France by some of the Pyrenean passes, in a more easterly direction. The brave, patriotic, and indefatigable Spanish General, Mina, had, by destroying bridges, breaking up roads, and in various other manners, obstructed General Clausel's movements, and obliged him to make considerable *détours* to reach different points.

We encamped near Muro on the 26th, and on the 27th marched through a good town called Tafala, where the people greeted us with joy and enthusiasm. After a long march through a fertile and beautiful country, we encamped near Olite, an old town with a wall round it. The whole of the 28th was spent in following the route by which it was expected we should come up with General Clausel; and worse or more rugged roads no one need wish to travel over. At midnight we bivouacked in some ploughed land on the banks of the Arragon, without baggage or provisions, and in tremendous rain.

We were ordered to halt on the 29th in our bivouac, it having been ascertained that a Spanish priest had given General Clausel information of the march of the three British divisions. This, by causing him to change his direction, prevented our taking him by surprise, and, in all probability, giving a good account of him. Clausel effected his retreat into France; and we returned on the 30th towards Pampeluna, bestowing sundry benedictions on the padre for having marred our plans, and given us three long marches to no purpose.

On the 3d of July we found ourselves within a few miles of Pampeluna again, where we remained until the 5th, assisting in the blockade. We then commenced penetrating into the Pyrenees, and on the 6th reached Lanz, amidst the most lovely scenery imaginable. The valleys, watered by the clearest streams, are well cultivated with Indian corn, and the mountains clothed to their summits with the most luxuriant woods.

SPLENDID PYRENEAN SCENERY.

A sharply contested affair between the advance of Sir Rowland Hill's corps and the enemy took place this day at or near the pass of Maya, in which the French were driven from the mountains into their own country. At daybreak, on the 7th, we quitted our beautiful encampment; but it was only to exchange it for one equally so. No country in the known world can afford scenery more interesting or more truly splendid. Here is all the wild magnificence of the Alps, without the eternal monotonous fir and larch. Oak, beech, birch, box, and various trees, flourish on the sides and summits of the mountains, in a manner which I have never seen in other regions of the kind, except on the Ebro.

We had scarcely taken up our ground for the night, near Gostello, when an order was sent for our battalion to move to San Estevan, a town about one league in front of the bivouac of the division, whence we were to push pickets on the roads leading to Vera and Echelar. If we were struck with astonishment and delight at suddenly looking down on the Ebro on the 15th of June, we were equally so, when, on crowning a mountain, we all at once beheld the vale of San Estevan beneath, with the Bidassoa flowing through it. But a truce with descriptions of scenery. Simply let me observe, that I consider this valley unequalled in romantic and picturesque beauty.

Our arrival excited great curiosity, as we were the first British troops that had ever visited this secluded spot. The inhabitants received us hospitably and kindly, although they at first doubted our being English, as we were not clothed in scarlet. The French had fortified San Estevan against any sudden attempt from the guerillas of Mina and Longa, who eternally hovered about the mountains, and threatened the garrison. The complexions of the women in this part of Spain are very unlike those of the southern provinces, where the heat is so much more intense. Here you see the bloom of the northern Europeans; and their features also are dissimilar to those of the south. The women wear their fine long hair plaited, which hangs down the back to a great length, and is tied at the bottom with ribands of the most gaudy colours. The peasantry are a remarkably handsome race. Of the Basque language I know nothing, further than that it is, in print, unlike any other I have seen. Half a dozen consonants without a vowel, is nothing uncommon; but it does not strike one as being inharmonious or harsh. The Spanish is as little understood by the peasantry as German or English; and even the better classes do murder the Castilian most cruelly.

We remained a week in San Estevan; and as it was the first halt of any consequence which we had made since the 21st of May, we enjoyed beyond measure our short sojourn there. We had dances every night, and received the greatest attention from the people of all classes. The tune of one of their provincial dances we converted into a quick march for the band; and I have never since heard it, without being instantly reminded of the few happy days which I passed in that delightful spot. Whilst there, I caught some uncommonly fine trout in the Bidassoa, which abounds with them.

On the 14th July, the Light Division marched towards Vera; and on the 15th approached that town, which the French occupied, as well as some walls and enclosures in its front. A part of the 43d regiment attacked the village, whilst our battalion was ordered to ascend the heights of Santa Barbara, and to drive off their pickets. From its summit we had a distant view of the ocean, which for several years we had not seen. A spontaneous and universal shout was raised by the soldiers, which must have astonished our French neighbours, who were separated from us only by a valley.

The French held the pass of Vera with a strong force, and had thrown up field-works of different kinds for its defence. The 1st and 5th Divisions were near St. Sebastian; on the left bank of the Bidassoa was the Light Division, fronting the pass of Vera, the 7th Division at the pass of Echelar, and the other four divisions further to the right, occupying Maya, Roncesvalles, and other passes. The greater part of the cavalry were cantoned towards Vittoria and the Ebro, it being impossible either to feed or to employ them in the mountains where the army was now posted, and whence we looked down on, and cast a longing eye at, France.

A few days after we had encamped near Vera, we saw a gay assemblage of French officers and well-dressed females dancing to the music of a band in front of their tents, on the other side of the valley. The distance across was so trifling, that we distinctly made out the tunes to which they capered away, and, with our telescopes, could see their faces. Here were two large armies so near to each other, that an order for either party to advance would have brought on an engagement in a few minutes. Still, so much were they at their ease, that one party looked on at the other quadrilling!

Sir Thomas Graham had commenced the siege of St. Sebastian with the 5th Division. The French army was entrenching itself in an extended position, with its right on the sea near the mouth of the Bidassoa, and the left stretching along the lower Pyrenees in front of the western passes. On the 25th, a breach in the walls of St. Sebastian was stormed by a party of the

5th Division, but unfortunately the attack did not succeed, and the assailants lost many men in their gallant attempt. On the same day, Marshal Soult, who had recently joined the French army from the north of Europe, and superseded Marshal Jourdan, attacked, with a heavy force, Sir Rowland Hill's corps at the pass of Maya; which, after a desperate resistance, and having suffered severely from numbers very superior, was obliged to fall back in the direction of Pampeluna. The other divisions also, which formed the right of the army, retired through the mountains, from position to position, after a variety of skirmishes, during several days in succession, and ultimately defeated Marshal Soult with great loss, in a desperate conflict in front of Pampeluna.

The 1st and 5th Divisions, during those operations remained near St. Sebastian, and the 7th and Light were ordered, on the 26th of July, to fall back from the passes of Echelar and Vera. But as, in the various intricate mazes and sheep-paths of the Pyrenees, through which we marched day and night, and floundered in the dark amongst precipices, from the 26th to the afternoon of the 30th, a man had quite enough to do to be able to ascertain the route taken by his own division, I shall not venture to detail the movements of the 7th Division.

Soon after we had arrived at Lecumbra, on

the 30th, we received the glorious intelligence of Marshal Soult's army having sustained a signal defeat in its repeated attacks on the right wing near Pampeluna, consisting of the 2d, 3d, 4th, and 6th Divisions, which four alone, and at a great distance from the others, had beaten Marshal Soult to his heart's content, and driven the remnant of his army back into France. The brunt of the battle was understood to have fallen on the 4th Division, which supported the high character it had acquired on various former occasions.

Marshal Soult, who had in his proclamation to the French army, a few days before, promised them that the English should be driven back over the Ebro, and the birth-day of the Emperor celebrated in the city of Vittoria, was obliged, for the present, to renounce his intentions, and to beat a rapid retreat into his own country. His loss during those operations has been rated as high as 15,000 men. He was followed by the right wing from Pampeluna, over the same ground nearly by which he had advanced; whilst the Light Division was directed to retrace its steps to the Bidassoa by forced marches, and to reach the bridge of Yanci. This was effected late in the afternoon of the 1st of August, after some harassing marches over the worst possible roads, impracticable for artillery. Many hundreds of men were left on the road thoroughly exhausted.

On arriving at the top of the mountain, which looks down on the Bidassoa, we found a large body of infantry strongly posted behind walls and rocks, opposite the bridge of Yanci, so as to render the passage of it impracticable. We perceived also a large French column marching, without much order, in great haste, and evidently much jaded, for the passes of Echelar and Vera, by the road which runs close along the bank of the river. Some companies of our regiment were instantly sent down the side of the mountain, with orders to blaze across the river at them. Our fire threw them into great confusion, which was increased by their being aware that the advanced guard of the 4th Division was following their track. Many of the French threw away their arms and knapsacks, and scrambled up the face of the mountain on their right, to get out of the scrape in which they found themselves, and for which there was no other remedy. They lost many men killed and wounded, and a great lot of baggage; but their troops posted for the defence of the bridge still held their ground, and did not abandon it until long after dark, when they followed their discomfited comrades to Echelar and Vera.

The next morning at daybreak, the Light

Division crossed by the bridge of Yanci, and advanced to Vera, where we found the French occupying precisely the same ground as they had done a week before. General Kempt's brigade was ordered to drive from a high mountain above the heights of Santa Barbara several French battalions. The 1st and 3d battalions of the 95th Riflemen, supported by the 43d regiment, climbed the mountain, and were soon warmly engaged. A thick fog suddenly came on, which obscured every thing from view; but the enemy kept up a continual fire at random. As soon as the mist cleared away, we again advanced, and finally succeeded in clearing the mountain, and hunting them down the opposite side of it into their own country.

Whilst we were thus engaged, the 4th Division was driving before it another body of the enemy from a mountain on our right. A brigade of the 7th Division, under General Barnes, consisting of the 51st and 68th regiments, made a gallant attack this day on a French corps, very superior in numbers and strongly posted, and drove them from their position in admirable style. It was asserted that General Barnes had twenty musket-shots through his clothes, hat, and saddle, without one of them touching his body. If, after such extraordinary escapes, that general should be a fatalist, who could wonder at it?

Soult's army was now fairly over the Pyrenees again, and re-occupied its former positions; and in this manner terminated his expedition to raise the blockade of Pampeluna and the siege of St. Sebastian, and to drive the English over the Ebro.

CHAPTER XVIII.

We celebrate the anniversary of the formation of our corps. St. Sebastian is stormed and taken. The French pass the Bidassoa near Vera. Part of the Light Division engaged in that town. The French attack the Spaniards, and are repulsed. They retreat to the Bidassoa, and force the bridge of Vera at night. Movements of the Light Division on this occasion. Lord Aylmer's brigade joins the army from England. The left wing of the army passes the Bidassoa. The Light Division and Spaniards storm the entrenchments in the pass of Vera. Gallantry of Lieut.-Colonel Colbourne's brigade. A French gun-brig destroyed by British cruisers, in sight of both armies. Horrible weather in our mountain encampment. Tents continually blown down. Violent snow-storm. Two Portuguese soldiers of the pickets die from cold. Pampeluna surrenders. The army invades France. Battle of the Nivelle. Approach Bayonne. French entrenched camp. Position of the allied army. Soult reconnoiters our line of pickets. Skirmishes. The Light Division drives back the French advanced posts in its front.

FROM the 3d of August to the 30th, nothing very particular occurred. A Spanish army blockaded Pampeluna; and Sir Thomas Graham carried on the siege of St. Sebastian. The French were busily employed in strengthening their position by numerous field-works, which we could plainly see without the assistance of our telescopes. The enemy being so near us, we could never venture to wander far from camp, not knowing the moment we might be attacked, either by day or night.

The 25th of August being the anniversary of the formation of our corps, the three battalions of it determined, if our French neighbours did not interfere, to dine together, on the banks of the Bidassoa, in our camp-ground. Having constructed a long rude table, with benches round it equally so, seventy-three officers sat down to such a dinner as we could scrape together, under a large hut made of the branches of trees, and within a short distance of the most advanced French sentinels. They looked down on us from the heights of Vera, but were too civil and well-behaved to disturb the harmony of so jovial a set of fellows. Neither vocal nor instrumental music was wanting after the feast; and, with the aid of cigars and black strap, we enjoyed the most extraordinary *fête champêtre* I ever witnessed;—as may easily be imagined, from the singularity of our situation, and the possibility of our being hurried from the festive board to stand to our arms.

On the 31st of August, St. Sebastian was stormed by the 5th Division, and by detachments from the Light, and some others. After a bloody and most severe conflict, in which more determined bravery and perseverance were never evinced, and wherein a most terrible loss was sustained, the town was taken, and the French retired into the citadel. There they maintained themselves until the 8th of Sept., by which time our mortar-batteries obliged them to capitulate, after they had made a noble defence.

On the same morning that St. Sebastian was stormed, the French presented at Vera, opposite to the Light Division, a force estimated at 15,000 men, which immediately commenced fording the Bidassoa below the town, and from thence marched in the direction of Oriazun and St. Sebastian; leaving, however, a sufficient number to guard the pass of Vera and the bridge. Throughout the day, the 2d battalion of the 95th and the 1st Caçadores were warmly engaged in and about the town of Vera and the churchyard, and suffered considerably. We lost some men also from several mountain-guns, which the French brought into the pass to cover their troops in fording the Bidassoa.

In the course of the day the French attacked some Spanish troops, who conducted themselves with great spirit, and repeatedly repulsed the enemy. Lord Wellington was on the spot, and headed the Spaniards in their charge. The

GALLANT DEFENCE OF THE BRIDGE OF VERA.

French, completely routed, fell back towards the Bidassoa; but heavy rains having swollen the river and rendered the fords impassable since the morning, they had no resource but to force the bridge of Vera about midnight of the 31st. This post was defended by two companies only of our 2d battalion, who, although they inflicted a severe loss on the enemy, as their dead bodies on and near the bridge plainly told the next morning, could not stop 10,000 Frenchmen. Captain Cadoux, who commanded the two companies, was killed in the gallant defence of the bridge, with many of his men.

Some hours before this attack at the bridge took place, General Kempt's brigade was ordered to cross the Bidassoa at the bridge of Lezacca, and to operate on the left of the river. I happened to have command of the pickets of his brigade that night, and was ordered to descend from the heights of Santa Barbara as soon as some Spanish troops relieved me, when I was to follow the brigade across the Bidassoa.

I have been out in all kinds of weather, in all seasons; but the thunder, lightning, and rain, the roaring of the Bidassoa and its tributary streams, the utter darkness which succeeded the vivid flashes of lightning, and made our descent down the sides of the mountains, by the narrow rocky paths, so slow and tiresome, rendered that amongst the most dreary nights which I can call to my recollection. In addition to this, we knew the enemy were near us in great force at different points; the two brigades were separated by a rapid river; we knew not what had been the result of the attempt to storm St. Sebastian in the morning, nor of the attack of the French on the Spaniards. In short, all was uncertainty and darkness, which we trusted the morning would do away with; and so it did. St. Sebastian was taken; and the Spaniards had defeated the French, who finally regained their old position in the pass of Vera, after losing many men in forcing the bridge. Here terminated Soult's second attempt, which was fully as unsuccessful as that which he made in July to relieve Pampeluna.

At this period Lord Aylmer arrived from England, with the 76th, 62d, 84th, and 85th regiments, which formed a brigade under his command, and was not attached to any division.

PASSAGE OF THE BIDASSOA, AND STORMING THE FRENCH ENTRENCHMENTS AT VERA.

The two armies remained tolerably quiet, after the late operations, until the beginning of October, when Lord Wellington made preparations for crossing the Bidassoa with the left wing of the army. Having established a pontoon-bridge near the mouth of the river, the 1st and 5th Divisions, and Lord Aylmer's brigade, under Sir T. Graham, attacked the enemy on the 7th of October, and forcing the passage of the river with great bravery and determination, carried all the works constructed for its defence, with the loss of many men. At the same moment, the Light Division, the Spanish army of Andalusia, and General Longa's guerillas, stormed the French entrenchments in the pass of Vera.

As our division was engaged many miles distant from Sir Thomas Graham, I am unable to detail particularly the operations of the left wing. I know, however, that Sir T. Graham planted the British standard that day on the soil of France. But a word or two about the work chalked out for the Light Division.

The business commenced by our 3d battalion climbing a small mountain, on which the French had a strong advanced post. After a sharp conflict, the enemy were driven from it; and if the evidence of impartial spectators may be credited, the business was done in handsome style. From the summit of this hill we were able to reconnoiter the whole of the French entrenchments in the higher mountains beyond it. Art and nature combined had certainly given it a formidable appearance, particularly that portion allotted to the 2d brigade of the Light Division to assault, commanded by Lieutenant-Colonel Colbourne, of the 52d regiment, an officer possessing the most cool and determined courage, coupled with excellent judgment and considerable experience. The Spaniards were already engaged on our right, and General Kempt's brigade was enabled, by a movement to its right and a flank fire on their entrenchment, to dislodge a strong force of French infantry, who must have been made prisoners, if they had not bolted like smoked foxes from their earths.

During those operations, Colonel Colbourne's brigade had a much more arduous task to perform. His opponents could not be taken in flank, and he was therefore obliged to advance straight against them, entrenched up to their chins. The impetuosity of the attack made with the bayonet by this brigade, headed by Colonel Colbourne, and its brilliant success, are like many other conflicts which took place during the Peninsular war, not coming under the head of general actions, but imperfectly known except to those engaged in the operations on the spot. A succession of redoubts and field-works were carried by the bayonet, and those who defended them were either shot, bayoneted, or driven off the mountain. The 52d regiment, the 2d battalion of the 95th, and the 1st Caçadores, which composed this brigade, suffered very severely.

The pass of Vera was now gained; but the French still held the mountain of La Rhune, which overlooked us, out of musket shot. The Spaniards skirmished with them at its base, and attempted to dislodge them; but night closed without their having accomplished it.

The 2d, 3d, 4th, 6th, and 7th Divisions made no movements that I am aware of on the 7th of October; but remained to guard the passes of Echelar, Maya, and Roncesvalles. The following day the French abandoned the mountain of La Rhune, seeing that Lord Wellington was arranging matters to drive them from it. Our division constantly afterwards had a picket of three companies on that mountain, amongst some ruins called the Hermitage of La Rhune.

Being under arms, as usual, an hour before daybreak, we heard one morning a cannonade at sea. Our glasses were pointed in that direction as soon as the daylight broke sufficiently, and we perceived a French gun-brig, which had endeavoured to escape out of the harbour of St. Jean de Luz, and to creep along the French shore, beset by a British gun-brig, and a man-of-war schooner. In a short time the French crew took to their boats and escaped ashore; and their vessel, in which they had left slow matches, blew up with a great noise. This hubbub was increased by our men cheering at the catastrophe of their French neighbours; and as we were not far from their advanced posts, they had the double satisfaction of seeing one of their vessels of war destroyed at the mouth of a French harbour, and of hearing thousands of Englishmen exulting at it.

Pampeluna, although closely blockaded, and the garrison nearly in a state of starvation, still held out; and it was pretty well understood, that we waited only for its surrender to advance into France. A continuation of tremendous gales of wind and rain tormented us for a whole fortnight, which blew down our tents as fast as we pitched them, and almost tore them to pieces; so that we were never dry.

Being on picket at the Hermitage of La Rhune early in November, as furious a gale of wind, with heavy snow, came on, as I ever recollect. To light fires was impracticable; and I believe that troops have but rarely been exposed for twenty-four hours to such weather on so unsheltered a spot. Two Portuguese soldiers belonging to the pickets were carried down to the hospital at Vera next morning in a state of insensibility, and died the following day.

The weather was so inclement during October and the early part of November, that were I to enter into detail, and to describe the actual state of our canvass habitations during the many weeks which we encamped on the pinnacles of the western Pyrenees, I might be accused of colouring matters too highly, except by those who were present. It is enough to say, that day or night we were never dry; springs bubbled up from the ground on which our tents stood, and we began to think it was really time to seek winter-quarters in more hospitable regions.

Pampeluna surrendered about the beginning of November, and the 10th of that month was the day appointed for the invasion of France, and a general attack on the enemy's position, which stretched from the sea near St. Jean de Luz, several miles along the front of the different passes.

To give a minute detail of the operations of each separate division, I do not pretend. The left wing was now commanded by Sir John Hope, who had succeeded Sir Thomas Graham, that officer having returned to England: it consisted of the 1st and 5th Divisions, and Lord Aylmer's brigade, with some Portuguese troops; and had its left on the sea, near the main road from Irun to St. Jean de Luz. On Sir John Hope's right, on La Rhune, was the Light Division; and on its right were the 2d, 3d, 4th, 6th, and 7th Divisions, and a large body of Spaniards. Each division was to form its own reserve, and was directed to attack the points specified for it on the chain of hills where the French were entrenched.

We were ordered to leave our camp early on the night of the 9th, and to approach, in great silence, as near as possible to their advanced pickets. No horses were to accompany the troops, lest their neighing might alarm the enemy's pickets, and put them on the *qui vive*. No fires were to be made, and every thing was to be as silent as the grave. The Light Division lay down at the back of some rocks, in front of which we were to sally forth at break of day, and to assault the enemy's advanced position on a detached mountain, called La petite la Rhune.

The signal for the whole army to advance to the attack, was a cannonade on a French redoubt, at Sarr, or Zara, opposite the centre of our army. We had been standing to our arms more than an hour before day dawned, straining our eyes towards the French position, and, as the light faintly appeared, momentarily expecting to hear the cannonade, as a signal for a powerful army of British, Portuguese, and Spaniards, to rush forward at the same instant from the different passes of the Pyrenees, and to invade the "sacred territory of France." Whatever fire-eaters and salamanders may say to the contrary, such moments as those which intervened from the time day began faintly to dawn, until it became sufficiently light for the signal of attack to be made, and for the army to be put in motion, are far more trying than the actual strife when once fairly begun.

BATTLE OF THE NIVELLE.

Nov. 10*th.*—The fire of artillery in the centre at length opened. The Light Division descended the face of the mountain in columns of battalions, our front covered by skirmishers, and crossing the valley which separated us from the French, instantly attacked La petite la Rhune, on which they had constructed a star redoubt of stone. The rapidity of the attack was such, that in less than half an hour from its commencement the enemy were driven off the hill, and the redoubt was in our possession. This success was not attained without a heavy loss. Our division reformed columns of attack on La petite la Rhune, whence we could now plainly see the whole chain of entrenchments filled with French infantry, the redoubts bristling with cannon, and every thing ready for our reception. The other divisions had also driven in the enemy's advanced posts, and a sharp fire of musketry for some miles to our right and left was kept up.

It is impossible to conceive a finer sight than the general advance of our army from the Pyrenean passes against the French position. Almost as far as the eye could reach, was seen one sheet of flame and smoke, accompanied with an incessant fire of light troops, and frequent volleys of musketry, as the lines and columns approached the entrenchments. An order now reached the Light Division to advance from La petite la Rhune, to cross the valley in our front, and to storm the enemy's works, in conjunction with the other five divisions, and the Spaniards which were on our right. Long and severe was the struggle; but each division succeeded in forcing the enemy from the numerous entrenchments which were met at every step, and in driving them off their strong position, with the loss of all the heavy artillery mounted in their works. A battalion of the French 88th regiment were made prisoners by the Light Division in a redoubt on the summit of the position.

The commandant of our battalion, Colonel Barnard, was shot through the body whilst leading it against the entrenchments. His instant death was expected, the ball having entered his breast and lodged under the shoulder-blade. No man would have been more universally or deservedly regretted, had the ball proved fatal; and his recovery caused the most lively satisfaction and pleasure to all under his command.

The troops on the left, under Sir John Hope,

drove the enemy before them; and by their intrepidity and determination overcame numerous obstacles, both natural and artificial, which they encountered in their advance. Marshal Soult withdrew his army across the Nivelle during the night, and destroyed the bridges over it near St. Jean de Luz, evacuating that sea-port. From thence he fell back towards Bayonne. The allied army bivouacked for the night on the heights which it had taken.

We moved forward the following morning by execrable roads, flooded with rain, and in a few days took up a line of posts within a few miles of Bayonne, in front of which Marshal Soult had formed an extensive entrenched camp. The allies were posted with their right on the river Nive, and the left on the sea at St. Jean de Luz, having a strong cordon of pickets along the front of the cantonments, which consisted of such villages and farm-houses as lay within the line. Field-works were formed in front of it also, at certain points, as a security from any sudden attempt which the French might make from their entrenched camp. The country was intersected, and the roads were of the worst and deepest description.

The Light Division was stationed at and near Arcanguez, the château of that name being allotted for our battalion, which we strengthened by digging trenches round it. The churchyard of Arcanguez was also converted into a sort of garrison by the 43d regiment. Marshal Soult reconnoitered our line of posts on the 18th of November, which brought on a skirmish with our pickets, as also with some troops of the 3d Division on our right.

On the 23d of November, the Light Division drove in the French pickets, and occupied a much safer and more contracted line for our own. Nothing particular occurred from that day until the 9th of December. We were always under arms an hour before daybreak, men and officers sleeping accoutred, being so near the French outposts.

CHAPTER XIX.

Sir Rowland Hill passes the Nive. Battles of the Nive. The French are beaten in every attempt against us. We dance-in the New-year of 1814 at Arcanguez. Reflections on the past and present situations of the two armies. Soult manœuvres near Dax. We take the field for a few days in very inclement weather. Return to cantonments. Heavy fall of snow in the Pyrenees. Capital woodcock shooting. The army moves to its right. Our battalion marches to St. Jean de Luz for its new clothing. Sir John Hope blockades Bayonne. He passes the Adour. The Guards repulse a sortie from the garrison. We march from St. Jean de Luz to rejoin the army. Orthes. Handsome peasantry. We rejoin the Light Division. Soult makes demonstrations against Sir Rowland Hill's corps. The 15th Hussars attack a French cavalry post and take some prisoners. The 7th Division is detached to Bourdeaux. Lord Wellington marches on Tarbes. Affair near Vic Bigorre. Action near Tarbes. The French retreat towards Toulouse. We follow them. A pontoon-bridge is established below Toulouse. The army crosses.

BATTLES OF THE NIVE.

On the 9th of December, Sir Rowland Hill's corps crossed the Nive by a pontoon-bridge, near Ustaritz. Those troops met with but little opposition, and were established in a position with their left on that river, and their right on the Adour; thus commanding the navigation of the latter, which was highly inconvenient to Marshal Soult. Whilst this was in progress on the right, the Light Division and Sir John Hope's corps drove back all the French posts in their front, under the protection of their fortified camp near Bayonne. Some hours were spent in a hot fire of light troops, during which Sir John Hope reconnoitered the French entrenched camp; and by this forward movement of his own corps and the Light Division, created a diversion in favour of Sir Rowland Hill, and facilitated his passage across the Nive. Towards evening Sir John Hope's corps and the Light Division fell back to their former ground.

At daybreak on the 10th, the French advanced in great force from their entrenched camp, driving back the pickets of the Light Division and of the left wing, under Sir John Hope. This was followed by several desperate attacks on the 5th Division, in all of which the French were repulsed with great slaughter, after much hard fighting, wherein the troops under Sir John Hope behaved heroically. During the remainder of the day, Marshal Soult confined his operations to a cannonade on the posts of the Light Division in the churchyard of Arcanguez, and a continual fire of light troops. One of my subalterns, Lieut.

Hopwood, was killed on this occasion. He was a good and gallant soldier, and a worthy fellow.

In the course of the night, three German regiments in the French service, who had served many years in Spain, deserted to us with their arms and baggage.

On the 11th, the French again attacked Sir John Hope's troops; but they were beaten back most gallantly at all points. Things remained tolerably quiet on the 12th, until the afternoon, when there was a brisk fire of light troops on the left. In front of the Light Division, during the 10th, 11th, and 12th, the French constantly employed a swarm of light infantry, with whom we waged a desultory warfare during the whole three days. The enemy constructed a battery for ten guns opposite the Château of Arcanguez, which proved to be precisely what many of us predicted —a mere sham. They had recourse to the same system of humbug at Buzaco and other places, previous to abandoning the position in our front. Soult withdrew, in the course of the night, his whole force from our front, and passing with it to the opposite bank of the Nive, made a furious attack on Sir Rowland Hill's corps, posted between the Adour and Nive. Nothing could exceed the bravery of the 2d Division, which, though outnumbered beyond all comparison, inflicted a terrible loss on its assailants, defeating them in every attack, and driving them back in confusion under cover of Bayonne, in sight of thousands of their countrymen, who witnessed their disastrous defeat from the walls of the fortress. Finding all his attempts fruitless, both on the right and left banks of the Nive, Marshal Soult allowed us to remain pretty quiet for some time afterwards. He withdrew into his entrenched camp, and the allies occupied their original positions.

On the last day of the year, we got together some females, French and Spanish, and danced in the new year at the Château of Arcanguez, in spite of our proximity to such queer neighbours as the French advanced posts consisted of.

On the 1st of January, 1814, nothing extraordinary occurred. We could not, however, but reflect, that the war, which had commenced on the 1st of August, 1808, in the Peninsula, was still going forward, and that there was no apparent chance of its termination. It was a great consolation to look back to the spring of 1810, when Marshal Massena boasted he would drive us into the sea, and to contrast that period with the present. Four years had now elapsed since that threat was held out; and, instead of finding ourselves performing the part of Newfoundland dogs off the coast of Portugal, the British army had expelled the imperial legions from the Peninsula, and planted its standard in France.

Early in January, Marshal Soult manœuvered on the right and rear of Sir Rowland Hill's corps, crossing the Adour near Dax. The 3d, 4th, and 7th Divisions moved against him, by which he was obliged to retire to his former ground. About this period, the Light Division moved nearer the Nive, and part of Sir John Hope's corps took up our ground. We were for several days called into the field, from cantonments, in dreadful weather, in consequence of some movements of the French beyond the right of the army; but, with the exception of some skirmishing between the light troops, nothing occurred worth noticing. Heavy snow fell about the end of January, which drove the woodcocks in great abundance from the Pyrenees into the low grounds, by which I profited, and had some capital sport.

About the middle of February the army was put in motion, the divisions following in succession to the right. The Light Division crossed the Nive on the 16th, and encamped near La Bastide, where we remained, in severe frosty weather, for several days. New clothing had arrived from England for the army; and as we were nearly in rags, and our wearing apparel patched with sundry colours, one regiment was sent back at a time, to St. Jean de Luz, to receive its clothing; and as soon as it rejoined the army, another was sent down, and so on in rotation.

On the 20th of February, the turn arrived for our battalion; and having received our clothing on the 23d, we posted back on the 24th towards the army, which was advancing on the Gave d'Oleron, where Marshal Soult was concentrating his army. Sir John Hope, with the 1st and 5th Divisions, Lord Aylmer's brigade, and some Spaniards, remained to blockade Bayonne. A part of his corps crossed the Adour below Bayonne by means of rafts and boats; and soon after they were over the river, the French made a sortie and attacked them, but were driven back with the greatest gallantry by the Guards.

Passing through Ustaritz, La Bastide, and Garris, on the 25th, 26th, and 27th, our battalion reached St. Palais on the 28th, on our way to rejoin the army. Here we were ordered to halt until relieved by the first regiment that should pass, and it occasioned our remaining there until the 7th of March, when we pushed on in all haste to the front. A multiplicity of rumours reached us every day and every hour while at St. Palais; amongst others, that a general action had been fought near Orthes. We could not, however, collect any positive information, and were consequently in a state of suspense and anxiety by no means enviable.

The 7th of March brought us to Sauveterre, a tolerably good town, standing in a fertile valley, through which the Gave d'Oleron flows. On the 8th we reached Orthes, a good town on the Gave de Pau. I there saw, in the market-place, as handsome a collection of female peasants, and with as beautiful complexions, as are to be found in England. The inhabitants every where received us with kindness and hospitality; and either were, or affected to be, heartily tired of war and conscriptions, and prayed for a new order of things and a new ruler.

The French Basques are a remarkably handsome race, and very like the Basques of Spain. In no part of France have I seen any people so good-looking, or whose manners I like so much. Their country is, in general, beautiful, and abundantly supplied with provisions, which we found exceedingly cheap, although the large armies of France, England, Spain, and Portugal, were congregated in that department. The Basques pay great attention to their horned cattle, which are worked in carts, and are generally, whilst in their stalls, covered with large white linen cloths, similar to those we use for our horses in the summer months.

We joined the Light Division on the 11th at

Barcelone, where we heard particulars from our friends of the battle of Orthes, which had been fought during our peregrinations in search of the clothing. Fate ordained that we should not take share in a battle which gave additional laurels to the army and to its consummate chief. The 2d and third battalions of our corps were present.

On the 14th, Soult made demonstrations against Sir Rowland Hill's corps on the left bank of the Adour, which caused the 3d and some other divisions to cross to his support, and the Hussar brigade and Light Division to be under arms the whole day on the right bank. Nothing of importance, however, took place.

On the 16th, some squadrons of the 15th Hussars, supported by the 2d battalion of the 95th Riflemen, attacked a post of French cavalry near the village of St. Germain, and took thirty prisoners. Our loss was trifling. About this period the 7th Division was detached to Bourdeaux, to feel the pulse of the people in that quarter. The 1st and 5th Divisions were blockading Bayonne, so that Lord Wellington had with him only the 2d, 3d, 4th, 6th, and Light Divisions. What cavalry regiments were with the blockading army before Bayonne, I do not know; nor whether any accompanied the 7th Division to Bourdeaux.

On the 18th of March, Lord Wellington advanced in the direction of Tarbes; Sir Rowland Hill's corps, with the 3d and one other division, marching by the left bank of the Adour; the Hussar brigade, the Light Division, and another, by the right bank.

On the 19th, the light troops of the 3d Division had some warm work near Vic Bigorré with the French rear-guard, which was falling back on Tarbes by the left bank of the Adour.

ACTION NEAR TARBES.

On the 20th, the Hussar brigade and Light Division continued their march on Tarbes, and we soon came up with the enemy, posted on a long ridge of formidable wooded hills near the town. The Light Division was directed to attack this position in front, whilst another division should outflank its right. Sir Rowland Hill was at the same time driving before him, on the other side of the river, a body of the enemy, which were also retiring on Tarbes. The fight soon began.

It so happened, that on this day the only troops of the Light Division engaged were the three battalions of the 95th Riflemen, which were let loose about the same instant, and ordered to attack the heights at different points; all of which fully succeeded, and the enemy was soon dislodged. The French being reinforced, tried to retake the ground which they had lost. We inflicted on them, however, a severe loss, and drove them back in great confusion. The vineyards near the scene of action were covered with their killed and wounded in all directions. They then retreated on their reserves, which were formed on another ridge about a mile distant. The contest was not of long duration, but it was extremely hot; and in less than half an hour, our corps lost eleven officers killed and wounded, and an equal proportion of men.

The troops with whom we had been engaged belonged to the division of General Harispe, which had recently joined Marshal Soult from Catalonia; and, having been accustomed for many years to oppose imperfectly organised Spaniards, probably did not calculate on so warm a reception as they met with at Tarbes.

Lord Wellington was about to attack the French again in their new position, but they would not wait for us; and retreated several miles until they reached another range of hills, very defensible, and covered by a small river. Night came on before arrangements could be made for turning them out of it; and they cannonaded us as we took up our ground opposite to them. The night was cold and dreary; and as the baggage did not arrive, we stretched ourselves on the ground supperless.

In the course of the night the French retreated, and we followed them several days in the direction of Toulouse.

It is impossible to conceive any people more diametrically opposite in manner, person, costume, language, and in every respect, than the Gascons (amongst whom we now found ourselves) and the Basques. The latter are in general tall, handsome, cleanly in their persons, and becomingly dressed; whereas the Gascon peasantry are short, ugly, ill-dressed, and dirty; and, moreover, speak a terrible jargon.

The rains continued to fall so heavily and incessantly, that we concluded the long-protracted contest between the French and allied armies would be terminated by a deluge, and our marches and countermarches cease. In spite of all these foretellings and prognostications, we still waded, day after day, through mud and water to the knees, and came up with the French rear-guard on the 26th between Plaisance and Toulouse, where our cavalry lost some men and horses in a skirmish. The next day our 3d battalion had a brush with the French light troops near Tournefuille.

The 29th brought the Light Division within two miles of Toulouse, and we occupied a straggling village called St. Simeon; a long chain of French pickets being near at hand, between our quarters and the city. The army remained tolerably quiet for a few days, when a pontoon-bridge having been thrown across the Garonne, some miles below Toulouse, two divisions of infantry crossed, and were followed some time after by the Spanish army of General Frere.

CHAPTER XX.

Battle of Toulouse. The French retreat to Carcassone. The allied army enters Toulouse. Despatches reach Lord Wellington from Paris relative to Bonaparte's abdication, and his departure for Elba. He transmits this information to Soult, who declines a cessation of hostilities. We march from Toulouse towards Carcassone. Count Gazan meets us with a flag of truce. Soult acknowledges the new order of things. Hostilities cease. The dismay of fire-eaters at the termination of the war in the Peninsula and south of France. Sortie of the French garrison from Bayonne. Some regiments embark at Bourdeaux for America. Five weeks at Castel Sarrazin. Soult's army reviewed at Montauban by the Duke d'Angoulême. We march to Bourdeaux. Take leave of our Portuguese allies. The parting. Arrive at Bourdeaux. Lord Wellington reviews the 43d, 52d, and 95th regiments. We embark for England.

BATTLE OF TOULOUSE.

By the morning of the 10th of April, the 3d, 4th, 6th, and Light Divisions, with the cavalry, were across the river; and Sir Rowland Hill's corps remained on the left bank, having closed near the suburbs. Lord Wellington immediately arranged matters for attacking the enemy, who was in a position on the heights above the city, covered with redoubts and different field fortifications, which had been constructed under the directions of General Cafarelli, an engineer of talent. The different entrances to the town were defended by artillery, and the head of the bridge, opposite to which Sir Rowland Hill's troops were stationed, had been rendered formidable also. The approach to the heights was, in most parts, a *glacis*, which, as it afforded no protection to the assailants, exposed them to a deadly fire.

Sir Thomas Picton's division occupied the ground from the Garonne to the great road leading from Bourdeaux into Toulouse. The Light Division covered the ground from the left of General Picton nearly to the base of the French position. On our left again were the Spaniards; and considerably further to their left was Marshal Beresford, with the 4th and 6th Divisions. Sir Rowland Hill threatened the city from the opposite side of the Garonne. The cavalry, I believe, supported Marshal Beresford's column.

The outline of the plan of attack was something like the following. The 3d and Light Divisions were to throw light troops along the canal, and by a constant fire to attract the enemy's attention on that point, and to threaten the entrance by the great road. The Spaniards were to attack the heights in conjunction with the 4th and 6th Divisions; but being nationally and by constitution obstinate and self-opiniated, they thought proper to ascend the heights long before Marshal Beresford's column had made a sufficient *détour* to enable it to attack the French right. The consequence was, that the Spaniards were driven back with great slaughter, and probably would not have halted until this time, if the Light Division had not advanced in line to cover their retreat, and enabled them to form behind it.

The 4th and 6th Divisions had now arrived at their destination, and with a bravery and resolution which was never surpassed, stormed and carried redoubt after redoubt, and finally drove the French with great slaughter from the heights into Toulouse. The loss sustained by the troops which stormed the heights was extremely severe.

The high ground looking into Toulouse was now entirely in our possession; and from it Lord Wellington had the power of making it too hot a position for the French army, if he had thought proper to use his artillery. Motives of humanity towards the citizens prevented his taking such measures. Both armies suffered severely in this bloody contest. The loss of the allies has been rated at nearly five thousand men, and that of the French (who lost several general officers) is stated to have been as great. Not a shot was fired on the following day; and in the night of the 11th Marshal Soult retired on the road leading to Carcassone.

The allied army entered Toulouse on the 12th (except the 4th and 6th Divisions, which were on the road by which the French had retreated), and was received with the greatest apparent joy. White cockades were in every hat, and white flags displayed from every house.

The same day despatches reached Lord Wellington from Paris, announcing the abdication of Bonaparte, and his being about to repair to Elba. A flag of truce was sent to Marshal Soult from the British head-quarters, to apprise him of the fact; but, as no official communication to that effect had reached him direct from the provisional government at Paris, he declined overtures for an armistice. In consequence of this, the allied troops left Toulouse on the 17th, and proceeded in the direction of Carcassone, where the French army was concentrated.

General Count Gazan, the chief of Soult's staff, met us with a flag of truce near Baziege; the purport of his mission being to inform Lord Wellington that Bonaparte's abdication had at length been officially notified to Marshal Soult, who was ready to conclude an armistice, and to appoint persons to fix on a line of demarcation between the French and allied armies. Thus we at length witnessed the termination of the war which had so long been waged in Spain, Portugal, and the South of France.

I believe it is common to human nature to forget hardships, privations, and fatigues, of however long continuance, soon after they have ceased, and are succeeded by the common comforts of life. This may account, in some measure, for the assertions which I have heard made by a few zealots and fire-eaters, who, long after the termination of the war in the Peninsula (and not until then), have declared that they were quite inconsolable when the armistice was concluded, and the prospect of no longer being targets for French bullets stared them in the face. But at the moment when hostilities ceased between the armies of France and England, I do maintain that the general and universal feeling was (amongst those, at least, who had been participators in the whole of the war in the Peninsula, from the summer of 1808 to the spring of 1814), that for the present we had had enough of campaigning, and that a little rest and time to refit would be desirable.

A few days after the battle of Toulouse, the French garrison made a sortie from Bayonne at night, and vigorously attacked the blockading army. There was a great deal of bloodshed on both sides; and Sir John Hope was made prisoner. It has been asserted that the French governor in Bayonne was well aware that Bonaparte had abdicated, and that hostilities had ceased between the French and allied armies. If this be true, hanging would be far too honourable a death for the man who could wantonly sacrifice so many brave soldiers, without any possible good to his country.

The war between America and Great Britain was still in progress; and no sooner had we done with fighting in Europe, than daily reports were in circulation of various regiments being about to embark at Bourdeaux for the western world. Many regiments did embark at that port for America, a few weeks after hostilities ceased in France; but our regiment did not receive orders to proceed across the Atlantic until a later period.

In the latter end of April the army was cantoned on both banks of the Garonne; the river Tarn being the line of demarcation between us and the French. The Light Division occupied Montech, Grizolles, Castel Sarrazin, and other towns. In the latter place the 52d regiment and our battalion were quartered; and we spent five or six weeks very pleasantly, receiving the greatest kindness and hospitality from the inhabitants. Dances, fêtes champêtres on the banks of the Garonne, horse-races, and various gaieties, filled up our time; and great regret was expressed when the order arrived which obliged us to leave our new French acquaintance; some of the fair females of whom had ruined the peace of mind (*pro tempore*) of many of our gallant gay Lotharios.

I went from Castel Sarrazin one morning to Montauban, to see the army of Marshal Soult, and a part of Marshal Suchet's, reviewed by the Duke d'Angoulême. The troops were drawn out in several lines, waiting the arrival of the duke; and I had an excellent opportunity of inspecting that very army which we had so often met in the Peninsula. Their general appearance was fine and soldierlike. The Spanish sun had left its mark on their countenances, which were for the most part lively and animated, without the smallest appearance of despondency or disappointment at the late change, or at the loss of their imperial master. Marshal Soult alone appeared sullen and dejected. But this possibly was his natural manner. Marshal Suchet, who sat on horseback on the duke's left hand, laughed and joked, and had every appearance of being perfectly satisfied.

On the 1st of June we bade adieu, with infinite regret, to our kind friends at Castel Sarrazin, and marched towards Bourdeaux.

On the 11th we arrived at Bazas, a small town on the left bank of the Garonne, where the Portuguese troops were to take farewell of their British allies, and to return through Spain to their own country. The 1st and 3d Caçadores had now served in the Light Division four years, and participated in its various successes. Many of the officers of the two corps were consequently known to us, and the best understanding existed between their soldiers and ours. There was a great deal of shaking of hands, accompanied by many *vivas;* and the parting was altogether affecting. At this place, also, the Portuguese and Spanish followers, both male and female, were doomed to take their departure from the British army. There was much weeping and wailing on the part of the signoras.

We reached Bourdeaux on the 14th of June, and encamped a few miles from the city. Lord Wellington took a last look, near the suburbs of Bourdeaux, at the British regiments of the Light Division, which were about to embark and to be dispersed. He departed amidst loud cheers of men and officers, many of whom had followed him through seven successive, and, I may add, successful campaigns in the Peninsula and the south of France. The cavalry marched from Bourdeaux to Boulogne and Calais, where they embarked for England; and the infantry waited at Bourdeaux for shipping to take them to England, Ireland, or America, as their destinations happened to be. Bourdeaux was thronged with British officers and soldiers, not in gay or flashy costumes, but in remnants of what had once been so.

After several weeks spent in this delightful

town, the 1st and 2d battalions of our corps embarked on board the Ville de Paris of 110 or 120 guns; and, after a ten days' voyage from the mouth of the Garonne, anchored at Spithead on the 22d of July, 1814. Nothing could exceed the kind attention of the officers of the Ville de Paris towards us; and I never passed ten days at sea so pleasantly. We marched from Portsmouth into Kent, and both the battalions wintered at Dover.

CHAPTER XXI.

Embark for Ostend. Proceed to Brussels. We are appointed to Sir Thomas Picton's division. Battle of Quatre Bras. Ligny. Predictions and foretellings *after* things have occurred, no uncommon practice. Fire-side tacticians and critics. The army falls back from Quatre Bras to Waterloo. The cavalry are engaged.

CAMPAIGN OF 1815 IN FLANDERS.

As the war with America still continued, the 1st and 2d battalions of our corps were under orders for embarkation, early in the spring of 1815, for the Western World, whither a considerable part of our 3d battalion had already been sent, and formed a part of the expedition against New Orleans. Napoleon's sudden flight from Elba, and his subsequent occupation of the throne of France, altered our destination; and by the end of April both our battalions were in Flanders. From Ostend we were conveyed without delay, in large boats by the canal, to Ghent, where we remained ten days, and thence proceeded to Brussels. There we were stationed in capital quarters for some weeks, until ordered out of them to take part in that battle which decided the fate of Europe.

During our stay in Brussels the 5th Division of the army was formed there, and consisted of the following regiments:—The 3d battalion of the 1st Royals, 28th, 32d, 42d Highlanders, 2d battalion 44th, 79th and 92d Highlanders, and 1st battalion 95th Rifle Corps. The 2d battalion of our corps, and two companies of the 3d battalion, were appointed to Sir Henry Clinton's Division. Sir James Kempt and Sir Dennis Pack each commanded a brigade in the 5th Division, which had for its chief Sir Thomas Picton. He did not arrive at Brussels from England until the 15th of June, on which day there were various rumours in circulation as to the movements of the French army.

It was known that Napoleon had driven back the Prussian outposts, and it followed, as a matter of course, that affairs would, in all probability, be speedily brought to a crisis.

Soon after dark on the evening of the 15th the drums beat to arms, and the bugles sounded to assemble the division; but as the soldiers were billeted in every part of the city, the night was drawing to a close and morning beginning to dawn, by the time the whole of the troops were collected and formed. We then advanced by the road through the forest of Soignie, and halted near the village of Waterloo, where the troops of the Duke of Brunswick (which had been cantoned for some time in the vicinity of Brussels), joined us.

No one who has campaigned need be told, that a multiplicity of rumours, reports, speculations, and calculations, most of them vague, contradictory, and unfounded, are the forerunners of the advance of an army. " The enemy is in position at such a point with so many thousand men, his front covered by a deep and impassable river," declares one; " the troops stationed at such a point must inevitably be overpowered and annihilated before assistance can arrive," says a second; " we shall have a brush with their advanced guard in less than an hour," declares a third; and so on: every man conjuring up something wherewith to throw a light, not only on the intended operations and movements of his own army, but, moreover, on those of the enemy. The *on dits* on the present occasion were by no means few; but the heads of the many which had been thus racked and tormented with conjectures, were ere long to be otherwise employed.

BATTLE OF QUATRE BRAS.

Our division and the Brunswick troops, after a halt of an hour or two near Waterloo, were directed to advance; and we arrived at Quatre Bras about two hours after mid-day. Long before we reached this point, which consists of a few houses at the junction of four roads, we were aware that something not of an amicable nature was in progress between the Belgian troops under the Prince of Orange and the French under Marshal Ney, as a number of wounded Belgians were proceeding towards Brussels, and an occasional cannonade was, moreover, heard in our front. The troops under the Prince of Orange had been driven back on Quatre Bras, after some resistance.

We found the Prince in possession of Quatre Bras, occupying also a wood on his right, and a farm-house in his front, as his advanced posts. The French were moving on in great force towards Quatre Bras, and to a wood on the left of the road, at the moment of the arrival of our division. The Duke of Wellington instantly directed our battalion to occupy and to defend this wood; and we kept possession of it throughout the day, in spite of the many attempts made by the enemy to dispossess us of it, who kept us constantly engaged until night.

The remainder of our division, during this period, were engaged on our right in a fierce and desperate struggle against some heavy bodies of infantry and cavalry. The approach of the latter force obliged the different regiments to form squares, which resisted, with the greatest steadiness and gallantry, the repeated attempts to charge and break them, and strewed the field with cuirassiers and horses. Neither the charges of their numerous and daring cavalry, nor the incessant fire of musketry, supported by a powerful artillery, enabled the French to gain one foot of ground, although, at the most moderate calculation, they outnumbered the British in the proportion of two to one. The Duke of Brunswick fell early in the action, whilst setting a glorious example to his troops, which were chiefly new levies.

The only cavalry which we had in the field were those belonging to the Duke of Brunswick, which were drawn up on the road towards the right of our division; and by their giving way, at the approach of the cuirassiers, the consequences would have been serious, had not the French cavalry received at that moment a destructive volley from a regiment of infantry (I think the 92d), which sent back those who escaped the fire fully as fast as they had advanced.

Several hours had been spent in this unequal contest; and although we were aware that reinforcements were marching from different points to our assistance, it was not until late in the afternoon that the head of Baron Charles Alten's division was seen approaching; and a welcome sight it was. Supported by this division, which was ushered into the field by a cannonade from the enemy, we drove back their light troops, with whom we continued engaged until night.

The post occupied by our battalion having been given over to General Alten's troops, we were ordered to rejoin our own division, which were lying down by their arms on the ground where they had been engaged throughout the day. Other troops of infantry reached Quatre Bras during the afternoon and evening of the 16th; and in the course of the night the whole, or the greatest part, of the cavalry joined us.

It will easily be credited, that, not having had one moment's sleep on the night of the 15th, and the whole of the 16th having been spent in marching and in engagements with the enemy, very little time was requisite to invoke the sleepy god, as about eleven at night we lay down by our arms for that purpose. But our slumbers were not destined to be of long duration; as we were suddenly broad awake and standing to our arms in consequence of the pickets of both armies blazing away at each other, from some unknown cause, which kept us on the alert until day dawned.

Whilst we were employed on the 16th at Quatre Bras, in the manner which I have attempted to describe, the Prussian army, under Marshal Blucher, was furiously attacked by the French under Napoleon in person, at the village of Ligny, some miles to our left. The tremendous and unceasing fire of artillery, and the constant roll of musketry, announced that a deadly conflict was going forward, which did not terminate until after dark. We were in anxious suspense as to the result of this battle; nor was the disheartening fact known to us until the morning of the 17th, that the Prussians had been completely defeated, and obliged to fall back from Ligny with a heavy loss.

The man of candour will not deny, be he ever so determined a fire-eater, that the news of this disastrous defeat of our allies was calculated to throw a damp on the prospects of the campaign; and notwithstanding I have heard some few individuals since declare that they never entertained the smallest doubt of our success, I never believed them. Nothing is more easy than to prognosticate occurrences which have already taken place. This may be a *bull*, but it is nevertheless a system which I have seen adopted by individuals from both sides of the Irish channel.

It is now time to notice the retrograde movement which the British army was obliged to make from Quatre Bras to the position at Waterloo on the 17th June, in consequence of the defeat, and

FIRE-SIDE TACTICIANS AND CRITICS. 379

subsequent retreat of the Prussians from Ligny, on the night of the 16th. Before I make the attempt, a word or two on another point may not be altogether amiss.

I have often been heartily tired of, and out of all patience with, the one engrossing question, ever uppermost, and ready to be let fly at any one who happened to have served with the Waterloo army, either by non-combatants, or by those who have never given themselves the trouble to investigate the real position of affairs at that period,—"Pray, sir, was not the Duke of Wellington taken quite by surprise, whilst he was at the Duchess of Richmond's ball at Brussels, by the sudden irruption of Bonaparte's army into Flanders?" Now, as every officer stationed in Brussels with Sir T. Picton's division knew, I presume, on the 15th of June, that the French army was in motion on the frontiers of Flanders, and that Prince Blucher's advanced posts had been engaged, it is utterly impossible but that those facts should have been known to the Duke of Wellington long before we could possibly have been informed of them.

I conclude, that those fire-side and feather-bed tacticians would have had the Duke of Wellington, the moment he heard of the affairs which had taken place at the Prussian outposts, mount his horse, draw his sword, and give the word of command himself to the troops in Brussels, to fix bayonets, shoulder arms, and march. I have never, however, distinctly understood to what particular point, or on which of the different roads by which Bonaparte had the option of penetrating into Flanders, these *savans* deemed it judicious that the duke should have ordered a concentration of his army, before he had obtained certain intelligence of the enemy's intentions. A very small share of intellect is necessary to comprehend that the British commander was obliged to canton the different divisions of his army along an extensive frontier, not only with a view of watching the roads by which his adversary might advance, but, moreover, for the purpose of more easily supplying them with provisions, particularly his cavalry and artillery. It would consequently have been a specimen of generalship not very creditable to him, had he directed his army to assemble at any one particular point as long as a doubt existed of the movements of his opponent, or whilst his intentions remained unfathomed.

It is doubtless a pleasant and edifying occupation, while sitting by an English fire-side, to criticise and calumniate that commander, who, in spite of his being " taken by surprise," contrived to gain the most splendid and decisive victory ever achieved by the British army or any other. Leaving those critics to rub their shins by a coal fire, and to finish half a dozen of port (on the qualities of which I should infinitely prefer their opinion than on the campaign of 1815 in Flanders), I must return to Quatre Bras.

The retreat of the Prussians from Ligny having rendered a corresponding movement on our part necessary, the Duke of Wellington put his army in motion about ten o'clock on the morning of the 17th, towards the position at Waterloo.

Our battalion, which was the last of the infantry that left the field at Quatre Bras, retired with the cavalry, who covered the retreat of the army. Tremendous rain commenced falling before we reached Genappe, where we were ordered to take such shelter as the houses on each side of the street at the entrance of the town afforded. Some shots which we heard exchanged between the advanced cavalry of the two armies, obliged us instantly to leave the hovels in which we had taken momentary refuge from the storm; and, as the cavalry very soon afterwards entered Genappe, we retired through the town with them. Our cavalry having formed on the most favourable ground beyond Genappe, became engaged with the Lancers and other corps of the French cavalry as they debouched from the town; and notwithstanding some loss was sustained on our side, and the enemy pressed and rather roughly handled the rear-guard, the household brigade, by their resolute and gallant conduct, soon retrieved matters, and drove back the French cavalry in such style, as made them keep at a much more respectable distance during the remainder of the day. The march from Genappe to Waterloo was little better than a mud-bath, owing to the deluge of rain which continued to fall.

About two or three hours before dark we reached that position which has been rendered so memorable for the sanguinary contest which took place on it the following day. The French occupied a ridge of heights opposite to us, and kept up an occasional cannonade until dark.

The two preceding days and nights having been spent in marching, fighting, and without sleep, the floods of rain that descended the whole night of the 17th, which we passed on the position lying down by our arms, did not disturb our repose. For myself, at least, I can answer, that I never in my whole life slept more soundly, although thoroughly drenched to the skin before I lay down on the ground, which was like a snipe-marsh.

CHAPTER XXII.

Sketch of the battle of Waterloo, but more particularly of the operations of Sir Thomas Picton's division. Death of Sir Thomas Picton. The 27th regiment. Advance of the Prussians. General attack on the French position, and their total defeat and route. The morning after the battle.

Our men lost no time after daylight appeared, on the morning of the 18th, in drying and cleaning their arms, and preparing for the battle which it was clear must inevitably take place.

So many detailed accounts of the battle of Waterloo have been already written by all sorts and descriptions of persons, civil and military, that it would be presumptuous in a regimental officer, who was necessarily tied to one spot with his regiment during the whole of the action, to endeavour to throw a light on a subject already so frequently discussed. I would fain, however, touch on some of the different occurrences which took place during the momentous struggle on the 18th of June, and more particularly such as happened between our division and that portion of the French army which was repeatedly sent to dislodge us from the ground on which we were posted.

Sir T. Picton's division was formed in two lines, with its right resting on the road leading from Brussels to Genappe, and extending its left along a ridge where there was a thorn hedge, which afforded little or no protection against musketry. The troops of the first line were stationed there.

Immediately in front of the extreme right of the position of our division was a hillock, and in its front and at its base was an excavation close by the road, from which sand had been taken; and this was occupied by two companies of our battalion, of which I had the command, supported by the remainder of it on the ridge above.

The farm-house of La Haye Sainte, about a quarter of a musket-shot distant, in front of the hillock, and on the other side of the road, was occupied by one of the light battalions of the German Legion belonging to Baron Alten's division. Several pieces of artillery were planted on the right near the road, and others further to the left. The only troops on the left of our division were some foreign battalions, which formed the extreme left of the Duke of Wellington's position, and they were supported, I believe, by some regiments of British cavalry. With the exception of Sir C. Colville's division, which was detached at a distance of some miles from the right of the position, to watch the enemy in another quarter, the remainder of the infantry, British, Hanoverian, Brunswickers, &c. &c., were formed on the right of the Genappe road, having the château of Hugomont in front of the right, which was defended by the British Guards. The mass of our cavalry were, I believe, in rear of the centre, and in reserve. There may undoubtedly be some inaccuracies in the rough sketch which I have attempted to draw; but I believe the general outline is not very incorrect.

On a ridge of hills higher than those on which our army stood, and immediately opposite to it, was the French position. The ground rose gradually towards each of the positions of the hostile armies from a broad and open valley, which might be termed neutral ground. Being entirely free from wood, with the exception of some trees near Hugomont, and having neither ditches, rocks, walls, nor enclosures, the field was particularly adapted for the operations of cavalry; and, moreover, the approach to each position being exposed, the effects of artillery could not fail to be severely felt by both parties.

BATTLE OF WATERLOO.

As I did not happen to consult my watch, I shall not be positive as to the exact moment at which the battle commenced; but I should say, that between ten and eleven o'clock our attention was first attracted by a heavy cannonade on the right of the army, followed by an exceedingly sharp fire of light troops, which proved to be the commencement of a desperate attack, made by a large force under Jerome Bonaparte, on the château of Hugomont. As it was impossible for us to see what was going on at that point, there being some higher ground between us and Hugomont, I shall not attempt to describe the many desperate and impetuous attacks made by the enemy, hour after hour, on this château, in each of which they perished in heaps by the fire of its undaunted defenders; whom neither the unremitting fire of shot and shells, from the numerous French batteries, nor the swarms of infantry which assailed it again and again, could dislodge from this important post.

As yet all was quiet in the immediate front of our division. But after a calm comes a storm. We perceived our adversaries bringing into position, on the heights opposite, gun after gun; and ere much time had elapsed, there were, at a moderate computation, fifty pieces of artillery in battery, staring us in the face, and intended particularly to salute our division, the farm of La Haye Sainte, and the left of Baron Alten's division. The enemy's columns were not as yet visible, being covered by some undulations of ground near the summit of their position. In an instant this numerous and powerful artillery opened on us, battering at the same moment the farm-house of La Haye Sainte. Under cover of this cannonade several large columns of infantry, supported by heavy bodies of cavalry, and preceded by a multitude of light infantry, descended at a trot into the plain, with shouts and cries of "Vive l'Empereur!" some of them throwing up their caps in the air, and advancing to the attack with such confidence and impetuosity, as if the bare possibility of our being able to withstand the shock was out of the question, fighting as they were under the immediate eye of their Emperor. But Napoleon was destined, in a few minutes after the commencement of this hubbub, to see his Imperial Legions recoil in the greatest confusion, with a dreadful carnage, and with a great loss in prisoners.

The fire of our two companies posted in the excavation near the road, and from the remainder of the battalion on the hillock, as also that from the windows and loop-holes, by the Germans, in La Haye Sainte, had already inflicted a severe loss on the enemy. In spite of it they pressed boldly and resolutely on, until met by our first line, which delivered such a fire, when they approached the thorn hedge, as shattered their ranks and threw them into disorder; and this was increased by the cheers, and an attempt of our line to close with them. At this instant the household brigade of cavalry coming up to our support, rushed gallantly amongst their infantry and the cavalry which were endeavouring to retrieve matters for them, and drove them back, man and horse, in terrible confusion and dismay, and with immense loss. It was, I think, about this time also that the brigade consisting of the Royals, Scotch Greys, and Enniskillen Dragoons, made so brilliant a charge, and took two eagles and seventeen hundred prisoners.

Accounts are various and contradictory as to the time and place of Sir T. Picton's death. I believe there are many living witnesses who will agree with me in the declaration, that immediately after we had repulsed the French in their first attack, and as Sir T. Picton rode forward to the crest of the position, amongst some of our skirmishers, to look at the retreating enemy, an unlucky straggling musket-shot put a period to his existence, and thereby deprived the army of one of its most gallant, experienced, and talented generals. His loss has been universally admitted and sincerely regretted. The command of the division now devolved on Sir James Kempt; an officer in whose brigade our battalion had served the last two campaigns in the Peninsular war, and whose zeal, gallantry, and abilities, are so well known and acknowledged, that any panegyric of mine might appear fulsome and superfluous.

The roar of cannon and musketry continued without intermission on the right; and although the lesson which the enemy had lately been taught by our division and the heavy cavalry, made them delay a considerable time before they renewed their attack on us in regular form, they kept up a constant and well-directed cannonade, from which we sustained a heavy loss, without the power of immediately retaliating, except from some pieces of artillery which the French batteries vastly outnumbered. After having endured for a length of time, and with a tolerable degree of patience, this eternal pounding of shot and shells, strong symptoms appeared of a second and equally formidable attack being about to commence on our division and on the farm-house of La Haye Sainte. The second edition of "Vive l'Empereur!" "En avant, mes enfans!" and other stimulating cries, burst forth as their masses of infantry and of cavalry again advanced in the most imposing and intrepid style, under cover of a terrible cannonade and of their light troops. The 4th, 40th, and 27th regiments, which had arrived on the field from Brussels, under Sir John Lambert's command, (I believe after the battle had commenced,) were sent to support us.

Nothing could exceed the determined bravery with which the Germans defended the farmhouse of La Haye Sainte; but in the desperate attack which was now made on it, having expended the whole of their ammunition, and there being no means of supplying them with more, they were driven out, and the house was instantly filled with the enemy's infantry. For several hours afterwards they kept up a dreadful fire from loop-holes and windows in the upper part of it, whereby they raked the hillock so as to render it untenable by our battalion. They were also enabled to establish on the knoll, and along the crest of the hill, a strong line of infantry, which knelt down, exposing only their heads and shoulders to our fire.

Thus the closest and most protracted contest with musketry perhaps on record, was continued for several hours; during which we were several times supplied with fresh ammunition. The artillerymen were swept from the guns which were within reach of the house and the hillock. The possession of La Haye Sainte by the French occasioned a vast loss to our division, which was so diminished in numbers, that all our reserves of infantry were brought up into our first, and now only line, as were also the 4th and 40th regiments.

Sir Andrew Barnard received a wound early in the action, and the command of our battalion then devolved on Lieutenant-Colonel Cameron. That officer was likewise severely wounded some time afterwards, and the command of the battalion fell to my lot during the remainder of the day.

The 27th regiment had its good qualities of steadiness, patience under fire, and valour, put more severely to the test than, perhaps, any corps in the field. It was formed in a hollow square, a short distance in rear of the right of our division, with one of its faces looking into the road, as a protection to it against any attempt which the enemy's cavalry might make by charging up that road. This brave old regiment was almost annihilated in square, by the terrible fire of musketry kept up on it from the knoll, whilst it was impossible for them to pull a trigger during the whole time, as they would thereby have been as likely to kill friends as foes. Those who may chance to visit the field of Waterloo, cannot fail to find on the spot which I have mentioned, near the road, and at a short distance from the thorn hedge, a small square of a darker colour than the ground immediately about it, marking the grave of this gallant Irish regiment.

Every kind of exertion was made by the French officers, during this blaze of musketry, to induce their men to advance from the crest of the ridge and from the hillock, to charge us; and although, by the daring and animating example shewn by many of them, they at times prevailed on a certain portion of their men to advance a few yards, the fire which we sent amongst them was such, that they were glad to get back under cover of the knoll; such of them, at least, as were not disabled. In this manner continued the contest on our part of the line hour after hour, without any appearance of its being decided as long as any one remained alive on either side.

The arrival of the Prussians had been long expected; but the only intimation we had of their approach was the smoke of a distant cannon occasionally seen far on the left. About seven o'clock in the evening a party of their Lancers arrived on the field to announce the approach of their army. It was about this time that the last and desperate attack was made by Napoleon with his guard, to annihilate us before the Prussians should arrive to our assistance. That this grand effort entirely failed, and that his Imperial Guard was driven back in irretrievable confusion and with immense slaughter, carrying with it over the field, like the receding waves of the sea, every thing on its surface, is universally known.

The Prussians were now commencing an

attack on the extreme right of the French, which the Duke of Wellington being aware of, and witnessing the immense loss which they had suffered in their last attack, as also their indescribable confusion, ordered a general advance of his whole army, to put the finishing stroke to the work of this bloody day. The lines moved forward rapidly and in fine order, loudly cheering; and the time only which was required for us to reach the enemy's position, sufficed to complete this most hardly contested, sanguinary, and important of battles.

Having principally touched on what took place on the left of the army under my own eye, it remains only to add, that the right and centre were exposed throughout the day to a constant and tremendous fire of artillery, to a murderous discharge of musketry, and desperate charges of cavalry; all of which combined proved insufficient to drive them from their position, or to break a single square, although the brave cuirassiers of the French fell in heaps in their strenuous and repeated attempts to do so.

Those amongst us who had witnessed in the Peninsula many well-contested actions, were agreed on one point, that we had never before seen such determination displayed by the French as on this day. Fighting under the eye of Napoleon, and feeling what a great and important stake they contested for, will account for their extraordinary perseverance and valour, and for the vast efforts which they made for victory.

The loss sustained by the army was such as might have been expected in so long and closely contested a battle. There was a sorry reckoning amongst the officers and soldiers of our battalion, as well as of our 2d and 3d battalions, which were in Sir H. Clinton's division.

Marshal Blucher having put his army on the enemy's track, with strict orders that not a moment's respite should be allowed them on their retreat, the Duke of Wellington's army bivouacked for the night on the ground which had been the French position during the battle. Here, amidst heaps of dead and dying, men and horses, captured artillery, ammunition waggons, &c. &c. &c. huddled together in one confused mass, we spent the night.

Soon after daybreak, the following morning, I mounted my horse for the purpose of glancing my eye over the field of battle. It was not the first of the kind on which I had looked; but the frightful carnage of men and horses lying in so comparatively small a compass, the thousands of the wounded of the two armies which had not yet been removed, together with their groans and lamentations, produced such an impression on the mind, as every writer who has attempted to bring it home to the conception of those who were not eye-witnesses of the bloody scene which this huge charnel-house presented, has failed to effect. I relinquish it, therefore, as a hopeless undertaking; and turn willingly from this scene (which in cold blood will not bear inspection) towards the French metropolis, on the road to which our army was put in motion about nine or ten o'clock on the morning of the 19th.

CHAPTER XXIII.

March to Paris. Cambray is taken by escalade. Letters from Highlanders to their friends in the North. Half a dozen lines only relative to Paris. Another half dozen as to the three years spent by the army of occupation in the north of France. On the distribution of medals. The army evacuates France, and is dispersed all over the globe. Reflections on this breaking up of old friends and comrades. A campaign amongst the Glasgow radicals. Proceed to Ireland. Guarding jails, hunting stills and white boys. A few words at parting with my military friends.

WE followed the wreck of the French army without delay, and without any attempt being made on their part to stop our progress, until we arrived, about the end of June, near St. Denis, which town they had barricaded, and appeared determined to defend. Montmartre was in some measure fortified, and looked formidable; but the Prussians having succeeded, after sustaining some loss, in crossing the Seine, and thereby menacing Paris from other points, Marshal Davoust, who commanded in the city, sent out a flag of truce; shortly after which the capitulation was agreed on which put the allies in possession of the capital.

A few days after the battle of Waterloo, Sir Charles Colville's division took Cambray by escalade, with trifling loss.

In the encampment near St. Denis I one day overheard the following curious dialogue between some soldiers of our division. An Irishman, who was washing his linen under a hedge close to my tent, observed to some of his comrades similarly employed, "I'm tould the newspapers is come out from England, and by J——s thim Highlanders have got all the cridit for the battle." To this, a Highlander, who was on the opposite side of the hedge, and had heard the remark, replied, "And sa they ocht;" meaning thereby, I presume, "so they ought." The Irishman, however, appeared by no means disposed to cede that point, and very naturally proceeded: "Sure, did'nt we do our duty as well as any of thim Highland regiments, and lose as many min?"

I much doubt, nevertheless, whether honest Pat's logic carried with it that conviction to the Highlander which it most indisputably ought to have done. They continued to discuss the point for a considerable length of time, and it terminated, I fancy, in the same manner as all arguments ever do, by each party retaining the same opinions with which they first set out. One cannot but applaud the feeling displayed by the

Irishman for the honour of his regiment; and, in good truth, the self-same feeling has manifested itself in hundreds of others, of all ranks and of different regiments, who fought on the bloody fields of Waterloo and Quatre Bras.

No man will deny that the Highlanders displayed invincible courage, and that they nobly upheld the honour of their country and of their respective regiments, in common with their brothers in arms from England and Ireland. The myriads of letters, however, with which the newspapers were constantly inundated for some months after the battle, from Highlanders to their friends in the north, actually had the effect of convincing nine-tenths of the people in England, and nine hundred and ninety-nine out of every thousand in Scotland, that the Scottish regiments were the only people who pulled a trigger on the left of the British position throughout the whole of that protracted struggle, and that they, unaided, defeated the reiterated attacks of the Imperial Legions at that point.

The candid and liberal-minded Scot will neither cavil nor take umbrage at my remarking, that Sir Thomas Picton's division was composed of eight British regiments, three of which were Highland, one (the 1st Royals) Lowland Scotch, and four English or Irish. Whoever has seen that part of the position which our division occupied, need not be informed that every regiment which composed it must necessarily have been exposed in an equal degree to the repeated attacks of the French; and it was therefore utterly impossible that one regiment should have had a smaller or greater degree of pounding than another.

Various panoramic exhibitions have also strongly tended to convince the good people of England, that John Bull and Pat were little better than idle spectators on the left of the British position. In a panorama at Edinburgh, some months after the battle, the Highlanders and Scotch Greys were depicted as giants, and placed in the foremost ranks, cutting, slashing, charging, bayonetting, and sending headlong to the devil, every thing in the shape of a Frenchman; whilst the other poor dear harmless little regiments of the 5th Division were represented as mere pigmies in size and stature, and placed in the back-ground. "Fair play is a jewel, and the devil should have his due." With a view, therefore, of rendering common justice to all hands who composed Sir T. Picton's division, I have been induced to touch on these matters; and I repeat, that no man of a liberal and unprejudiced mind will misconstrue, pervert, or twist my remarks into any thing approaching, in the slightest degree, to an invidious feeling towards those distinguished Scottish regiments who fought side by side with us on that memorable occasion.

It is unnecessary that I should dwell for an instant on the wonders of Paris: its Louvre, Palais Royal, Boulevards, and a multiplicity of other things of high interest, are too well known to the myriads of my countrymen, who have since seen them, to need description. The swarms of officers and soldiers, British, Hanoverians, Prussians, Russians, Austrians, Dutch, Belgians, Brunswickers, and others, with whom Paris was inundated, and who choked the avenues of the Palais Royal by day and night, were by no means the least interesting objects at that period. Crowds of English families flocked to Paris before we had long occupied it; and there John Bull might be seen, in all his glory, gaping and staring, in every part of the city, at those continental novelties.

I now take flight from Paris, after a six months' sojourn there, to the north of France, which we marched to about the end of December. The 1st and 2d battalions of our corps formed a part of the army of occupation; and our 3d battalion was sent to Ireland, with various other regiments. The three following years passed by the army of occupation in Cambray, Valenciennes, and other towns and villages in that part of France, furnished no materials of consequence for journalising. Our summers were spent in camp, and

DISTRIBUTION OF MEDALS. 401

we had annually some grand reviews, in presence of emperors, kings, archdukes, and a variety of big-wigs of different kinds.

Those who were fond of field-sports indulged in them to their hearts' content; and I was among the number who did so. Game was very plentiful, and a finer country for coursing is no where to be found. There were several packs of fox-hounds and harriers belonging to different divisions of the army, and greyhounds without number. At Valenciennes we had races frequently, and some decent nags found their way out from England. Champagne, Burgundy, Claret, and other orthodox fluids, were abundant; and the greater part of the army would willingly have protracted their stay a dozen years longer in those quarters.

A few months after the army of occupation had reached the north of France from Paris, medals were sent out from England, and distributed amongst the regiments which had fought at Waterloo. Every man on whom this honourable mark of distinction was conferred, must undoubtedly have felt extremely gratified, conscious that he had lent a hand in gaining a battle more sanguinary and obstinately contested, perhaps, than any to be found in the annals of history, and one on which the fate of Europe depended. The mode of distributing this badge was such as no one could object to; for it was not conferred on the few, and withheld from the many; but the very same description of medal was, on this occasion, suspended at the breast of the Commander-in-chief and the private soldier.

No one, however, can be surprised, that the regiments which had taken an active part in the many battles and sieges in the Peninsula, and had struggled, year after year, with all the dangers, hardships, and fatigues, which those campaigns brought in their train, (but whose fate it was, not to have been present at Waterloo), should have felt sadly galled on finding themselves, at the termination of a long and bloody war, without even a bit of copper, by way of badge, to commemorate their services. Many men, on the contrary, who had, perchance, commenced their military career in England a month or two only before the battles of Quatre Bras and Waterloo, and until the night of the 16th of June, 1815, knew not what it was to sleep in a bivouac, enjoyed the marked and distinguished privilege of wearing a medal for a battle, which, sanguinary, long-protracted, and decisive, as it was, surely ought not to cast oblivion on the many blood-stained fields of Portugal, Spain, and the south of France.

The mode which was concocted at home of distributing medals to the Peninsular army, has, with great reason, created surprise, and, I may add, discontent. I could name many officers who disembarked with the army in Portugal on the 1st of August, 1808, as captains or subalterns, and served throughout the whole of those seven years, without having received a single badge. And why? Simply because they held no higher rank than that of captain or subaltern during that succession of campaigns, and consequently never commanded a battalion in a general action. On the other hand, some of those who joined the army for the first time in the end of 1813 or the beginning of 1814, as field-officers in command of regiments, or holding some staff situations, found themselves bedizened with medals in the course of a few months.

For example: if a regiment arrived in the Pyrenees in the autumn of 1813, (being its first appearance on that stage,) and happened to be engaged in the battles of the Nivelle, Nive, Orthes, and Toulouse, the whole of which were fought between the 10th of November, 1813, and the 10th of April, 1814 (a period of only five months), the field-officer who commanded this newly arrived corps would receive four medals, and be created a K.C.B. into the bargain. The captain or subaltern, however, unless he happened, by some stroke of good fortune, to command a regiment in a general engagement, although he could boast of having fought at Roleia, Vimeira, Corunna; the passage of the Douro, Talavera, Buzaco, Barossa; in Massena's retreat out of Portugal, at Fuentes d'Onoro, Albuera, at the sieges of Ciudad Rodrigo, Badajoz, Burgos, or St. Sebastian; at Salamanca, Vittoria, and in the Pyrenees, (*the whole of which, with an infinity of minor actions, took place before the arrival of this new regiment from England,*) and in spite of his having also fought at the Nivelle, Nive, Toulouse, and Orthes, returned to England in 1814, as he first entered Portugal in 1808—badgeless!

If the dictionaries of Johnson or Sheridan do not acknowledge the word which I have just made use of, I must take the liberty of coining it for the occasion. Whether a medal be of gold, copper, tin, or iron, is a matter of no importance whatever; and I feel well convinced, that one metal would be appreciated equally as much as another. Every private soldier in the Prussian army who fought in 1813, 1814, or 1815, had a copper medal, with the date of the campaign in which he served inscribed thereon.

I can scarcely believe that the expense attending a similar distribution of badges to every man who took a part in the Peninsular campaigns, would be attended with consequences so ruinous to John Bull's finances as some people may imagine; for I am quite sure that, from a few pieces of artillery, out of the one hundred and fifty which we captured at Vittoria, might have been cast brass medals sufficient to satisfy those who so naturally and laudably wish to possess some trifling mark of having fought in many a bloody field.

The rising generation of soldiers will listen with about as much patience to details of Peninsular exploits, as we of older standing do to tales of Minden, Dusseldorf, or Bunker's Hill; and ere many years elapse, if the names of Vimeira, Talavera, Salamanca, Vittoria, &c. &c. should be partially remembered, the actors in those scenes (with a few exceptions) will be entirely forgotten.

The beginning of the winter of 1818 witnessed the evacuation of France by our troops, which were immediately afterwards scattered all over the world, like dust before the wind. A few regiments went to England, many to Ireland, and still more to the East and West Indies, Canada, the Cape, the Mediterranean; and, in short, to every creek and corner where we had colonies or garrisons. Thus was dispersed an army, many regiments of which had been together from the year 1808 to 1818; the whole of which time, with the exception of the few months that Napoleon spent at Elba, was passed in the Peninsula and in France. It was the breaking up of a large family, which was, or ought to have been, bound together by those ties which the various scenes inseparable from the life in which they had been actors, might naturally be expected to create. It was impossible to witness, without feelings of regret, this thorough dispersion of regiments and of individuals so long known to each other; and who, in all human probability, would not be re-assembled under similar circumstances of interest and excitement.

No long time had elapsed, after leaving France, before our battalion was despatched, post haste, from England to Scotland, for the purpose of keeping in order the radicals of Glasgow, Paisley, and the vicinity. It was by no means a delectable service, for we found them a most nefarious crew. After one year spent in this manner, we were removed to Ireland; where still-hunting, white boy hunting, and guarding county jails, were the amusements substituted for over-awing cotton-spinners and colliers in Caledonia. And thus, in Old Ireland, I now find myself employed, after having served three long apprenticeships in the army.

I am free to confess, that I feel no particular *penchant* for passing the remainder of my days in marching off guards, going grand rounds and visiting rounds, and performing other dull, monotonous, and uninteresting duties of the kind, on which such great stress is laid, and to which such vast importance is attached, in various stiff-starched garrisons; but, on the contrary, prefer to range, henceforth, free and unfettered by military trammels, wherever my fancy leads.

And now I would offer a few words of advice at parting with the members of that corps, whose uniform, during the many years which I served in it, was seldom exchanged for a plain coat. It is true that I never held a staff appointment, nor enjoyed the benefit of having the theoretical principles of my profession hammered into my brain either at High Wycombe, or at any other military college; but, on the contrary, have merely twenty-one years of practice to boast. May those who hereafter rise to command its respective battalions, ever bear in mind, that although it is necessary for riflemen to be thoroughly grounded in the drill of infantry of the line, and able to go through correctly, in presence of the inspecting general, that series of manœuvres recently introduced,—our corps gained the reputation, which it wrung from friends and foes, *not by aping the drill of grenadiers,* but by its activity and intelligence at the outposts; by being able to cope with, in all situations, the most experienced and best-trained light troops which the continent of Europe could produce; and by the deadly application of the rifle in action. In making this assertion, I defy contradiction, even from those who, jealous of its fame, would most readily and delightedly, if they were able, detract from its hard-earned renown. I will further assert, also, that when called on to storm the breaches at Monte Video, Ciudad Rodrigo, and Badajoz, the corps proved itself equally efficient in the form of grenadiers, as any of the other brave regiments employed on those occasions.

It is, doubtless, vastly pretty to see officers march by and salute gracefully, — to see formations from line into column, and from column into line, executed with accuracy and promptness; but I hold all these to be very secondary considerations indeed for a rifle corps, although I am far from thinking that they should be neglected. Too much time and attention, however, ought not to be employed on them. The great and important points, before which all others should succumb and sink into comparative insignificance, are, to attain the most perfect use of the arms they bear, which can only be effected by constant and unremitting attention and practice; to become thoroughly master of all matters connected with outpost duties, pickets, flank patroles, advanced and rear-guards; to direct the attention, and to practise the eye, of officers and non-commissioned officers, to the selection of positions advantageous for posts and pickets; and to instil into the mind of the soldier, that he must act for himself, and on his own judgment, in taking every advantage of the ground on which it may be his lot to engage the enemy; and that, in the desultory nature of our warfare, it is impossible that an officer or sergeant can always be at his elbow to set him right. I maintain that this can only be learned by constant practice.

In my opinion, by far the most useful and profitable drill for riflemen is, that of sending out one or more companies to take up a defensive position, and to attack them with the remainder of the battalion: and I would, if possible, select the most intersected, intricate, and difficult ground for that purpose. He who fancies that these matters are to be learned in a day, a month, or a year, will find himself egregiously and wofully mistaken; as he in like manner will, if he flatters himself, that occasionally trotting out one of his flank companies to a skirmish in front of the battalion, in a clean-swept, smooth barrack-square, without inequality of ground, or any elbow-room for light movements, is all that is requisite to make first-rate light troops. Any company of any regiment in his Majesty's service surely can extend in skirmishing order in front of a line, and fire advancing and retreating; unless, indeed, their training has been much neglected.

When war shall again appear, and either, or both, of the battalions of the rifle brigade find themselves in boats, with orders to gain some hostile shore—to land—to attack—and disperse the light troops of an enemy ready to dispute the disembarkation of the army, it will then be found that every perfection, as light troops and marksmen, will be expected from them; and that the slower and more compact movements in masses, however requisite for infantry of the line, will, as far as they are concerned, become little better than a dead letter.

The opinions on the training of Riflemen, which I have here offered, may possibly be deemed little short of heresy by those who either *cannot*, or *will not*, perceive the immense distinction which ever exists between the duties of infantry of the line, and those of the *lightest of the light*, when an army takes the field in good earnest. If the theoretical soldier, who has never seen a rifle or musket discharged at any object more formidable than a target, is disposed to question the accuracy of my doctrine, I must attribute it to his total want of experience in such matters. The practical soldier, however, if he has candour, will scarcely place his hand on his heart, and assert that he believes my opinions on this subject erroneous.

May the muster-rolls of the corps never be so

unfortunate as to bear on their strength tacticians with new-fangled doctrines, whose vanity and presumption may induce them to attempt to overturn the good old-established system of the regiment, which, both in garrison and in the field, has hitherto been attended with complete success!

But I will not anticipate evils which I most sincerely hope may never be realised. That every success may attend both its battalions, and glory continue to mark their paths, is my most ardent hope!

In the 70th regiment there is not now an officer who was with us at the period of our embarkation for the West Indies, and, in all human probability, not one individual. My best wishes, nevertheless, attend the regiment to whatever part of the globe the Fates may call it.

My military infancy was passed in it—days which will never be effaced from my memory. All the friends of my early life are entombed in Antigua.

THE END.

FORTESCUE'S HISTORY OF THE BRITISH ARMY: COMPLETE SET - 14 VOLUMES + MAPS
9781474537780

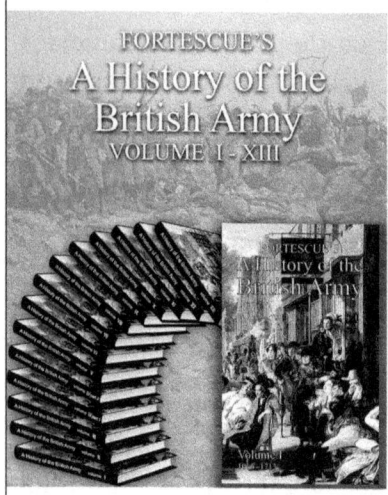

This work, which is a classic, covers the history of the British Army from the Norman Conquest down to the Cardwell reforms of 1870, when commission by purchase was finally abolished. The very last chapter of the work looks at the British Army up to 1914.

Naval and Military Press have reprinted this valuable and timeless work in its entirety, faithful to the originals in all respects. The contents of the individual volumes are as follows:

Vol. I - from the Battle of Hastings to the end of the Seven Year's War (1713). Includes such battles as Bannockburn, Crecy, Agincourt, Flodden, the battles of the English Civil War, Dunkirk Dunes, Tangiers, and the battles during Marlborough's campaigns. The volume also traces the development of European Armies, infantry, cavalry and artillery, and the specific changes in Britain during the period.

Vol. II - covers from the 1713 to 1763 and includes the Jacobite Rebellion of 1715, the scandals of the reign of King George I, the war with Spain and the dispute over the Austrian Succession, and the Battles of Fontenoy and Culloden. It also covers the situation in India and the contest for mastery with the French. The expansion into North America is described and the differences that arose between the French and the British, together with Wolfe's campaigns in North America. The volume includes much material on the development of the British Army, and the problems that arose with regard to recruitment and conditions of service at that time.

Vol. III - continues the story from 1763 to 1792. The continuing problems in North America are joined by the growing pains of Empire. The loss of the Americas is covered in detail, as is the state of the British Army, especially in the light of Cornwallis' disastrous contributions to the American failure. Developments in India follow, and again Cornwallis makes a contribution to failure.

Vol IV Part I - Deals with the French Revolution from 1789 to the Treaty of Amiens in 1798. It includes British operations in the Netherlands, the West Indies, South Africa and Ireland. The whole European area is described with the French and Allied nations included. Naval matters are also included, and the campaigns in Egypt and the Mediterranean are treated in detail. At the same time a close eye is kept on developments within the British Army.

Vol. IV Part 2 - continues the theme of the previous part, and goes up to 1801. The examination of the British Army is also expanded, and an important appendix gives exact details of British Army pay.

Vol. V - the period 1803 to 1807. Detailed treatment of the situation and operations in the East Indies and Ceylon, the West Indies, Europe and the Mediterranean. There are important chapters on conditions at home,and the air of war-weariness that was appearing. Finally, there is a description of operations in South America.

Vol. VI - 1807-1809. The Napoleonic War continued, with further details of operations in Egypt and in the Mediterranean. The Swedish situation is covered, the British expedition to Copenhagen and operations in Portugal. The Spanish theatre is also examined in fine detail.

Vol. VII - 1809-1810. This volume is concerned mainly with these two years in the Peninsula, but also covers the expedition to the Scheldt, and operations in the East Indies, Mauritius and Java.

Vol. VII - 1809-1810. Maps

Vol. VIII - 1811-1812. This volume covers two more years of the campaign in the Peninsula, together with the War with the United States. There are details of many battles, including Barosa, Badajoz, Fuentes de Onoro, Albuera, Ciudad Rodrigo, Salamanca and others of fame during the Peninsula War. the United States. There are details of many battles, including Barosa, Badajoz, Fuentes de Onoro, Albuera, Ciudad Rodrigo, Salamanca and others of fame during the Peninsula War.

Vol. IX - 1813-1814. The French invasion of Russia is

followed by descriptions of the situation in the Peninsula, and in North America. Throughout developments in Europe are covered so that the picture of the war for the reader in these years is complete, and second to none in detail.

Vol. X - 1814-1815. The whole of Europe was aflame in these two years, and Fortescue writes most effectively of the military activity and the political background. Italy, the Peninsula, the Low Countries and the American War are all interwoven from the British point of view in a tour de force of military history. He then includes a really valuable summary of events in Europe from 1803 to 1814 before setting out to describe the culminating battle at Waterloo. From the Duchess of Richmond's Ball to the exhaustion on the night after the battle, Fortescue maintains a pace and directness which is fascinating to read.

Vol. XI - 1815-1838. Fortescue looks at the British Army in 1815, and particularly the recruit in England. Every detail of his life is included, and the picture is an important one for all who are interested in this period of military and social history. The War with Nepal, the Pindari War, the War in Ceylon and the War with Burma all occupy the subsequent pages followed by the Ashanti campaign and the Kaffir War of 1834-35. This volume also includes details of Home Affairs and Foreign Policy.

Vol. XII - 1839-52. This volume is mainly concerned with India, and covers operations in Afghanistan and on the Khyber Pass, together with internal security operations in India itself. There is also a section dealing with the revolt in Australia and operations in New Zealand. Finally there is a description of the Kaffir War and the Boer revolt.

Vol. XIII - 1852-1870. This volume includes the Crimean War, the War in Persia and the Indian Mutiny and the campaign in China. It then goes on to look at the Ambela and Abyssinian campaigns, and the Wars in New Zealand. Finally Fortescue looks at affairs in Great Britain and the position of the East India Company. He then turns his attention to the new army from 1870 to 1914, and includes the territorial system, the new social engineering going on for men's wefare in the army, The series ends however with an important look at the end of the era of purchase, and what the army was going to do next.

Map Compendium - includes all six separate map volumes that came with the original work in one binding.

www.ingramcontent.com/pod-product-compliance
Lightning Source LLC
Chambersburg PA
CBHW070916180426
43192CB00037B/1186